Building Influence for the School Librarian:
Tenets, Targets, & Tactics

Second Edition

Gary Hartzell

Library of Congress Cataloging-in-Publication Data

Hartzell, Gary N., 1943–
        Building influence for the school librarian : tenets, targets &
tactics / by Gary Hartzell.— 2nd ed.
            p. cm.
        Includes bibliographical references.
        ISBN 1-58683-161-5 (pbk.)
        1. School libraries--United States--Marketing. 2. School
libraries--Public relations--United States. I. Title.
Z675.S3H268 2003
027.8--dc22

                                                    2003016416

Published by Linworth Publishing, Inc.
480 East Wilson Bridge Road, Suite L
Worthington, Ohio 43085

ISBN: 1-58683-161-5

5 4 3

Table of Contents

Preface
to the Second Edition

I'm going to make an assumption: If you're reading this book, you've already decided that you want to think about increasing your influence at work.

Library advocacy efforts were just beginning to accelerate when the first edition of *Building Influence for the School Librarian* came out in the middle 1990s. Many librarians had not yet given a lot of thought to how they could—or even if they should—deliberately go about changing the way others perceived them, their libraries, and their library media programs. About a third of that edition was devoted to the argument that librarians could and should build an influence base in their schools. Now, a decade later, library advocacy and librarian influence are leading edge topics in the field. I don't think it's still necessary to try to convince most readers that they should consciously set about shaping other people's perceptions of them and their programs. Consequently, instead of deeply investigating *why*, this edition much more concentrates on *how* school library media specialists can use what is known about workplace influence from research and theory to improve their own situations.

The Perspective of This Book

There are two things about this edition, however, that have not changed from the first, and that readers new to the study of influence need to know in advance. The first is the book's perspective and the second is its target audience.

The Perspective

This book is different from most others that have been written for school librarians in that it doesn't approach its subject from the librarian's perspective. Instead, it flows from an organizational influence perspective. This point is important because it relates to the fundamental principle of influence: **Influence is derived from the perceptions of the person to be influenced, *not* from the perceptions of the person doing the influencing. The key to building your influence lies in your ability to shape the perceptions of others.**

The ways in which teachers and administrators, and students and parents, perceive you, your library, and your program dictate how they treat you. Not to put too fine a point on it, and certainly not to be offensive, but the larger part of the truth is simply that your perceptions of the library and of what constitutes quality librarianship are almost irrelevant in the determination of someone else's behavior, *except* for ways in which your perceptions impact how that person perceives you and what you do. You truly might be the single best school librarian to ever work in your district, but you won't be treated you that way unless *others* perceive you as such.

I have never been a school librarian, but I have been a high school teacher, vice principal, and principal. I value the library as a central piece in the quality structure of a school, and I value the librarians with whom I have worked because I perceive them as essential players in my professional success and in the success of the students under my charge. Research and experience argue that if you would increase the influence you have in your school you will have to build that same perception in the school people who surround you.

Because this book is written from an administrator's perspective and not from a librarian's, some readers may encounter positions and suggestions that they will feel are simplistic, obvious, or biased. But these interpretations will not necessarily negate the value of the idea in question. I would argue that the viewpoints expressed in the book represent perceptions held by many, if not most, educators *outside* the library, and accepting that fact is the starting point for changing them.

The Target Audience

The target audience of this book is obviously school librarians. The problem is that, since readers may range from library science students still in university training programs to long-time school library veterans, it is impossible to predict any given reader's training, background, experience, or attitude. This is important to know because readers have a role in determining the value of a book like this since both it and they are locked into particular contextual boundaries. Individual readers come to it carrying their own unique backgrounds, experiences, and knowledge. They bring these things to bear in assessing whatever perspective the book offers and make credibility judgments by filtering and refining the presented material as they examine it through the lenses of their own personal experiences.

A given reader may well discount some portion of the book's content and argument. However, because experience is individualized and subject to individual interpretation, different readers will discount different elements. The result is that there may be ideas or suggestions that seem painfully simple, maybe even insultingly obvious to one—"Don't *all* librarians do that?"—while the very same idea or suggestion may be enlightening or may appear very challenging to another. The contents of this book can potentially be applied to a wide range of library environments and librarian experiences, and you will have to deliberately view the contents in the light of your own experience and surroundings.

The Book's Content

The book's content is largely drawn from research and theory not commonly applied to libraries and librarians. Many of the authorities cited and much of the research described come from sources probably unfamiliar to most school librarians. Still, these investigations were conducted among and across enough diverse organizations to support generalization.

The book is organized into three parts. Part I outlines the tenets of influence, providing a general understanding of the nature and operation of workplace influence with particular attention paid to what these principles and theories imply for school librarians. Part II zeros in on specific influence targets in the school. It examines why these people are important to school librarians and suggests ways to capture their support. The final section offers a small collection of influence-building and influence-enhancing tactics that specifically address elements of school librarians' work lives.

A Concluding Thought

Schools are organizations in the same sense that businesses, medical facilities, public agencies, and governments are organizations. The forces that drive and shape school operation are shared by all complex organizations, and we can learn from observing them. Moreover, schools are intensely human enterprises, and exercising influence is a singularly human activity.

As the school librarian, you have an important and critical role to play as a full partner with teachers and administrators in bringing educational opportunities to students. But, given most schools' traditions and structures, the chance to be a full participant will not be delivered to you. You will have to seek it out; perhaps create it. The irony of the school librarianship is that the people who are the beneficiaries of your knowledge and skills are often the very people who either don't recognize it or who discount and resist it. As Phillip Turner observes, they are simultaneously the challenge, the frustration, and the reward.[1]

I think it's true, as John Kotter says in *Power and Influence*, that it's naive to think that reading really can change the way a person perceives his or work place and co-workers. But a book can suggest some new ways of thinking about your relationships with work and colleagues. It can focus or refocus your attention on important issues and can help you to rethink professional and personal priorities.[2]

Achieving such priorities frequently results from organizational influence. The hope is that this book will encourage you to think about your role in the school in a new way and will help you discover more effective ways to make the important contributions of which you are capable—inside and outside the library media center.

References

1 P. M. Turner, *Helping Teachers Teach: A School Library Media Specialist's Role, Second Edition* (Englewood, CO: Libraries Unlimited, Inc., 1993), p. xiii.

2 J. P. Kotter, *Power and Influence* (New York: Free Press, 1985).

Section I
Tenets of Workplace Influence

This section of the book outlines the tenets of workplace influence. Our understanding of workplace influence is informed by the results of about eight decades of organizational and behavioral research defining its value, nature, and operation. The five chapters in this section each address a particular dimension of what we know and how it applies to school librarians.

Chapter 1 offers a rationale for why you should build your influence at school. The bottom line is that because you have no power, influence offers your only avenue for making a positive difference in what goes on there.

Chapter 2 is a reality check—influence comes at a price. The price includes attitude readjustment, redefined relationships, work that is both more and different from what you've done before, and subjection to greater scrutiny as you assume a larger role in school affairs. The trade off, of course, is that you will have a more powerful voice in school affairs.

Chapter 3 describes what we know to be the attributes of influential people— those personal characteristics that cause others at work to listen to influential people and most often to comply with their suggestions and requests. Without ever quite saying so, the chapter also asks, how many of these characteristics describe you?

Chapter 4 introduces the notion of judgmental heuristics—what some researchers call the "tools" or even the "weapons" of influence. Heuristics are unconscious rules-of-thumb that guide the way we interpret our interactions with others at work. By surfacing them, we can see ways they can be used to encourage others to go along with our ideas.

Chapter 5 closes out the section with a closer look at the library's organizational position. There are some positions in every organization that allow the people who hold them more influence building opportunities than are afforded to people occupying other positions in the same organization. In schools, the library is one of the former.

Chapter 1
Workplace Conditions Create the Need for Influence

As a school librarian, you're an educator in the full sense of the word—a fact, unfortunately, too often not fully realized by others. When this is not realized, you're unable to fully exercise the power and influence you should, both in regard to your own role in the school and to how the school functions as a whole. The question is, should you try to do anything about it? The answer is yes for three powerful reasons.

The Need to Have Some Control of Your Life and Job

The first is psychological. Some sense of power is a human need. We all share the desire to have influence and control in our work lives. Possessing influence is one of the pillars of psychological health.

We've all heard Lord Acton's dictum that absolute power corrupts absolutely. The emphasis should be on the word "absolute," and not on the word "power." History, psychological research, and simple experience all tell us that powerlessness is equally, perhaps more, damaging. Just look at the histories of women and minorities all over the world.

People need to feel they have influence over their lives and their work accomplishments. Our culture links strength with self-esteem. In the workplace, strength means the ability to make a difference, and making a difference clearly is linked with professional self-esteem. Research shows that people who believe that their actions affect other people and events in lasting and varied ways are more satisfied with their lives *and* are more productive than those who don't share similar beliefs.[1] Power and influence are central to defining self-esteem at work, just as they are in the larger world beyond the organization.[2]

Schools Are Bureaucracies

The second reason for seeking workplace influence is the simple fact that schools are bureaucracies. Bureaucratic organizations are built on an interlocking dependency concept; you can't do your job by yourself because bureaucracies don't allow people to have everything they need in order to do their best work. It's not an accident that you must depend on other people in order to be able to do your job. Even in a position with the autonomy and isolation of the library, you cannot operate in a vacuum. You're structurally tied to other parts of the organization and to the people who populate them. Whenever you're dependent on others for what you need to succeed, your ability to control your own destiny is reduced. Influence is a mechanism for countering dependency.

Schools, like most organizations in business and government, are structured as "rational bureaucracies."[3] A rational bureaucracy is designed to prevent the concentration of power in the hands of a single person or in the shared possession of a very few. The objective is to keep powerful people from acting upon arbitrary and unpredictable whims by preventing such behavior at its source. Power, responsibility, and resources are deliberately divided among employees across the organization. Each person holding a position in a bureaucratic structure is given authority over particular areas and made to be accountable to certain other people for the use of that power. The division of labor and power sees to it that no one has all the skills or resources needed to carry out job responsibilities alone. The result is what you see in your school and district organizational charts—hierarchical structures with levels of authority and responsibility, each limited in its scope and function and linked through a chain of command.

There is, however, an irony in bureaucracies. The greatest source of current problems, someone once said, lies in the solutions to past problems. In trying to create situations where employees are not made dependent upon any other single individual, bureaucracies also create systems that make you dependent. You're vulnerable to people from whom you need cooperation or resources, but over whom you have no direct control. In one sense, bureaucratic organization increases your need for influence because it puts you in a situation where you must maintain positive and influential relationships with several people at a time instead of with just one.

To cope with this, and particularly if you decide you want increase your influence in the bureaucratic setting, you need a working sense of which people are most important to you. That is to say, those upon whom you're most dependent. Some are obvious, but the identities of others are not always so apparent. They can, however, be made visible with a little concentrated thought. John Kotter of Harvard has suggested a good way to conceptualize the complex network of power and influence that affects you as a school librarian. He advises that you try to map the people and positions upon which you depend.[4]

Using the model on the next page, draw a diagram of your organization. Put your library media center in the center circle. In each of the orbiting circles, place the name of a person or group upon whom you're somehow dependent for an element of your success as a school librarian.

In the open space on each line that connects an orbiting circle to your position in the center, indicate the intensity of your dependency on that person or group by writing "high," "medium," or "low" as an evaluation. High indicates that their support is absolutely necessary to your success. Medium indicates that their support makes a critical difference in your ability to perform. Low indicates that their support is important in the quality of your performance.

Clearly, the principal will appear on your map and be ranked as high. Which other people or groups deserve a position? A few ideas to get you started might include:

- Assistant principal(s)
- Department chairs
- Parents
- Students
- Clerical staff
- Grand funding agency or foundation
- District Library Coordinator
- Curriculum specialists, supervisors, or directors

- Teacher or teachers who have considerable informal power or influence
- Superintendent
- Board of Education
- Union
- State Government
- Federal Government
- State or national library association

Figure 1.1: Bureaucratic Dependency Map

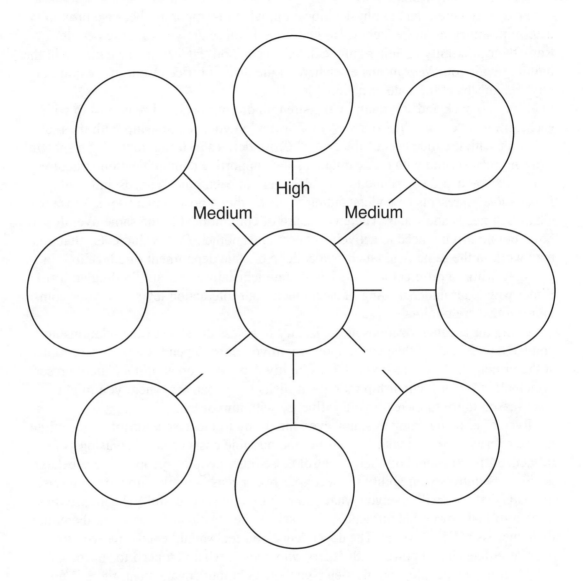

It's probably best if you complete this exercise on a separate piece of paper onto which you can draw many more orbiting circles.

Republished with permission of the publisher, from *Power in Management* by John Kotter, © 1979 AMACOM, a division of the American Management Association; permission conveyed through Copyright Clearance Center.

Once you have constructed the map and have rated your dependence level on each entry as either high, medium, or low, go back and try to sort the people and groups into two other useful categories: their proximity to you and the strength of your current relationship.

Proximity here refers to physical location, which is important because proximity determines interaction frequency. How physically close are you to these people? Rank their proximity as either "immediate," "near," or "far." *Immediate* means in the building with you. *Near* means elsewhere in the district office or out in the community. *Far* means at the state or national level.

Next, go back and sort them by the strength of your personal relationship with each. Are you "close," "reasonable," or "distant" in your relationship with the individual or with the members of the group? *Close* defines a strong, mutually respectful working relationship with clear, frequent, and supportive communication structures. You understand and contribute to the fulfillment of each other's needs and goals. *Reasonable* represents an understanding of each other's position and some sense of what each needs and wants. There is a sense of commitment to the same overall purpose, but no driving need to actively support one another. *Distant* indicates that you may work in the same field (such as a college or state department of education) or you may work in different fields (such as state legislature or grant funding entity). Either way, your understanding of each other, your interaction level, and your communications are minimal.

Using these categorizations as a base, try to assess the state of the relationship you have with each of the people upon whom you most depend. Look, for example, at the principal. If you rated yourself as highly dependent on an immediately present principal, but your relationship rating was distant, you can see where you might have reason to try to increase your influence with him or her.

Even after recognizing this, however, the desire to increase your influence might not be overwhelming in you, so consider the possible costs of not increasing your influence. If you cannot officially control these other people—people whose behavior in part controls your ability to meet your own needs at work—how do you raise the odds that they will give you what you require to be successful? The answer has to be informal power and influence—in a sense, the creation of a belief in them that their success is tied to yours. The dependence you feel should encourage you to acquire influence and power with others who control what you need to succeed.

To influence people, you must engage them. Without engagement, there is no recognition. Part of the danger for you rests in the isolation of your job. If you're not engaged in a variety of activities outside the library media center itself, you run the risk of coming to focus on just your own little part of the bureaucracy. Looking inward, your definition of effectiveness can become rooted in making the library as efficient and smooth running as possible, and you may come to define its challenges and problems in a narrow and internal sense. This isn't all bad. You may become very good at not only meeting these challenges and problems but at anticipating them. You may be able to routinize the library's activities and systems in order to have greater control.

In the long run, however, this behavior is counterproductive. It reduces the amount of control you actually have because it reduces the amount of attention outsiders pay to library operation. Without attention, the library's ability to attract resources and support on its own is diminished. This happens because, lacking engagement, other people simply are not aware of the library's value. They don't see the library as integral to their success and they don't perceive its need for additional resources. Over time, this increases your dependence on others because possession and control of resources are what allow independence of action. Autonomy begins to erode.

The lesson is this: quiet competent behavior just sustains your dependency. People don't get much credit or notice for doing what is expected or mandated. Influence, power, and opportunity flow to people who display enterprise or creativity, and to those upon whom others depend. If your library only operates "smoothly," people will wonder if you're doing anything really worthwhile. As Leonard Sayles, a prominent organizational researcher, has demonstrated, quiet efficiency is deadly; routine work produces powerlessness.[5] Unless you stand out in some way, it is very difficult to be perceived as an integral element of the operation.

When situations arise which require outside support and the infusion of resources, isolation can be ruinous because it reduces informal influence opportunities. Presenting your case through formal channels is frequently not enough. Formal and informal relationships are rarely separable. The informal influences the formal. Isolated people without powerful sponsors, peers, or subordinates get overlooked.

Schools Are Changing

The third reason encouraging you to build your influence at work is that schools are changing rapidly. Change inherently involves conflict. Don't be fooled: when people invite you to be part of a change effort, they're really inviting you to a fight. There always are winners and losers in change situations. You need to be aware of the forces swirling around you if you're going to be able to maintain, let alone enhance, your ability to have a say in what you do and how you do it.

There is neither space nor need here to talk about the "education bashing" of the last decade or the accelerating pressure for change in schools. The important point is that change, whatever form it may take, is always accompanied by a redistribution of resources, power, and influence. In effect, such redistributions inevitably alter the culture of the building and the district. Cultural change has far reaching consequences.

As Tom Donahoe of the Far West Laboratories for Educational Research and Development has observed, changing culture is a wrenching experience. As he puts it:

> But culture—the values, beliefs, behaviors, rules, products, signs, and symbols that bind us together—is not something we can change like a flat tire. Culture is organic to its community. If culture changes, everything changes.[6]

In the process of these changes, conflict and competition are inevitable. The competition is not only for resources. It is also for philosophical dominance. As culture is redefined, the operative questions become: "What are we to be?" and "Who will decide what and who we are?"

Those questions will be answered. The answers may be allowed to emerge through trial and error or they may be shaped and directed by those who will constitute the organization itself. Either way, the process will distress people. Stephen Robbins, an organizational researcher, has offered an explanation of why change generates such strong feelings and causes the stress it does. His description helps to put the process in perspective.[7]

First, he says, change stirs powerful feelings in individuals because it threatens what they know, and threats almost always stimulate resistance. The dynamics of that resistance help to shape the final form of the change.

Second, Robbins says, change stresses the organization itself as an entity, and it is stirred to resistance.[8] It helps sometimes to think of organizations as artificial people that exhibit many of the same characteristics as the humans who make them up—energy, lethargy, inventiveness, traditionalism, enthusiasm, anxiety, compliance, and resistance. Organizations are among the most conservative of entities. Change poses a threat to established structures, systems, group standards, notions of expertise, resource allocation methods, and power relationships. It is worth taking a moment to examine each of these a little more closely.

Organizations have internal environment-stabilizing mechanisms built into their structures. Just think of the rules and policies that govern your school with the single purpose of instilling order. These are designed to combat the threat of disruption.

Organizations are systems made up of several subsystems working in concert. One cannot be changed without affecting others. Even improvements in one can pose threats to another. For example, increasing high school graduation requirements threatens elective programs. In other instances, group norms may restrain people from engaging in change efforts. Robbins cites the example of an individual who may want to change, but the norm in the teachers' union to which she belongs is to reject administrative initiatives, so she resists. To change is to threaten the role and practice of the union. Successful change requires major effort, coordination, and a systems perspective. Without these, resistance in one part of an organization may mean that changes in another never reach fruition.[9]

Changes in structure and function may also cause stress. Such changes can render a particular skill or knowledge set obsolete. Obsolescence reduces status, and power and influence are lost. Newly valued expertise will cause previously marginal groups to emerge, seizing the power and influence formerly held by others. Look, for example, at how the status of technology people has changed in the last 20 years.

Change also poses a threat to resource control. One of the rules to remember about organizations is that someone always benefits from the status quo. Since resources are integral to power, those who stand to lose control of resources will resist change strongly.

Changes in these five elements—structure, system, norms or standards, expertise, and resource allocation—combine to bring the sixth element into effect: the threat to established power relations. Think back to your own dependency map. In some combination and at differing times, you, like everyone else in the organization, need resources, someone else's expertise, the support of the group, the interlocking activities of the system, and the support of the structure to provide a calm environment in which to work. The fact that some measure of these things is controlled by each of the people and groups on your dependency map is what earned them the positions they have there. If power and influence are defined by the resources people hold and by the nature of their dependent relationships, to change the elements is to change the power distribution. If the people on your dependency map were stripped of the resources or authority they control, you could erase them in a moment.

The objective in a changing environment is to protect your resource base, increase it if you can, and reduce the level of your dependency while raising the level to which others are dependent upon you. The key in accomplishing that is rooted in how resource, system, normative, and expertise decisions will be made and who will influence the way they are finalized.

Fomenting change means getting people to act in new ways. That always involves influence. And not all of it is always visible. As a participant in change, you have to take into account what some researchers call the "hidden" face of power.

One of the most common errors people in bureaucracies make is the assumption that power is only exercised overtly and openly. Often it is, sometimes bluntly. Nevertheless, the hidden practice of power is always in operation. In unobserved ways, powerful people quietly, and unobtrusively, influence the normal, everyday actions of others by giving or denying resources, authority, expertise, support, and information to certain people. Research suggests that this is really the "normal" mode of exercising power in organizations: unseen actions generally determine how visible decisions are made. The term for this is organizational politics.

As distasteful as organizational politics may be to some, they are inescapable. Every organization is political. Recognizing this fact, the question becomes not how to avoid or to do away with organizational politics, but how to deal with them. Geoffrey Bellman, a corporate consultant, offers some guidelines that may be comforting.[10] They help explain how the reality of organizational politics can be faced without sacrificing your own values.

First, he advises, know what you value and what you want; know what your principles are. Consciously and regularly review them.

Second, acknowledge the reality of politics, and, third, know that you're a part of the process. Understand that there is no way to avoid being a player. You cannot secede from the game. Whatever you do or don't do, your behavior figures in the outcome.

Fourth, understand that anything important will be considered politically as well as objectively by others. People may very well resist any proposal that promises to bring overall improvement to the organization if it also promises to reduce their personal status and power. No matter how good the idea, political support may still be required for its success.

In deciding whether you should act politically, Bellman suggests that you use the measures of moral and professional importance to guide you. Think about what will or will not happen in the organization if a given idea doesn't get the required political support and fails. Fold that vision into your calculations about how you should behave.

Lastly, he comes around to make a connection with the first piece of advice: be clear about your limits, about what you will and will not do to accomplish your goals. To the extent that you can work this out in advance, your comfort level should be increased.

You don't have the choice of standing outside other peoples' plans and calculations, but you do have the choice of engaging or not engaging. If you elect not to engage, you'll probably lose your opportunity to significantly impact the decision-making process. It will go on without you. As schools reinvent themselves, there will be changes specific to your interests. Organizational research continually demonstrates that the more someone's performance depends on the behavior of others, the more important it is for that individual to be involved and to be able to influence those others. It is possible to integrate politics and principles, but in a changing environment, it can be very difficult to sustain principles without politics.

A Conceptual Summary

There are three reasons why a school librarian should think about building a stronger potential for influencing what goes on at work:

1. It is psychologically healthy. The ability to influence our own destiny is a human need at work as well as in the larger realms of life.

2. Schools are bureaucracies. Bureaucracies deliberately create interlocking dependencies. Power and influence are mechanisms for reducing dependency and increasing personal control.

3. Schools are changing and change involves the redistribution of power. Unless we take part in shaping the changes, our vulnerability is increased. Without the formal authority of high office, influence is the only available tool for improving our position.

References

1   M. Parks, "Interpersonal Communication and the Quest for Personal Competence." In M. Knapp and G. Miller (Eds.), *Handbook of Interpersonal Communication*, (Beverly Hills, CA: Sage Publishers, 1985).

  D. Kipnis, *The Powerholders*, (Chicago: University of Chicago Press, 1976).

2   A. J. Grimes, "Authority, Power, Influence, and Social Control: A Theoretical Synthesis," *Academy of Management Review*, vol. 3, no. 4 (October 1978), pp. 724–635.

  R. W. White, "Motivation Reconsidered: The Concept of Competence," *Psychological Review*, vol. 66, no. 5 (1959), pp. 297–333.

3   M. Weber, "Bureaucracy." In O. Grusky and G. A. Miller (Eds.), *The Sociology of Organizations: Basic Studies, Second Edition* (pp. 7–36) (New York: Free Press, 1981).

4   J. P. Kotter, "Power, Success, and Organizational Effectiveness," *Organizational Dynamics*, vol. 6, no. 3 (Winter 1978), pp. 27–40.

5   L. R. Sayles, *Leadership* (New York: McGraw-Hill, 1979), p. 96.

6   T. Donahoe, "Finding the Way: Structure, Time, and Culture in School Improvement," *Phi Delta Kappan*, vol. 75, no. 4 (December 1993), pp. 298–305.

7   S. P. Robbins, *Essentials of Organizational Behavior, Third Edition* (Englewood Cliffs, NJ: Prentice-Hall, 1992).

8   Some interesting conceptions of organizations as systems and entities can be found in works like Peter Senge's *The Fifth Discipline* (New York: Doubleday, 1990) and *Schools That Learn* (New York: Doubleday, 2000).

9   There are some interesting reflections on this in Karl Weick's idea of "loosely-coupled" schools. See "Educational Organizations as Loosely Coupled Systems," *Administrative Science Quarterly*, vol. 21, no. 1, pp. 1–19, and "Administering Education in Loosely Coupled Schools," *Phi Delta Kappan*, vol. 63, no. 10 (June 1982), pp. 673–676.

10 G. M. Bellman, *Getting Things Done When You're Not in Charge: How to Succeed From a Support Position* (San Francisco: Berrett-Koehler Publishers, 1992).

Chapter 2
Influence Has a Price

Please Answer These Questions Before Reading This Chapter

Before you read this chapter and begin to think about how important power and influence may be to you, please take a moment to complete this exercise. Your responses to these four questions will help to put what follows into perspective and help you to take the first steps toward developing an informed answer to the question of whether you understand what you're really getting into when you decide to work at becoming influential in your school.

Figure 2.1

1. How Do You Define "Political Behaviors at Work"?

> Please take a moment and write out your own definition of "political behaviors at work." Please don't consult a dictionary or ask anyone else's opinion. Just define the term as you understand it in a few sentences.
>
> _____
>
> _____
>
> _____
>
> _____
>
> _____
>
> _____
>
> _____

2. What Is Interpersonal Influence?

> Please take a moment and write out a definition of influence in your own words. Don't consult a dictionary or ask anyone else's opinion. Just define interpersonal influence as you understand it in a few sentences.
>
> _____
>
> _____
>
> _____
>
> _____

3. How Do People at Work Try to Influence You?

Please take a moment and write a short description of how someone at work tried to influence you to do something. Please consider only an influence attempt by another adult employed in your school. Please describe four things: (1) What the issue was; (2) What tactic(s) the person used in trying to influence your behavior; (3) How successful the person was in his or her attempt to influence you; and (4) How you felt about the influence attempt, both while it was going on and when it was over.

(1) _____

_____

(2) _____

_____

(3) _____

_____

(4) _____

_____

4. How Do You Try to Influence People at Work?

Please take a moment and write a short description of how you last tried to influence someone at work to do something. Please consider only an influence attempt you targeted at another adult employed in your school. Please describe four things: (1) What the issue was; (2) What tactic(s) you used in trying to influence their behavior; (3) How successful you were in your attempt to influence this person; and (4) How you felt about the influence attempt, both while it was going on and when it was over.

(1) _____

_____

(2) _____

_____

(3) _____

_____

(4) _____

_____

Please keep these answers in mind as you read the following chapter. We'll come back to them at the end.

The Realities of Building Your Influence

Becoming influential in your school may be difficult. It certainly will be hard work. Not only will you make increased physical investments of time and energy, you'll also make emotional and psychological investments as you reassess and redefine your role as a librarian, as an educator, and perhaps as a person. While the rewards of influence and power can be professionally and personally fulfilling, they come at a price. Only you can decide if it is within your ability and willingness to pay.

The Price of Power and Influence Is Political Behavior

"Information Power" does not directly translate to organizational or personal power. The skills and knowledge that make you a technically excellent librarian will not alone make you an influential one. Power and influence in professional settings derive from a different, and possibly unfamiliar, set of behaviors. These behaviors are political, in the best sense of the word, and not bibliotechnical.

Political behaviors are "those activities that are not required as part of one's formal role in the organization, but that influence, or attempt to influence, the distribution of advantages and disadvantages within the organization."[1] Political behaviors, then, occur outside any job description. They aim at influencing the goals, the operations, the evaluative criteria, and the decision-making processes across the organization, not just in the part where your job is found. In effect, political behaviors are what fill the blank spaces between the boxes on the organizational chart of your school.

Politics, goes the old saying, is the art of getting things done. Changing the system is more difficult if you don't understand how the system works. Effective political behavior, which is the vehicle of effective influence, is in part based on knowing with whom you must work and how you must work with them. As Geoffrey Bellman has observed, you can stay out of the politics of your organization, but you cannot stay *outside* of them. Whether you include yourself or not, others in the organization will include you, your resources, the value of your cooperation, and your capacity to resist in their political calculations and planning.[2]

Political behaviors are value-neutral. That is, they are tools, and may be used either to advance or retard change—and they can be used both ethically and unethically. For example, providing pertinent information to decision-makers is as much a political act as withholding it. Both are aimed at affecting the way a particular issue is decided. Likewise, it is no less a political act to build a good relationship with the media in order to improve public relations than it is to leak confidential information in order to harm someone. It is as much a political act to obstruct organizational policies as to openly work to change them, and it is as political to lobby for the promotion of certain people as it is to lobby against them.

The vast majority of political activities in any organization are legitimate. This is because most people are ethical and because the price of being caught in illegitimate activities can be so high. Still, the general connotation of politics is negative. Gantz and Murray's study of over 400 managers in different occupations illustrated this nicely.[3] More than 90% of their research subjects felt that politics are a part of their work experience, and almost 90% felt that successful executives had to be political. At the same time, almost 60% felt that organizations without politics would be happier places, more than half felt that politics were detrimental to organizational efficiency, and almost half said that top management tenets should try to rid their organizations of political behaviors. Their summary conclusion was that people are aware of political behaviors in their systems, seem to regard them as necessary, but simultaneously say they don't like them and don't want to engage in them.

Whether we like it or not, the reality is that organizations are political systems. Schools would be much better places if they could be counted on to be non-political and to be supportive, just, harmonious, and cooperative—but they are not. Adopting a non-political view of schools can lead people to believe that others will always act in the best interests of the institution, when the truth is that people frequently act in their own best interests. In contrast, a political view explains much of what seems to be the unfair, even irrational, behavior of the people with whom we work.

Many educators, however, are not comfortable with a political view of schools, and find it difficult to develop one. It means surrendering the idea that teachers, administrators, and parents are allies in some worthwhile enterprise that puts student interests before all others. In its place they have to adopt an idea that goals and decisions emerge from an ongoing process of negotiation and bargaining among the participants in the enterprise. It can be hard to do that, especially if you're an idealist, and it is important to know how you feel about doing it.

Look back now to the definitions of political behaviors and interpersonal influence you wrote before beginning this chapter. Was the definition you wrote of political behaviors value-neutral, or did the meaning you assigned the term also convey a positive or negative feeling? How did you define interpersonal influence? Did you regard it as a morally neutral process, or would your definition encourage or discourage the use of influence for some reason?

It is as important to understand how you feel about politics, influence, and power as it is to understand what they are. Carl Jung, the great psychologist, once observed that we cannot understand the world only through the intellect, and we shouldn't pretend that we can. We comprehend it just as much by feeling. Intellectual understanding is only half of the truth.[4] Building power and influence exacts a cost in time and behavior. If you pay those costs, you want to feel good about what you are getting in return.

The Cost of Building Influence

Almost everybody wants to be more influential at work. Having control to a greater or lesser extent is a human psychological need.[5] As with most things in life, however, there are costs in building and exercising power and influence. You need to ask yourself whether you are willing to trade your traditional position's security and familiar routines—but also its powerlessness—for the unfamiliar challenges, risks, and opportunities of a non-traditional position of influence. If you decide that you do want to make the trade, you'll immediately be faced with a series of operational tradeoffs. Exercising influence and power will put you in a better position to make an important difference in your school and to realize your personal goals, but it also will change your relationships with certain people, make you subject to closer scrutiny, and increase your responsibilities.

In deciding whether or not to pursue influence and power in your work environment, you need to consider the specific behavioral changes you'll have to make in your everyday activities. Influence is both built and exercised through continual interaction with others. People are more likely to come to you once you possess power and influence, but you most often have to go to them while you're building it. Having to go outside the library to engage people in different arenas is just the cost of doing business.

Going out of the library and into the school will give you a wider stage on which to perform. You can showcase your talents and advertise your resources. The price is that large parts of this stage, at least at first, will be unfamiliar territory. Meeting with people in their classrooms and offices instead of in yours will change the dynamics of certain encounters.

There will be new roles to learn as a participant on a committee, task force, planning team, advisory or public liaison group, or as a member of the department chairs' council or the principal's cabinet. Learning these new roles will increase your influence, but there is an effort cost involved. Sociological and organizational research has consistently demonstrated that learning new roles and how they fit into an unfamiliar work environment is one of the most difficult tasks employees face in changing the way they work.[6]

Through increased involvement with others, you will become more visible, and so attract more attention. The cost you'll have to accept is that some of it will be negative. Involvement means you will be able to play a greater role in shaping decisions that affect everyone in the school. You'll be able to make larger and more significant contributions than you could previously, but you also will experience more conflict than you have in the past. You'll continually have to deal with others who also care about the direction taken by the school, but whose perceptions and values differ from yours.

Finally, as your influence grows, so will your responsibility. When people recognize you as a leader, they'll look to you for leadership. Leadership is arduous, time consuming, and subject to criticism. It is immensely rewarding, but it also is immensely demanding.

Deciding Whether the Pursuit of Influence Is Worth the Price

Involvement at this level opens a new realm to you, but the thought of entering it may raise your anxiety. School librarians are not routinely trained in the skills required for success in political situations, and you may not be attracted by the idea of having to learn them. If you have these feelings, the first important thing you have to do is to acknowledge and confront them. One of the critical elements in building influence is certifying the will to do it.

In measuring your will, you have to consider at least two things: (1) whether or not you really believe in the new, fully involved school librarian role outlined in the literature and in the mission statements of your professional organizations, and (2) if this is something your personal make-up will allow you to do. You must examine your feelings about participating in organizational politics and decide whether you can feel comfortable doing so.

These are not easy questions, and there are no generally right answers. The right answers for one person may be completely different from the right answers for another. You have to decide what is right for you.

Causes of Discomfort

There are at least three reasons why undertaking a conscious attempt to build influence and power may be discomfiting to you and many other librarians. They have nothing to do with potential resources or opposition and everything to do with attitudes and feelings.

First, any systematic influence building attempt demands that you engage in political behaviors. You must surrender any lingering notion that your merit as a librarian alone will earn recognition and bring you influence. Gaining respect and recognition for quality library work requires you to do things that may have no direct link with library work.

Second, you have to face the fact, which emerging teacher leaders also must learn, that most school cultures don't support powerful people who emerge from the ranks but don't leave them for administration. You have to come to grips with the fact that, in many organizations, one person's gain in power means another person's loss. Attempts to gain and conserve power often create interpersonal conflicts and tensions. The idea of moving outside the relative harmony of the library to engage in such activities is not appealing to everyone, and may not be to you.

Third, and perhaps most important, you must deal with whatever ambivalence you may feel about the whole idea of power and influence. On the one hand, most people appreciate what power and influence can do for them, but, on the other, they have deep concerns about the ethics of power and influence and the damage they can cause. You have to decide what your feelings are.

All these concerns must be examined, wrestled with, and accepted or resolved before you can generate the commitment necessary for building influence. You will have to think them through more deeply than space will allow us to do here, and you will have to consider each in the context of your specific school and work situation. Nonetheless, the following overview of these concerns may help you in your deliberations.

The Idea that Merit Renders Political Behavior Unnecessary

Because politics have such a negative image, many people prefer to believe that the recognition of merit inherently bestows a measure of influence on the meritorious. We all are attracted to the notion that something of quality will enjoy support just because it is so obviously right. Research and experience show this is a wonderfully attractive, but fundamentally flawed idea.

People who believe they do a good job, especially if there are no problems in their areas of responsibility, often tend to think that the boss is aware of what they do. This may not at all be the case. The absence of problems allows supervisors, if they want, to ignore particular programs and people. It is not that they deliberately don't pay attention; it is that their attention is taken up by other things—problems or opportunities that require recognition because someone deliberately or unwittingly has put them before the supervisor and kept them there. You can think of it as the adult version of the teacher who concentrates on academically or behaviorally substandard students and ignores the "good kids" in a class.

Even the principal's awareness of a particular program or person is not sufficient. In order for simple existence to be enough to garner support, there has to be near perfect alignment of how the boss and subordinate see the subordinate's tasks, the importance level of those tasks, and the measures of quality. There are few situations like that in reality.[7]

It is a basic organizational error to think that merit alone will supply either power or influence. A high quality media center operation that is smooth, efficient, responsive, and up to date certainly is necessary if you want to be influential. People are attracted to competence, but competence and quality are not sufficient by themselves. If they were, many more librarians would exercise much more power and influence in their schools than they do presently.

Merit can serve as one part of a foundation upon which power and influence may be built, but it cannot deliver them by itself. The reason for this is painfully simple: despite the way the concepts are commonly expressed in the English language, power and influence are not actually possessed by anyone; rather, they are created, granted, and endorsed through the perceptions of others. You have power and influence only so long as others believe that they should accommodate your requests, work cooperatively with you, and seek your involvement, favor, and support.[8] They perceive it in their own best interests to do so because you either have or control access to something they need, whether it be money, material resources, knowledge, information, skill, or other people.

You have power and influence to the extent that others believe that you can help to make them, or something they value, successful. You may have the most wonderful library media center in the country, but if people do not perceive it as integral to their own and the school's success, you won't have a great deal of influence with them. Research shows that most students, teachers, and administrators don't usually perceive libraries and librarians this way.[9] Since the critical task in building influence rests in building perceptions of indispensability, your goal has to be to change others' perceptions of you and your program.

It takes work to change people's perceptions; not just more work, but work that is qualitatively different from that required to create and operate a technically sound media center. You cannot build an image of indispensability by increasing the library's collection, streamlining purchasing, making cataloging more precise, or improving inventory systems. It cannot be done by having more colorful displays, running noontime film programs, or attracting students to the library with games and prizes. It can't even be done by getting more teachers to bring their classes to the library or by raising circulation figures. These things help, certainly, but they are only tactics in a larger strategy.

Power and influence are created through focused engagement in activities specifically designed to positively alter how the people who matter in the school perceive you and your library. These activities are not a part of your job description; they are political behaviors. The influential librarian has to be as continually involved in interpersonal and political activities as in technical.

Non-Supportive School Cultures: Norms, Power, and Conflict

The second basic fact to be dealt with is that to be influential you have to challenge the traditional school culture, and that your efforts will to some extent be resisted.

The primary organizational unit in most schools tends to be the isolated activity staffed with one adult and a given number of students.[10] Look around your school. The most common organizational configuration you'll see is one adult in one room with one group of students for one period of time. The period of time may differ from elementary school to secondary school, but the basic model doesn't. Even some of the things we tout as innovations or refinements, such as block scheduling or smaller class sizes, only tinker with one of the paradigm's elements. They don't change the basic model. The classroom, of course, is the most common example, but the single library and librarian also fit the model, as does the individual counselor and the individual activities-director working alone in an office.

Spending the day with students and having much less adult interaction than do people in most other lines of work, teachers and other faculty usually have had little experience in leading other adults. Consequently, they rarely think of themselves as leaders, and even less often think of each other as leaders. They are not particularly open to suggestion, let alone direction, from their peers.

Teaching has an egalitarian culture.[11] With very few exceptions, there are no formal ranks among teachers. Promotion is possible only by leaving teaching. In most schools, a 65-year-old teacher with 40 years experience performs the same duties as a first-year 23-year-old fresh from the university. Salary schedules are built on a blend of educational level and years of experience. They do not differentiate on the basis of subject taught, students taught, or the quality of performance.[12]

As a result, in most schools, the ideal colleague is the person willing to offer help, but not to give direction. Unlike in medicine, law, architecture, or other professions where it is routine to seek second opinions, employ specialists, or work from a team concept, to admit a need for help on a problem in teaching is to admit a personal weakness or incompetence.[13] The norm in education prohibits teachers from criticizing each other and from telling or showing each other how to better do things. As one researcher has pointed out, the only really acceptable way one teacher has to tell another to do something differently is to pass along the non-threatening information that alternative methods exist and are being used in other schools—preferably at a considerable distance.[14]

To emerge as a leader is to challenge these behavior patterns. Recognizing faculty members as leaders introduces the notion of status differences based on knowledge, skill, and initiative—not just on organizational position. The status differences are not formalized by any change in the organizational chart, but they are real just the same.

Status differentiations most often are unwelcome in cultures structured to suppress them.[15] The involved school librarian described in *Information Power* by definition violates the egalitarian norms. The information specialist, teacher, and instructional partner roles require librarians to attack teacher isolation through partnerships, collaborative programs, and instructional consultation. Librarians are asked to provide leadership instead of just support by not only teaching students but by teaching teachers.

It is patent foolishness to believe that the school librarians of the world want to take over and control what goes on in classrooms. Nonetheless, there are faculty members who will perceive your entry into curriculum and instruction discussions and into planning sessions as just that. They'll regard such activities as academic incursions and interpret them as encroachments on their autonomy by an arrogant peer.

Classroom isolation provides teachers with a great deal of autonomy in the completion of their work. They decide the nature and the flow of events in their classrooms.[16]

The thought of having to negotiate and share this control threatens their autonomy, and they resist.

Librarians actively seeking to influence curriculum and instruction will sooner or later, and more than once, hear "Just who do you think you are?" If it isn't said directly, it will be translated into "Who does she think she is?" and said in the cafeteria, in the parking lot, or in a tavern or home after school some Friday evening.

The administration may even initially react that way too. Except in schools practicing or moving toward site-based management, most schools still hold a zero-sum view of power and influence. The zero-sum view contends that there is a fixed amount of power and influence in any organization; it cannot be expanded. To add to one person's power is to subtract from another's. Principals steeped in this view may not be very open to the emergence of faculty members as decision-makers.

It is probably impossible to avoid these kinds of situations. Someone always benefits from the status quo, and threats to it, even when they are perceived rather than real, will generate resistance. When and where the resistance will come from and exactly what shape it will take is not always predictable. Resistance can be open or hidden, immediate or deferred. Emotions related to change can build up in people and then explode in situations that seem totally unrelated and out of proportion to current conditions.[17]

Research offers reasons why you might find people challenging the role you're building for yourself.[18] First, people shape their worlds through their perceptions. Once they have created their own version of the universe, they resist changing it. They selectively process information in order to defend their established perceptions. They see and hear what they want and ignore or discount information that runs counter to their beliefs.[19] Activities that challenge the norms of school culture, and continually argue that there are better ways of doing what has traditionally been done only one way, will very likely meet with resistance.

Second, human beings are creatures of habit.[20] Once people develop an individualistic teaching style, a particular way of dealing with students and other faculty members, and a certain role and status in the school, they may find it very difficult to seriously consider other ways to approach their work lives. Change requires that long practiced habits be abandoned and new behaviors and relationships be established. This is always uncomfortable and sometimes very difficult to sustain. These activities move people out of certain, known, and familiar work patterns into ones that are not.[21]

This is why change most often is perceived as a kind of loss, and our reactions to it are not unlike our reactions to other kinds of loss. Much of the meaningfulness of life depends on predictability.[22] The discrediting of familiar assumptions and habits shatters our ability to predict how events will play out. This is painful, and we resist it.[23]

Third, people resist change for what they perceive as security reasons.[24] Changes in the ways jobs are performed and evaluations are conducted threaten feelings of safety. Moving into untried behaviors and unknown relationships entails a risk of failing. We often are concerned that we don't have the skills to succeed in the new environment and fear that we might not be able to acquire them. This can create high anxiety in teachers who are used to working alone and for whom individual competence is the measure of their worth.

These fears can be well grounded. Every change poses a challenge to our competency, and virtually everyone experiences what Michael Fullan calls the "implementation dip," that period when our efficiency and effectiveness are reduced as we learn the ins, outs, and nuances of the process, structure, or environment.[25] It's not uncommon for people to feel as if they will never be able to master the new situation in which they find themselves and the demands it places upon them.

Lastly, people often resist changing how they work because of who else is involved. There are two reasons why this is a particularly important point for you to consider. First, teachers don't think of librarians as one of their own.[26] The traditional librarian's role and function have been so different from that of the classroom teacher that a sense of shared experience and understanding is rare. The thought of taking any kind of instructional direction from a librarian can be unacceptable to many teachers.

Second, as Shakespeare tells us, what's past is prologue. All the past experiences others have had with school librarians have to be taken into account. Their tendency to resist involvement with you might be increased if faculty members endured conflict, miscommunication, or other negative experiences with your predecessor, or with librarians in other schools, or even with librarians while they were students.

Last, some teachers may be concerned that participating in a changed relationship with *you* may affect how other staff members will view them and what it may do to *their own* perceived status. How we are perceived is important to all of us. One of the fundamental characteristics of a good work place is having the respect of those with whom you labor.[27]

Taken together, school culture and human nature predict that you'll inevitably encounter resistance if you set out to build influence in your school. How much resistance you are willing to confront, over how much resistance you think you can prevail, and what support you can expect from others are all things you need to consider in your planning.

Ambivalence About Seeking Power and Influence

Before you can successfully commit to a conscious effort to become influential, you must deal with any ambivalence you may have about the nature of power and influence and the ethics of seeking them. Ambivalent feelings about overtly seeking power and influence are common. We understand the value of power and influence, but, at the same time, some of us cannot help but sense them as somehow corrupt and corrupting. Jeffrey Pfeffer of Stanford University points out two reasons why people are so wary of power and influence.[28]

First, he says, is the general association of power and influence with unsavory, even evil, events in history and modern society. Power and influence are used just as readily for evil ends as for good, and the former seems so much more visible than the latter. As a result, we have come to think of power and influence as tied to corruption.

This association of power with evil is unfortunate because a close examination reveals that influence and power are every bit as closely tied to positive events. The progress and accomplishments of the last century in environmental, racial, and gender issues, for example, are directly attributable to the exercise of power and influence by people of good will and strong conviction.

Pfeffer concedes that there is no doubt that power and influence can be acquired and used in the pursuit of evil ends. The problem, however, is with the user, not with the power. Armies carried the cancer of Nazism across Europe; other armies destroyed it. People die in automobile accidents every day, machinery of almost every kind can be dangerous, and drugs created as medicines can be addictive or deadly when wrongly used, but we will not forego any of their benefits because of their dangers. Instead, we develop training programs so that people may recognize the dangers, channel the power of these items toward productive ends, and protect themselves from harm. We need to do the same in thinking about organizational power and influence.

The second reason we are wary of power and influence, Pfeffer argues, is that we are conditioned in school to think of life as a matter of individual effort. Our schools teach us that we are each exclusively engaged in our own efforts to master certain knowledge and skills. What and how well those around us do should not affect our performance. In fact, to involve ourselves in what peers are doing is likely to be regarded as cheating. We should challenge the material to be learned on our own.

The problem is that this is not the way it is in real life, and certainly not the way it is in the work place. Individual success in job situations most often results from working with and through other people, and the success of the whole organization often depends on how well the activities of all its individuals are coordinated. In an athletic metaphor, Pfeffer argues that work activities in most organizations resemble football more than golf. You can't play football by yourself.

If we all could agree on which goals to pursue, on the best method for accomplishing those goals, and on the best way of measuring success, there would be no need for influence. Since that is not our situation, we depend upon persuading others that the course we have chosen is appropriate. Then we work to get others to commit to it with us. This is the exercise of power and influence. To be successful individually, and in turn to make our schools successful, people with important knowledge and good ideas must be successful in exercising power and influence.

Conclusion

While most everyone wants to feel a measure of control in their own professional lives, and most want to have an influence on the way things operate where they work, these things are more important to some people than they are to others. How important they are to you is a significant factor in deciding how hard to pursue them.

It takes energy, ability, commitment, and time to build influence and power in a school when you are not at the top of the hierarchy. Power and influence come at the price of organizational engagement and political behavior, things about which many people are ambivalent. You have to decide how comfortable a new role will be for you and how able and willing you are to pay its costs.

It is difficult to measure desire and commitment when they haven't been tested in the reality of the work place, but you can get some glimpse of how you feel by setting aside time for reflection and by asking yourself to examine how you really feel about power and influence.

You can begin by taking a moment to review the two descriptions of influence episodes you wrote at the beginning of the chapter. Run a short content analysis and try to identify any attitudes or value judgments imbedded in those descriptions. Look particularly at the last part of each.

How did you feel during and after each influence attempt? Did you feel resentful, angry, frustrated, or irritated by the other person's attempts to influence you? Did you feel manipulated? Or were you open and accepting, fully aware of what he or she was trying to do?

How did you feel about your own attempt at work place influence? Did you feel comfortable doing it? Were you confident? Were you frustrated by the other person's responses? Were you successful in getting what you wanted?

A second way to get a glimpse of how you think and feel about influence, power, and conflict is to take some of the attitude inventories available in the literature or from research companies. None of them will define your nature. No instrument will do that. However, they will give you some hints about how you see situations, and they help to surface some of your feelings about interactions with others.

If you're in a high school, it's probable that you already have a variety of attitude inventories in the books making up part of the psychology or business sections of your library's collection, especially if you're in a school where psychology is taught or there is a management emphasis in the business education department. Additionally, or if you're in an elementary school or middle school, you might find that one of the counselors in your school, or someone in your district office, perhaps in personnel or psychological services, already has copies of some of the respected inventories. If they're not available, you can order them through your library budget or borrow them from high school or public library through interlibrary loan. And, of course, there's always your local college or university library.

How well you relate to power and influence, both as a target and as a practitioner, is an important consideration in your decision of whether or not to pursue them. Before passing on to the sections that follow, you might profit from taking the results of these inventories, or of similar inventories of your choice, and seeing if any particular characteristics consistently appear throughout.

With that information in hand, complete the last, and maybe most important, exercise of this chapter. If you like your answers, then go on to the following chapters. If you don't like your answers, you may want to stop and seriously rethink whether consciously attempting to increase your workplace influence is the right thing for you to do right now.

A Conceptual Summary

Building influence has a price. It requires you to invest time and energy, to reassess what you do and why you do it, and to take on new behaviors and responsibilities. For some people, these are uncomfortable. You have to decide for yourself whether you are willing to make the investment.

There are three reasons why some school librarians may feel uncomfortable in their decision to attempt influence building. These are:

1. Influence building requires you to engage in political behaviors.
2. Most school cultures are not particularly supportive of powerful people who emerge from the ranks but don't enter administration.
3. We have largely been taught that power and influence are associated with corruption, and the pursuit of them generally carries a negative connotation.

Before you can make a firm commitment to an effort to increase your influence at work, you need to resolve your feelings about these issues.

Figure 2.2: Ask yourself why you think you might want to be more influential at work by answering these questions.

If you had more power and influence, how would things be different?

_____

_____

_____

_____

_____

_____

What would you want to accomplish?

_____

_____

_____

_____

_____

_____

What could you do that you cannot do now with the relationships and resources you have?

_____

_____

_____

_____

_____

_____

References

1   S. P. Robbins, *Essentials of Organizational Behavior*, Sixth Edition (Upper Saddle River, NJ: Prentice-Hall, 1992), pp. 161–165.

2   G. M. Bellman, *Getting Things Done When You Are Not In Charge: How to Succeed from a Support Position* (San Francisco: Berrett-Koehler Publishers, 1992).

3   J. Gantz and V. V. Murray, "The Experience of Workplace Politics," *Academy of Management Journal*, vol. 23, no. 2 (1980), pp. 237–251.

4   C. G. Jung, *Psychological Types* (New York: Harcourt Brace, 1923).

5   David McClelland did some interesting work in this area in the 1970s and '80s, and some of his ideas have emerged again in Daniel Goleman's work. See, for example, McClelland's *Human Motivation* (Glenview, IL: Scott, Foresman, 1985) and Goleman's *Working With Emotional Intelligence* (New York: Bantam, 1998).

6   D. C. Feldman, "A Practical Program for Employee Socialization," *Organizational Dynamics*, vol. 5, no. 2 (Autumn 1976), pp. 64–80.

    D. C. Feldman, "The Multiple Socialization of Organization Members," *Academy of Management Review*, vol. 6, no. 2, pp. 309–318.

    D. C. Feldman and H. J. Arnold, *Managing Individual and Group Behavior in Organizations* (New York: McGraw-Hill Book Company, 1983).

    M. R. Louis, "Career Transitions: Varieties and Commonalities," *Academy of Management Review*, vol. 5, no. 3 (1980), pp. 329–340.

    N. Nicholson, "A Theory of Work Role Transitions," *Administrative Science Quarterly*, vol. 29, no. 2 (1984), pp. 172–191.

7   J. P. Kotter, *Power and Influence* (New York: Free Press, 1985).

8   R. B. Cialdini, *Influence: Science and Practice*, Third Edition (Glenview, IL: Scott Foresman, 1993).

    J. R. P. French, Jr., and B. Raven, "The Bases of Social Power." In D. Cartwright (Ed.), *Studies in Social Power* (pp. 150–167) (Ann Arbor, MI: University of Michigan Institute for Social Research, 1959).

9   N. E. Gast, *The Role of the High School Librarian as Perceived by High School Librarians, Principals, and Teachers in the State of Oregon* (Doctoral Dissertation, Portland State University, 1984).

    W. A. Scott, *A Comparison of Role Perceptions of the School Library Media Educators, School Librarians, Principals, and Classroom Teachers* (Doctoral Dissertation, Vanderbilt University, 1987).

10 J. B. Davis, "Teacher Isolation: Breaking Through," *High School Journal*, vol. 70, no. 2 (1987), pp. 72-75.

    A. Lieberman, "Why We Must End Our Isolation," *American Teacher*, vol. 70, no. 1 (1985), pp. 9–10.

    Although the conditions of isolation and departmental organization are being challenged in middle schools across the country, the bulk of junior high schools and certainly the overwhelming majority of high schools suffer from this organizational structure. For a better understanding of the impact of organizational structure on secondary schools, see works such as E.L. Boyer. *High School: A Report on Secondary Education in America* (New York: Harper and Row, 1983); L. S. Shulman. "Teaching Alone, Learning Together: Needed Agendas and the New Reforms," in T. J. Sergiovanni and J. H. Moore (Eds.), *Schooling for Tomorrow: Directing Reforms to Issues That Count* (pp. 156–187) (Boston: Allyn and Bacon, 1989); and M. C. Wittrock (Ed.), *Handbook of Research on Teaching*, *Third Edition* (New York: MacMillan, 1986).

11 V. Troen and K. Boles, "Teacher Leadership: How To Make it More Than a Catch Phrase," *Education Week*, vol. 13, no. 9, November 3, 1999, pp. 27, 29.

12 P. R. Burden, "Career Ladders: Retaining Academically Talented Teachers." In H. C. Johnson (Ed.), *Merit, Money, and Teachers' Careers* (pp. 197–207) (New York: University Press of America, 1985).

S. L. Jacobson, "The Distribution of Salary Increments and Its Effect on Teacher Retention," *Educational Administration Quarterly*, vol. 24, no. 1 (1988), pp. 178-199.

R. J. Murnane, "Understanding Teacher Attrition." *In Teaching in the Eighties: A Need to Change* (pp. 29–34) (Cambridge, MA: Harvard Educational Review, 1987).

D. Stern, "Compensation for Teachers." In E. Z. Rothkopf (Ed.), *Review of Research in Education, Vol 13* (Washington, D.C.: American Educational Research Association, 1986).

13 D. Lortie, Schoolteacher: *A Sociological Study* (Chicago: University of Chicago Press, 1975).

G. McPherson, *Small Town Teacher* (Cambridge, MA: Harvard University Press, 1972).

S. B. Sarason, *The Culture of the School and the Problem of Change, Second Edition* (Boston: Allyn and Bacon, 1982.)

C. B. Silver, *Black Teachers in Urban Schools* (New York: Praeger, 1973).

14 J. Newberry, *The First Year of Experience: Influences on Beginning Teachers.* Paper presented at the annual meeting of the American Educational Research Association, New York, April 1977. ERIC Document number ED 137 299.

15 V. Troen and K. Boles, "Teacher Leadership: How To Make it More Than a Catch Phrase," *Education Week*, vol. 13, no. 9 (November 3, 1993), pp. 27, 29.

16 P. W. Jackson, *Life in Classrooms* (New York: Holt, Rinehart, and Winston, 1968).

17 J. P. Folger, M. S. Poole, and R. K. Stutman, *Working Through Conflict* (New York: Longman, 1997).

18 H. Margolis and J. McGettigan, "Managing Resistance to Instructional Modifications in Mainstreamed Environments," *Remedial and Special Education,* vol. 9, no. 4 (1988), pp. 15–21.

W. C. Piersal and T. B. Gutkin, "Resistance to School-Based Consultation: A Behavioral Analysis of the Problem," *Psychology in the Schools*, vol. 20, no. 3 (1983), pp. 311–320.

S. P. Robbins, *Essentials of Organizational Behavior, Sixth Edition* (Upper Saddle Creek, NJ: Prentice-Hall, 2000).

R. F. Waugh and K. F. Punch, "Teacher Receptivity to Systemwide Change in the Implementation Stage," *Review of Educational Research*, vol. 57, no. 3 (1987), pp. 237–254.

E. Aronson, *The Social Animal, Third Edition* (San Francisco: W. H. Freeman and Company, 1980).

19 S. P. Robbins, *Essentials of Organizational Behavior, Sixth Edition* (Upper Saddle Creek, NJ: Prentice-Hall, 2000).

21 D. Yankelovich and J. Immerwhar, *Putting the Work Ethic to Work* (New York: Public Agenda Foundation, 1983).

22 P. Marris, *Loss and Change* (London: Routledge and Kegan Paul, 1986).

23 R. Evans, *The Human Side of School Change: Reform, Resistance, and the Real-Life Problems of Innovation* (San Francisco: Jossey-Bass, 2001).

24 R. Evans, *The Human Side of School Change: Reform, Resistance, and the Real-Life Problems of Innovation* (San Francisco: Jossey-Bass, 2001).

S. P. Robbins, *Essentials of Organizational Behavior, Sixth Edition* (Upper Saddle Creek, NJ: Prentice-Hall, 2000).

25 M. Fullan with S. Stiegelbauer, *The New Meaning of Educational Change* (New York: Teachers College Press, 1991).

26 W. C. Buchanan, "The Principal and Role Expectations of the School Library Media Specialist," *The Clearing House*, vol. 55, no. 6 (February, 1982), pp. 253–255.

F. C. Pfister, "Library Media Specialists: What Role Should They Play?" In D. Loertscher (Ed.), *School Library Media Centers: Research Studies and the State-of-the-Art* (pp. 31–40) (Syracuse, NY: ERIC Clearinghouse on Information Resources, 1980).

27 J. Van Maanen, "Experiencing Organizations: Notes on the Meaning of Careers and Socialization." In J. Van Maanen, (ed.), *Organizational Careers: Some New Perspectives* (pp. 15–45) (London: Wiley, 1977).

28 J. Pfeffer, *Managing With Power* (Boston: Harvard Business School Press, 1992).

Chapter 3
The Attributes of Influential Colleagues

Ever wonder why some people just seem to have more influence at work than others do? Some of their influence is derived from calculated behavior, but more of it flows from how others perceive them as persons and as professionals. Before you begin this chapter, stop for a moment and think about people who have or have had influence with you at work and ask yourself what characteristics they share.

Don't think about authority; think about influence. Some people can affect your behavior because they have the authority to direct your activities or to evaluate you or to reward you or punish you. Don't think about them. Think about people you listen to because there is something in or about them that appeals to you. These people may have authority, but their authority isn't what draws you to them.

Pick three of these people and ask yourself, "What is it about these people that makes me listen to them?" Try to put those attributes into words. Can you name five characteristics about each that together explain that person's ability to have influence with you? Take just a few seconds and try to complete the sentences in Figure 3.1 about each one:

Figure 3.1 Charactericstics of Three People Who Influence Me

Person #1:

Person #1 is _____

Person #1 is _____

Person #1 is _____

Person #1 is _____

Person #1 is _____

Person #2:

Person #2 is _____

Person #2 is _____

Person #2 is _____

Person #2 is _____

Person #2 is _____

Person #3:

Person #3 is _____

Person #3 is _____

Person #3 is _____

Person #3 is _____

Person #3 is _____

Go back now and look over what you wrote for each of these three people. As you review your lists, the odds are that you will discover that the people who influence you share one or more attributes in common—and, most likely, not all of what attracts you to them was necessarily a gift of nature.

If you're like most people, you've listed characteristics that say these individuals are likeable, good at what they do, have integrity, are committed and energetic, and are sensitive to the context of others' lives, especially—in this case—yours. Some of these traits are a result of heredity, but others are not.

Research shows that we all exhibit three basic types of attributes, and all are integral to making us what we are. Some we are born with, others develop according to our life histories, and some we deliberately create. In short, personal attributes, positive and negative, derive from three sources: genetics, experience, and will. It's important to understand this if you want to expand your influence at work. Influential attributes are made as well as born, and you can add to yours if you wish.

Attributes shaped by genetics, of course, are basically unchangeable. Raw intellect is an example. Physical attractiveness is another. Other attributes, however, are subject to modification. Our personal levels of generosity, patience, and commitment, along with our attitudes, values, and work ethics, develop over time and—under certain circumstances—can be reshaped. These attributes largely evolve from the experiences and training we receive while growing up. Unlike physical attributes, these can be adjusted or even completely changed through persuasion, choice, and effort. Sometimes a watershed event will effect a change, sort of like Ebeneezer Scrooge's experience in *A Christmas Carol*.

More under our control are those attributes we can will into existence. Expertise is a good example. We can deliberately set out to become an expert at something, a common desire among school people who so value education.

In summary, two things are apparent. First, depending on whether the beholder perceives them as positive or negative, personal attributes either draw others to us or cause them to keep a distance. The relationships others are willing to establish with us are based in what they think we're like, what they sense we are able to give, and what they calculate we need from them. Just as a mix of personal attributes activates the chemistry we have with friends and lovers, attributes also play major roles in the development and dynamics of work place relationships and influence.

Second, some of our attributes are within our ability to develop and improve. As the positive force of our personal attributes increases, so does our potential for influencing others.

The Attributes of Influential People

Being perceived as possessing positive personal attributes increases the odds that others will listen to us and comply with our wishes. This, in turn, allows us to capitalize on opportunities to make a difference in our work environments.

Because every work setting and work group is unique, the most important attributes in one situation may not be the most important in another. Still, research has identified at least five that appear consistently important in virtually every kind of organization. These clearly have implications for school librarians. These are likability, expertise, integrity, committed energy, and sensitivity to the context of others' lives:

Likability

Why likable people have such power over us is sometimes difficult to explain. We like to think that we base our decisions on rational judgments, especially on the job. Research shows, however, that our reactions to other people often are influenced by elements largely separate from the merits of their work performance. The simple fact is that we are given to saying "yes" to people we know and enjoy. For some reason, we regard them as more honest, trustworthy, talented, and dependable than others. As a result, just as in our private lives, we are more likely to be persuaded by them and to consent to their requests.

Social psychologists define this attribute as "Likability," a composite term describing several attributes that, taken together, create a personal attractiveness powerful enough to influence our perceptions.[1] These attributes are logically linked and recognizable to all of us. We are drawn to people we find to be:

- Physically attractive

- Similar to ourselves

- Complimentary to us

- Familiar to us

- Associated with positive memories

No one necessarily needs to exhibit all these characteristics to be likable, but the more they exhibit, the greater the odds that we will like them.

Physically Attractive

The Concept

Psychological research shows that most of us unconsciously tend to link physical attractiveness with attractive personality characteristics.[2] Even without specific demonstrations of their talents or strengths, we're prone to give people we regard as physically attractive credit for being successful, in control of situations, and able to combat negative environmental forces.[3]

The research literature is filled with evidence that physically attractive individuals receive more attention and opportunities than do the less attractive. They're more likely to get hired, be credited with higher performance evaluations for the same work, receive higher salaries, marry more often above their social class, get elected to organizational offices more readily, and suffer lighter punishments for transgressions.[4] From an influence perspective, this is important because the evidence shows that they're also more likely to secure help when they need it and are more persuasive in changing the opinions of others.[5] Just like everywhere else, research evidence shows that this dynamic is at work in schools for both adults and students.[6]

Researchers debate why physical attractiveness has such an effect. One plausible explanation is that physical attractiveness is linked to self-esteem, and self-esteem to confidence. Attractive people may be more likely to feel good about themselves and to have more self-confidence than less attractive people, especially if their looks have contributed to a track record of successes.[7] Self-confidence is an attractive feature in its own right.

Implications for Librarians

The power of physical attractiveness says two things to school librarians. The first and overwhelmingly obvious, of course, is to maximize your personal appearance.

The second is to be aware of the impact others' personal appearance may have on your reactions to whatever they may propose. It is fair to ask yourself a question whenever you are attracted to a particular idea or proposal: "To what extent am I actually drawn to the idea itself and to what extent to the person who proposed it?" Reviewing proposals in writing, where they can be separated from the person advancing them, always helps you to remain objective.

This defense has greater application than just against the influence of personal appearance. When all the elements of likability combine, their power is multiplied. It is a good idea when approached by someone who wants something from you, especially someone you really don't know very well, to stop and assess your feelings for him or her. If you find that you like this person more than you would expect to under the circumstances, it might be a good idea to step back for a moment. As Robert Cialdini, who has made a career of researching influence, advises, "separate the requester from the request."[8] You do this intuitively when you are approached by salespeople. Consider doing it with your co-workers.

Similar to Us

The Concept

How much we tend to like someone also is influenced by the extent to which we perceive that person to be similar to ourselves.[9] Sociologist Elliot Aronson offers three reasons why we have this reaction.[10] First, we like people who are similar to us because we expect that they will like us. You might remember being told when you got your first job that you were going to have to work with people you didn't like. What you probably weren't told, however, and had to learn the hard way, was that the most difficult person to work with is someone you think doesn't like you. Similarities raise the odds that any two people will like each other.

Second, people who share our opinions and interests provide us with a sort of social validation. They support our notions that our beliefs are correct. People who disagree with us or don't value the same things can evoke fear that we may be wrong. It's not a comfortable feeling.

Third, Aronson contends, it is human nature to make negative inferences about the character of people who disagree with us on important issues. He argues that we tend to feel that if we disagree on anything fundamental, it becomes more likely that we will disagree on other issues. The effect can establish a self-fulfilling prophesy. You can see evidence of this in your private life. How many really close relationships do you have with people who have views fundamentally and passionately different from yours on issues like abortion, capital punishment, race relations, or gun control? The same dynamic operates in the workplace. It is very difficult to establish a close professional relationship with someone who has fundamentally different views of schools and schooling, students, teachers, and administrators.

Part of the reason similarity increases our attraction to others is that it makes social interaction easier.[11] The experience is reinforcing because we like to be around people with whom we can be comfortable.

Many people recognize the power of similarity and set out to deliberately construct linkages with others. Interpersonal similarity connections can be drawn from age, gender, race, religion, politics, dress, social status, hierarchical position, or recreational interests.[12] Similarities can be real or they can be created. It is no accident, argues Stanford University's Jeff Pfeffer, that bank staff members in Silicon Valley tend to be younger than the banking staffs in other areas; their clientele is younger.[13] Cialdini cites studies showing that people are more likely to loan money to, sign petitions for, or help others who are dressed like they are. Salespeople are trained to look for ways to build similarity links with their customers by seeking information about jobs, cities of origin, recreational interests, and children. Many sales training programs teach personnel to match the customer's body language, verbal style, and mood.

The similarity principle is recognized in education. It's part of the thinking behind concerns that the proportion of minority teachers is declining as the proportion of minority students increases. There are staff development programs for administrators that encourage them to build personal and professional similarity, shared goals, and congruent value perceptions when they conduct teacher evaluation conferences or deal with irate or troubled parents.

Implications for Librarians

You can build a sense of similarity among teachers and administrators by stressing the characteristics you share with them. Conversations about common educational backgrounds, visible regard for quality teaching, expressed concern with shared working conditions, demonstrated interest in the content of particular courses, and social and recreational interactions can all help forge connections with others on the staff. Teaching a class, team teaching, or being deeply involved in some other instructional activity can be particularly powerful in establishing linkages with teachers. The administrative functions you perform and the organizational boundary spanning you do to interact with parents, business community members, and the general public are fodder for establishing bonds with the administration.

The overall message is that teaching concerns, student needs, and other universally shared relationship elements should be the leading edge in interactions you have with non-librarians in the school. Talking about the library only reinforces perceptions of difference. Let talk of the library flow from and follow subjects that affect a broad spectrum of school people.

Complimentary

The Concept

We all relish recognition, and we're all vulnerable to attention, praise, and flattery, even when they are delivered indirectly. Attentiveness conveys the impression that our feelings are important enough to concern someone else. It is natural to like people who value us. This is particularly true when that someone holds rank above our own.[14]

Jeff Pfeffer offers an explanation of why praise and even clear flattery are so effective in causing us to like someone. We have, he says, a built-in motivational bias to accept praise and to believe that any compliment is sincere.[15] If we believe it is true, the praise makes us feel good about ourselves. If we believe the remark to be nothing more than an instrument to get us to do something, we begin to wonder what the other person thinks of us. Specifically, we wonder why he or she feels the need to flatter us and why someone should think that we would be taken in by it. This line of thinking doesn't promote positive thoughts about ourselves, so we generally choose to accept the compliment as sincere.

Moreover, rejecting a compliment raises questions about the whole workplace relationship. If we decide that the person giving us the compliment doesn't really understand the differences between good, mediocre, and poor performance, then we begin to wonder about his or her competence and expertise. If we are certain that the person does know the difference between good, mediocre, and poor in this instance, then we have to question his or her integrity. Compliment rejection creates discomfort on several levels.

The power of praise is such that it sometimes can render us almost helpless in resisting the influence of others.[16] Cialdini cites an illustration from research in which a group of men received comments about themselves from someone who wanted a favor from them. Some participants received only positive comments; some only negative; some a mixture. The person was most liked when delivering only praise, even though the participants knew that the flatterer wanted something. Most importantly, Cialdini reports, the compliments and praise did not have to be accurate to have effect. All they had to be was positive.

Implications for Librarians

As a school librarian, you interact with others all across the school organization. You are in an ideal position to discover quality performance and to deliver sincere compliments to members of the administrative, certificated, and classified staff. You can have access to information about curriculum and instruction, for example, in virtually every grade, program, discipline, and department in the school. You can directly compliment a teacher who has developed a particularly interesting project, taught an outstanding lesson, given intriguing assignments, or somehow supported the library's activities. You also can make complimentary contacts with people who been active in faculty affairs, community relations, or in any other way made a distinguishing contribution to the school.

Done a certain way, there also can be an additional influence building benefit in complimenting people who do good work across a wide spectrum. You can multiply the power of those compliments by sharing them with people in authority. For example, let's say that you see Mrs. Smith conduct a perfectly outstanding lesson. Instead of writing a note to Mrs. Smith praising the specifics of her performance, write the note to the principal and send a copy to Mrs. Smith. Mrs. Smith will be grateful, and you will have enhanced your relationship with her. The compliment will likely be repeated when Mrs. Smith next encounters the principal because both will know that Mrs. Smith is aware that the note was sent to the office. When the principal says, "I'm hearing good things about the work you're doing," the compliment has been doubled—and this time delivered by her supervisor. You can only benefit from this.

There is the possibility, however, of an even greater benefit to you over time. If you subtly repeat this behavior every three or four months over two or three years (don't flood your principal with these notes; he or she will get suspicious of your motives), you'll slowly bring your principal to realize that you understand and value education beyond the library and have an eye for quality work in curriculum and instruction. This increases your influence potential and may increase your opportunity to be involved in school-wide projects where you can showcase more of what you and your library have to offer.

Familiar to Us

The Concept

The fourth component of likability is simple familiarity. People are more inclined to like people with whom they are familiar.[17] Consequently, we're more likely to have influence with people we see regularly. Shared experience is the key to interpersonal connection. Research on cohesive groups supports this notion.[18] Groups become more cohesive when their members spend more time together, including time together away from the job. Shared goals or a common enemy help to bind people together, and shared successes tighten the links even more. This is one of the reasons, for example, that causes Cialdini to argue that instructional techniques like cooperative learning will probably do more to reduce racial tensions between students than simple school integration can ever hope to do.

Implications for Librarians

Familiarity is linked with visibility. School library media specialists are often isolated. To capitalize on the value of familiarity means that you have to be aggressive in establishing ongoing relationships with other staff members. Being a member of the principal's cabinet, a member or chair of a continuing committee, a teaching partner, or a regular fixture at the faculty lunch table will all contribute to increasing the level of familiarity you have in the school.

This is not as easy as it sounds. The keyword in all of this is *ongoing*. Building influence cannot be a one- or two- year project. It has to be a continuing project. Once people begin to look to you for certain things in your relationship, you cannot disappoint them. If you do, you'll rupture the relationship and end up with less influence than you would have had with them had you never tried to increase your familiarity or draw closer to them. There's abundant evidence of this in our private lives. Just think of your dating days. How many false starts and painful endings did you have in your relationships? More profoundly, look at most divorced couples. They're a lot farther apart than they were in the early days of their relationship. The same thing can happen in the workplace.

Associated with Positive Memories

The Concept

Lastly, psychological research shows that we interpret current situations through the screen of past experience.[19] We make sense of the world by forging links between the new things we experience and learn and the things we already know and feel. It is human nature to make associations. The irony is that we also make associations between things that are not necessarily related. A certain song or scent, for example, can bring back vivid memories of an especially good or bad experience, even though the song or scent really had nothing at all to do with the quality of that long ago moment. It was just there, part of the environment in which the experience unfolded.

If you want to test the power of something as simple as a song, just ask yourself why there are so many "oldies" music stations on the radio.

Research suggests that the same thing can happen with individual people. An innocent association with either good things or bad will affect how we feel about others.[20] We associate others with attitudes, emotions, and events.

Linkage with negative events and memories stirs dislike. Human beings simply dislike bad situations, being in them, and even hearing about them. In fact, we resist being told bad news at all and tend to dislike the people who deliver it to us—even when they didn't cause it.[21] Remember your reaction to your parents when they explained one of life's lessons to you, to teachers who gave you lower grades than you wanted, or to that librarian who told you that there was no way to get the book you really needed for your project? Or now, think about how you react to administrators who deny your budget requests?

At some level, we're probably all pretty much aware of the unpleasant associations that result from mixing good people and bad news. This might explain another characteristic most people share: we don't want to deliver bad news to others. We especially don't want to deliver it when we are visible to the recipient.[22] This is what motivates many organizations to send you a form letter telling you that you didn't get the job or the grant, or that you're going to be laid off, instead of phoning you or having someone tell you face-to-face.

On the other hand, people we like are often associated with pleasurable and positive events: promotions, births, weddings, athletic triumphs, dances, dates, any number of pleasures small and large. Even the simplest of things can have an effect. Eating, for example, is pleasurable. This explains why having lunch or going to dinner is so common in both social and work relationships. It also explains why there are fund-raising dinners. The association with good memories tends to cause people to like us more. This, in turn, makes it more likely they will comply with any request we may make.

Implications for Librarians

The implications of this are pretty straightforward: carve yourself a role in every positive event you can. Aside from spreading as much good news as possible and showing up at awards ceremonies, parties, weddings, and other social occasions, try to secure a place for yourself in enterprises that promise wide exposure *and* have a high probability for success.

Research demonstrates that people who share success in projects at work establish much closer bonds than people who share in failures. Failure causes people to question the wisdom of further association, and they don't want to be reminded of failures. It's easier to just avoid others who were involved. Success, on the other hand, provides a strong attraction. People like to revel in their accomplishments with others who helped to make the successes possible. This provides all the more reason for you to carve out significant roles for yourself in committee work, classroom instruction, and public relations.

There's also a lesson here that might make some people uncomfortable. All of this implies that you should be very selective in your initial attempts at collaboration with other faculty members. Try to work only with the brightest, most talented, positive, innovative, and resourceful teachers on your staff. There's a missionary impulse in many educators that needs to be controlled. Avoid the temptation to collaborate with mediocre or substandard colleagues. The odds go up that your project will fail or at least only be minimally successful. There are no secrets in schools over time, and the word will seep out that working with you didn't pay any dividends. Conversely, working with a high quality teacher increases the odds of project success and spreads the word that working with you is a good experience.

Taken together, physical attractiveness, similarity, compliments, familiarity, and association with positive memories are powerful forces in causing people to like us. To whatever extent you can develop and expand your likability, you raise the odds of being able to line up allies who will support you both within and outside the library.

Expertise

Expertise runs close to likability in promoting your workplace influence. Being regarded as an expert is a powerful source of influence, especially in organizations experiencing periods of uncertainty—and what school isn't?

The reason for this rests in the nature of workplace relationships. Workplace relationships are different from private social and love relationships. Sometimes it's easy to miss this relatively subtle fact because our working and our private relationships often look much alike at the surface. Beneath the surface, however, they differ profoundly.[23]

First, our social relationships exist because we want them to exist. Apart from certain family members, we pick and choose with whom we will associate. Work relationships, on the other hand, exist because the organization exists. The forces that bring us into relationships at work spring from the organization's goals, not from our own desires. Workplace relationships come into being in order that some task may be accomplished, and the organization decides with whom we will work and in what relative positions.

Because we're focused on a task to be accomplished, we tend to interpret individual attributes differently than we might in a purely social relationship. We perceive more value in work-related qualities and less in qualities that might be very important in a friendship or love affair. In fact, we're often willing to overlook individual traits that would flatly be undesirable — perhaps even unacceptable — in a purely personal relationship, so long as the other person delivers on a strong set of task-related attributes. Most of us can remember times when we've said to ourselves or to others something like, "Oh, yes, he's unpleasant and hard to get along with, but he really knows how to get things done." Our assessment of the other person's value in a workplace relationship is driven by our perceptions of his or her ability and commitment. Ultimately, these perceptions affect how much each of us is willing to invest in the relationship, how much trust develops between us and, ironically, over time, how much we may even come to like each other.[24]

Workplace expertise operates at two levels and is compelling at both. The first is the actual knowledge and skill level an individual may possess; the second is the extent to which someone is perceived as an expert. They may not be identical.

We are drawn to people who possess needed knowledge and skills. Despite the power of liking, and the aversive power of disliking, employees still sometimes request assignment with someone who has a reputation of being unlikable and hard to get along with just because of that person's acknowledged expertise.

The Concept

Most people abhor uncertainty and feel driven to reduce it.[25] An individual who controls unique information, particularly information that can clarify situations and help in making important decisions, has considerable influence. Highly technical environments where knowledge is routinely specialized into categories are also settings in which expertise offers opportunities for influence.

On the other hand, experts must guard against becoming too narrowly focused. A severely restricted expertise can be a problem in building wide spread influence in most organizations. It's sometimes easy to be compartmentalized if the expertise isn't viewed as having multiple connections to the mission of the enterprise.

Expertise can be a product of formal training or on-the-job experience, but its strongest forms are most often a result of the two. For expertise to remain an effective source of influence, its image has to be managed in the perceptions of others. People tend to judge expertise much more by behavior than by academic degrees, credentials, certificates, or years of experience.[26] An expert image is damaged by an inability to speak and write well, or to convince people that the knowledge possessed is widely applicable. An expert's resistance to change can cause others to develop the erroneous, but still compelling, impression that the master's knowledge and skills are dated. Together, these behaviors can reduce, or even destroy, the influence potential of expertise.

Generally, the value of expertise as an influence producer is linked to one or more of four conditions. First, how critical a particular expertise is to the solution of either an immediate problem or the accomplishment of a long-term goal. Second, what proportion of people in the organization has need for a particular expertise. Third, the visibility of the expertise, and, fourth, the extent to which the expertise resides in a single person or small group. If a given expert is the only source of the needed knowledge or skill, he or she becomes irreplaceable, and the potential for exercising influence is increased.[27]

Implications for Librarians

Right now, conditions in school favor your ability to capitalize on perceptions of your expertise. First, schools are in great flux, causing educators to deal with both immediate concerns and to rethink long-term plans. School violence, teacher shortages, multiplying mandates, changing demographics, expanding technology, changing curricular and instructional approaches, and shrinking budgets all generate both immediate and long-range information demands. Second, there is a growing trend toward data-driven and research-informed decision making in education. Third, things like high-stakes testing, standards proliferation, changing calendars and daily schedules, growing immigrant populations, and new teaching techniques are flooding school life. This means that most educators are—or soon will be—working in new environments, facing new challenges, and encountering new problems different from those they experienced in their own lives as either students or educators. Last, and very importantly, no other educators, including administrators, have access rivaling yours to research reports, theory, informed opinion, and model program descriptions. You can reach out to the whole round world for information in ways that no one else can.

This opportunity for building influence can be maximized by doing everything possible to further the development of these trends. It will require you to learn more about the specifics of particular disciplines, and certainly to keep on the cutting edge of developments in library media resources and techniques, but—if properly marketed with the faculty—the payoff can be substantial.

The concept of marketing raises a red flag, however. You can negatively shape others' perceptions of your expertise without ever realizing it. An example of this, I think, is using terms like "library media specialist," "information specialist," or "information manager" to describe yourself—and "information center" to describe the library.

Each of these metaphors is an excellent example of organizational researcher Gareth Morgan calls a metaphor's "one-sided insight."[28] Each does highlight a very important part of what your library is and of what you do in it, but each also obscures other very important aspects of what the library is and what the librarian does. The information center metaphor emphasizes collection over connection, evoking images of materials and retrieval processes — but not of learning. In that concentration, it neglects and obscures a great deal of what libraries are about today and defines the library as apart from the classroom rather than integral to it.

The manager metaphor suffers the same problem. "Information manager" bespeaks specialized knowledge and skill, even status, but it doesn't so much as whisper collaborator, teacher, consultant, or partner. It obscures those roles that really define quality library media performance and leadership. The greater parts of librarianship are beyond managing a collection and facilitating others' access to what it contains.

Metaphors may be figures of speech, but they have real consequences because they shape our perceptions, construct our sense of something. Faculty members perceiving you as the information manager in the information center may come looking for assistance in finding information—but they won't be predisposed to ask for help in defining their information needs, nor to look to you for advice or assistance in interpretation or application. The information center/information manager metaphors obscure those parts of your professional role. In a real sense, these metaphors— though perceived as improvements by many librarians—actually may serve to perpetuate the stereotype. They lay claim to a place in schools, but not in schooling. They invite people to say, "Help me find what I want and then check it out to me; I'll take it from there." And that does not communicate a comprehensive sense of your expertise.

Integrity

The Concept

Integrity's role in influence should take no explanation. However much I may like you or however much I am impressed with your expertise and competence, I won't be positively influenced by you if I don't feel that I can trust you. It's that simple.

Integrity is defined by most as truthfulness, honesty, and a consistency between word and deed[29]—and this includes not telling lies to yourself.[30] Integrity involves discerning your duties and obligations, mustering the courage to fulfill them, and being willing to acknowledge failure, tender apologies, and make amends.[31] You are a person of integrity if you are guided by commitments and ideals that pull together the diverse strands of your life and give it meaning. These guiding ideals grow out of family relationships and friendships, out of political, social, and religious commitments, and out of individual talents and skills.

Deciding that another person possesses integrity depends on your perception that his or her ethical views are fundamentally congruent with yours. To be perceived as having integrity, a person must not only adhere to a set of principles, but those principles also must be acceptable to the person asked to confer the trust.[32] Behavior decisions are guided by a set of core beliefs or values that describe what should be done and how a person should behave in a given situation. These core beliefs and values are related to a larger network of perceptions and attitudes that define a person's behavior pattern.[33] When we share common values, we are more able to predict another person's behavior and so feel more comfortable in trusting him or her to do the right thing.[34]

Implications for Librarians

All of this speaks to the need for clear communication between you and your supervisor and colleagues. Through information exchange and shared experiences, you and your co-workers increase your mutual ability to identify and develop more common values.[35] Integrity demands simple forthrightness and an honest expression of how you feel about a given idea or issue. It demands dependability and trustworthiness. And it demands an honest accounting of everyone's contribution in every interactive project. For those ideas that begin with you and which you assertively promote, you need to be sure that roles, responsibility, and recognition are equally distributed. Close cooperation with the librarian may be a new experience for some teachers, and cynics may ask what you are going to get out of it. Whatever their initial reservations, if the people with whom you work can be assured that their part in any enterprise is significant and important, and that they are part of a team effort, the odds of being able to persuade them to commit to a course of action are enhanced. In effect, influence is increased to the extent that power, credit, and ego gratification are shared.[36]

Energy and Focused Effort

The Concept

David Mechanic, in a classic study done in the 1960s, observed a direct relationship between the amount of effort people put into an area of activity and the influence they can wield.[37] The influence potential is multiplied if the effort is focused in an area that is critical to the organization. It is multiplied again if the area is one in which other members of the organization, especially higher-ranking members, are reluctant to participate. A job well done in such a situation creates a sense of obligation in others.

This is another instance where visibility is paramount, however. If you put in a great deal of effort, but no one knows that you do, the work will not produce an influence dividend. Perception is everything in building influence and your supervisor and colleagues must perceive you as exceptionally hardworking and committed to the same things they are. Visibility and perceived commitment are perceptual companions.

Implications for Librarians

You can accrue four benefits by showing energy and commitment in a job effort. First, by working harder in a position, you inevitably learn more about it. This increases your expertise and that, as you know, is an influence source in itself. Second, continued involvement with a job, especially a service position, increases the number of contacts you have with other workers. These contacts, in turn, increase opportunities to gather information informally and to develop networks. Third and fourth, hard workers provide role models for those around them, and the investment of a great amount of labor in a particular activity sends the message that the activity is meaningful.[38] These are serious considerations because inspiration is influential, and the perception that something is important promotes the perception that the person doing it is important.

Researchers have argued for a long time that no organization can be maximally effective unless many employees, perhaps even most, are willing to work above and beyond their job descriptions.[39] It's common knowledge that a significant part of a school's ability to complete all of its work rests on contributions people make outside their core responsibility areas. This is pointed up sharply in a crisis. Take, for example, when salary negotiations reach an impasse. Unions commonly call for an organized "slow-down" to demonstrate the intensity of faculty feeling. Far from being a strike, a slow-down doesn't ask members to withhold services, only to limit their contributions to the terms of their contract. In other words, *only* to do what they were hired to do—and this is perceived as *punishing* the district.

You need a visible presence in the larger school environment if you're going to convince people that you're highly committed to the school. Because extra work and activities beyond your job description are not required by the organization, your participation becomes a salient behavioral clue to your attitude.[40] And it's important that you be seen as consistently involved. There is research evidence that managers tend to link participation frequency with participation motives. The more you participate, the more likely it becomes that your principal and others will attribute your behavior to altruistic and commitment-driven motives similar to their own.[41]

Curriculum committees, technology project teams, program committees, attendance and behavior policy task forces, and other such permanent and temporary bodies usually work on issues or processes that affect the school as a whole. These are important activities because, when taken all together over time, they make a real difference in the school's ability to accomplish its goals and to enhance its overall performance.[42] This kind of service signals commitment to the school as a whole, not just to your individual part of it—both because it is work beyond the confines of your specific job and because it's geared toward improving overall system effectiveness. This kind of service is the mark of the "good employee."[43] Your participation is important, completely apart from any contact, networking, competency display, or influence opportunity it may provide for you, just because it sends this message to your principal and your co-workers.

Sensitivity

The Concept
A final key attribute in influential people is the ability to discern the needs and feelings of others. One of the ironies of influence is that the capacity to identify with others is a critical element in getting the things you want for yourself.[44] It's not altogether unlike the line from Meredith Wilson's *The Music Man*: "You have to know the territory!" The territory of influence is other people.

Being sensitive to others means knowing the nature of the work they do and the pressures they feel. It doesn't necessarily mean committing yourself to solving all their problems, lightening their loads, or meeting all their desires. But it does mean understanding their ambitions and having some sense of their limitations. In short, it means being able to recognize the context in which they live, the things they want, and the things they deem important.

Implications for Librarians

A key to influence building is being able to see things from the other person's perspective. Learning these things requires a great deal of interaction. More than that, it requires close observation of people and strong listening skills. Dante's advice is good: "Go right on and listen as thou goest."

Influence depends upon effective communication. Learning how best to approach another person is discovered through observation and listening—and through asking questions. People often hesitate to ask many questions of others, fearing they will be perceived as intrusive. But sincere questions regarding work and interest areas, questions that are not too personal, are much more likely to be interpreted as true concern.

You probably have more opportunities to engage in discussions of this type than most other people in the school. Teachers are alone in their classrooms through most of the day, but your contacts with teachers are probably more frequent than many teachers have with each other. Teachers come into the library regularly with their classes or in pursuit of something for themselves. The opportunity to talk between student questions can be substantial, and it's an ideal time to inquire about a teacher's particular professional needs, desires, and material concerns. You also have an entree to people's particular personal interests through their reading selections.

But the contexts of our professional lives are affected by all kinds of things supposedly completely separate from our professional domains. We are unable to shed our personal concerns, responsibilities, and feelings when we come to work. A good guess would be that probably close to half of the staff members with whom you interact each day are distracted by, if not focused upon, some personal situation.[45] Who hasn't gone to work worried about finances, an aging parent, a sick child, a recent diagnosis, an impending divorce or some other weighty matter? Or gone to work consumed with delight by a new love, an impending marriage, a new baby, or some other wonderful life-changing experience?

These people have professional pride and want to maintain their performance quality, but they must give priority to other issues. If you can identify people going through personal transitions, you may be able to offer real assistance through your library resources. Since it's unlikely that people will open discussion of these subjects in a library full of students and other teachers, you'll need to find other ways to gather such information. One good way is through student activities. You'd be surprised what someone will tell you when it's just the two of you—outside your hierarchical position—standing at the door to the auditorium taking tickets to the school play.

Another way to increase your sensitivity to the work life contexts of the teachers in your building is to consult the research on the work-life cycle of educators. Research has demonstrated that work-lives have a pattern of growth and development, direction finding and direction change, peaks, valleys, aging and decline just as our personal lives do.

Where our individual goals and concerns change in each stage of our personal lives, so do they change in each stage of our professional lives. What is important, even critical, to a beginning teacher may not be to a teacher with five years, 10 years, or 20 years experience—and vice versa. The research that identifies these evolving life span concerns is having a growing effect on staff development planning, but it can serve your purposes just as well. If you begin with something like Ralph Fessler's and Judith Christensen's *The Teacher Career Cycle: Understanding and Guiding the Professional Development of Teachers* (Boston: Allyn and Bacon, 1992), you can quickly get a sense of what is most important to teachers of differing ages and experience.[46] You may have a good handle on what beginning teachers face because you once were one. But because you left the classroom for the library, you're never going to experience what it's like to be a 50-, 55-,or 60-year-old teacher. Delving into the research on veteran teachers can provide some insight.

It's important to remember here that perception always outshines reality. It's not enough in itself for you to know the work others do, the pressures they feel, and the context of their lives. Knowing these things only pays influence dividends if they believe that you know these things. This is a challenge you share with counselors and administrators. Most teachers believe that when you leave the classroom—whether you're a counselor, an administrator, or a librarian—you almost immediately forget what it's like. You must engage in activities that demonstrate you understand what others face every day.

Conclusion

Positive personal attributes should be recognized for the powerful potential influence sources they represent in any organization. It's a good idea to examine what particular attributes you have going for you and work to maximize their effect. By strengthening them, you strengthen the probability of convincing others that the things you propose or support are worthwhile.

You surely have a sense of your attributes as they exist at the moment. The question is whether the people you would seek to influence have the same sense of your qualities. One way to make a quick assessment is to imagine a scenario where some people you would like to influence are discussing the quality of school personnel over a bottle of wine. When your name comes up, what adjectives will they use to describe you? Which would you want them to use? If the two lists are not the same, you have another question to ask yourself: Are the lists different because I really do or don't have a particular attribute, or are they different just because of what I've allowed them to see of me? Either way, you will understand the work you need to do.

It is difficult to see ourselves as others see us, but it is important to make the effort. People do not necessarily react to us as we are, and certainly not as a result of what we think we are. They react to us on the basis of what they *think* we are. Managing the perceptions others have of us is essential in maximizing the benefits of the attributes we really do possess.

The instrument at the end of this chapter offers an opportunity to take a look at yourself. It is a lot of work to complete, but the results will arm you with a much better understanding of what you have to offer to others and how you show it. With that as a foundation, you can plan whatever steps you feel you need to take to increase the impact of the attributes you possess.

Figure 3.2: A Self Assessment Instrument

Directions: This instrument has two parts to it. Please do the parts in order. The intention of the first part is to get you thinking about how you behave so you will be able to more accurately answer the questions in the second part.

Part I: I am and I am not

Directions for Part I: Close your eyes for two minutes and think about yourself in terms of what you are like at work. Then complete the following sentences. This will probably take you about 15 minutes.

I am _____

I am _____

I am _____

I am _____

I am _____

I am _____

I am _____

I am not _____

I am not _____

I am not _____

I am not _____

Now review what you have written and ask yourself the following questions:

____ Are all of these statements honest?

____ Do these statements describe me as I think I am or as I think others think I am?

____ Do these statements describe me as I am or as I would like to think of myself?

____ Are there both positives and negatives?

____ Have I denied any virtues out of false modesty?

____ Have I denied any faults?

One of the points of this exercise is to get you warmed up for the more involved questions that follow, but another is to demonstrate that no one is perfect — nor needs to be. If your principal completed this same exercise, the results would not describe the perfect person either. There is an important point in this: working relationships, like all others, are made up of the interactions of two imperfect and fallible people. Success is measured over time, not in a given specific incident.

Now, with this preface, answer the questions below as honestly as you can.

Part II: A Deeper Look

Directions for Part II: One of the purposes of this inventory is to allow you to better understand how you react and behave in particular organizational settings. If you are aware of your usual patterns, you have a better chance of controlling your reactions and of making conscious choices. To accomplish this, you need to be able to prove to yourself that you do, indeed, behave in a particular manner.

We all sometimes have a tendency to answer questions like those that follow with a description of how we would like to be rather than how we actually are. Please be as honest with yourself as you can, then test your answers against your memory. To test your answers, *please supply at least one specific example for each from your own experience.*

The examples should be drawn from your work setting if at all possible. Please only use examples involving *adults*. Please stay away from using any examples involving students.

If you cannot think of an example from your professional experience, please try to prove your statements with examples from participation in social, political, community, religious, family, or other groups. Please remember: the topic is your relationship with other *adults*. In your work, you will be called upon to exert influence and leadership in your relationships with administrators, teachers, support staff, parents, and members of the larger community.

It's best to write out the answers if you have the time. If you only answer these in your mind, complete with examples, it will probably take you about an hour to complete this section. If you write out your answers, it will probably take you at least twice as long. Writing out the answers will not only force you to think a little more specifically, it will also give you a document to use again at a later time.[47]

1. Can you develop a firm vision of what you want the library media center or the school to be like next year? in five years? If you have such a vision, is it stagnant? Can you deliberately change it or does it evolve on its own? Is it focused? (Note: this does *not* ask you what your vision of the library or school is. It asks whether or not you think in visionary terms.)

2. Exercising influence involves a great deal of ambiguity. That is, you are called upon to frequently make decisions without having full information and without knowing exactly what the outcome of your decision may bring. What is your tolerance for ambiguity? What is your need for structure? How well can you operate in unstructured situations? (Remember to give an example from your experience to prove to yourself that what you describe is, indeed, how you act.)

3. People who are involved in many activities in a school often find their work lives marked by variety, brevity, and fragmentation. In this context, variety means dealing with a wide range of topics in a single day, maybe in a single hour or in a space of minutes. Brevity means that your involvement with any given issue or person is usually very short, most often just a few minutes. Fragmentation means that you cannot begin a project and see it through. You must work on something, then work on something else, then something else, etc., and sometime later get back to one of the things you started earlier. How well do you handle situations like that? (Remember, there is no right or wrong answer here, or any answer that is better than another. The objective is to identify for yourself what you are like at this time.)

4. In what kind of organizational environment do you not function well? In which do you thrive? Do you need to pay more attention to task or more attention to people? What conditions can you identify that make a significant difference to you?

5. Does your style of working and dealing with people support or conflict with your pursuit of your objectives? For example, are you directive, collaborative, or non-directive in the way you deal with people in working situations? Are you detail oriented? Are you a "do it now" type person? How do you work? How well has your work style served you in getting your own tasks accomplished and in getting other people to do their share? (Think of the last project you worked on with other people, perhaps a committee assignment. Describe that experience to yourself as proof that you behave as you say you do.)

6. How much planning do you do? How far in advance? How good are you at dealing with unplanned situations? (Remember to give yourself proof by example.)

7. What attitude do you deliberately try to communicate to other adults in the work place? Are you all business? Messages about yourself, your values, your personality do you communicate? How do you know if you are successful?

8. What attitude do you think you may communicate unintentionally to other adults at work? Are you sometimes surprised by how people react to you? Do people read things into what you say or how you behave? How do you know?

9. How well do you communicate with other adults at work? What physical methods do you employ? writing? telephone? in person? With what level of intensity do you usually communicate? Do your methods change with changing situations? Are they effective? How do you know?

10. How well do you receive communication from other adults at work? What communication form do you most like to receive? writing? telephone? in person? Can you read "between the lines" of what co-workers say to see the feelings behind the message? How do you know? (Think of the communications you've recently received at work. Have there been any surprises where you later discovered something you should have seen when you first received it?)

11. Do you "level" with people? That is, do you tell people the blunt truth? For purposes of this question, "leveling" means something like sitting a person down and saying: "Look, this just isn't working, and it isn't working because of your . . ." When? Under what circumstances? How successful has it been? (Remember to provide proof for yourself by citing an example from your past.)

12. Do you really want others to "level" with you? Consider superiors, peers, and subordinates. How do you handle negative information about yourself? How do you handle positive information? (Remember to provide proof for yourself by citing an example from your past.)

13. What kind of an image do you try to project to other adults at work? We all practice "impression management." How do you do it? How successful are you?

14. How do you structure situations to make use of your talents? How do you try to influence situations so you can showcase your abilities? (For example, do you avoid certain responsibilities? Do you volunteer for certain things? If you are asked to handle a meeting, how do you behave?) (Remember to provide proof for yourself by citing an example from your past.)

15. How do you try to charm people, build rapport or empathy? How successful are you? (For example, think of the last time you met a new teacher or administrator in your building, or the last time you were at a professional conference. What kinds of things did you say or do?)

16. When do you trust other people? Think of the people at work whom you trust. Do they have one or more characteristics in common? How good is your track record in deciding whom to trust?

17. How sensitive are you to errors that you might make in your work? What is your method for minimizing or avoiding errors?

18. How do you deal with the errors others make? How do you react when someone makes a mistake or lets you down? When someone does it repeatedly? We all like to think we are forgiving and helpful. Are you? Think of the last time someone really screwed up. Specifically, what did you do and say?

19. What kind of a sense of humor do you have? Do you like jokes and stories? If yes, what subject matter? Do you make puns? Do you have a quick wit? How do you use your sense of humor? How well has it worked for you? How do you know?

20. How do you handle competition? Think not only of the sports type but when you apply for a job, or for recognition for accomplishment.

21. How do you handle controversy? Think of two kinds of controversial issues:
    (a) where you have to work in the setting or where you have to represent the decisions of the organization to the public (for example, certain curriculum decisions, ability grouping in schools, standardized testing, campus clinics, bussing, tenure, large pay raises, inappropriate personal behavior on the part of another employee) and
    (b) controversies of which you are a part (for example, book censorship attempts, union actions, conflicts with other educators over policy, appropriateness of your behavior as an individual or of the group to which you belong).

22. What is your strong suit? What trait, characteristic, or talent is your strongest? Can your strong suit lead you into problems? Can you give an example?

23. What is your major area of weakness in your relations with other adults at work? How do you handle (confront, avoid, structure) situations so you don't get hurt by them? How successful have you been? (Remember to provide proof for yourself by citing an example from your past.)

24. When do you take risks at work? Under what conditions are you willing to take a risk? Are they the same when you are risking something for the benefit of others as they are when you are risking something with a potential to benefit you? (Remember to provide proof for yourself by citing an example from your past.)

25. Do you feel like you need clear rules and regulations at work, or do you prefer a loose environment? Under what conditions do you decide, if you ever do, to bend or break the rules at work? Can you give an example from your experience? How do you relate to rules when it is your responsibility to enforce them?
26. Do you need to be recognized for what you do, or are you willing to share credit with others, or even go without any acknowledgement? (Remember to provide proof for yourself by citing an example from your past.)
27. How do you handle failure? This means both (1) how well do you handle it emotionally and (2) what kinds of activities, if any, do you engage in? (Remember to provide proof for yourself by citing an example from your past.)
28. How do you handle success? Consider the same two kinds of questions: emotions and activities. Is success or failure more motivating for you? (Remember to provide proof for yourself by citing an example from your past.)
29. How well do you handle criticism? Does criticism equate to rejection for you? (Remember to provide proof for yourself by citing an example from your past.)
30. Do you want personal relationships with the administrators you work with, or do you want only professional relationships?

References

1 R. B. Cialdini, *Influence: Science and Practice, Third Edition* (New York: Harper Collins, 1993), p. 136.

2 A. H. Eagly, R. D. Ashmore, M. G. Makhijani, and L. C. Longo, "What is Beautiful is Good, But…: A Meta-analytic Review of the Research on the Physical Attractiveness Stereotype," *Psychological Bulletin,* vol. 110, no. 1 (1992), pp. 109–128.

3 K. K. Dion, E. Berscheid, and E. Walster, "What is Beautiful is Good," *Journal of Personality and Social Psychology*, vol. 24, no. 3 (1972), pp. 285–290.

4 L. Baird, R. W. Beatty, and C. E. Schneier, *The Performance Appraisal Sourcebook* (Amherst, MA: Human Resource Development Press, 1982).

E. Berscheid, and E. Walster, "Physical Attractiveness," In N. N. Berkowitz (Ed.), *Advances in Experimental Psychology* (pp. 159–215) (New York: Academic Press, 1974).

A. H. Eagly, R. D. Ashmore, M. G. Makhijani, and L. C. Longo, "What is Beautiful is Good, But…: A Meta-analytic Review of the Research on the Physical Attractiveness Stereotype," *Psychological Bulletin,* vol. 110, no. 1 (1992), pp. 109–128.

C. P. Fleenor and M. P. Scontrino, *Performance Appraisal: A Manager's Guide* (Dubuque, IA: Kendall/Hunt Publishers, 1982).

D. Mack and D. Rainey, "Female Applicants' Grooming and Personnel Selection," *Journal of Social Behavior and Personality*, vol. 5, no. 5 (1990), pp. 399–407.

J. Ross and K. R. Ferris, "Interpersonal Attraction of Organizational Outcomes: A Field Examination," *Administrative Science Quarterly*, vol. 26, no. 4 (1981), pp. 617–632.

5 S. Chaiken, "Communicator's Physical Attractiveness and Persuasion," *Journal of Personality and Social Psychology*, vol. 37, no. 8 (1979), pp. 1387–1397.

S. Chaiken, "Physical Appearance and Social Influence," In C. P. Herman, M. P. Zanna, and E. T. Higgins (Eds.), *Physical Appearance, Stigma, and Social Behavior: The Ontario Symposium, Volume 3* (pp. 143–177) (Hillsdale, NJ: Lawrence Erlbaum Associates, Publishers, 1986).

R. B. Cialdini, *Influence: Science and Practice, Third Edition* (New York: Harper Collins, 1993).

R. M. Perloff, *The Dynamics of Persuasion* (Hillsdale, NJ: Lawrence Erlbaum Associates, Publishers, 1993).

6 L. Baird, R. W. Beatty, and C. E. Schneier, *The Performance Appraisal Sourcebook* (Amherst, MA: Human Resource Development Press, 1982).

K. K. Dion, "Physical Attractiveness and Evaluation of Children's Transgressions," *Journal of Personality and Social Psychology*, vol. 24, no. 2, (1972), pp. 207–213.

J. Rich, "Effects of Children's Physical Attractiveness on Teachers' Evaluations," J*ournal of Educational Psychology*, vol. 67, no. 5 (1975), pp. 599–609.

A. D. Tieger, *A Descriptive Study of Selected Characteristics and Educational Values of Principals and Assistant Principals in the Los Angeles Unified School District* (Doctoral dissertation, Pepperdine University, 1986).

7 G. R. Keats and K. E. Davis, "The Dynamics of Sexual Behavior of College Students," *Journal of Marriage and the Family*, vol. 32, no. 3 (1970), pp. 390–399.

8 R. B. Cialdini, *Influence: Science and Practice, Third Edition* (New York: Harper Collins, 1993), p. 168.

9 E. Aronson, *The Social Animal, Third Edition* (San Francisco: W. H. Freeman & Company, 1980).

L. Baird, R. W. Beatty, and C. E. Schneier, *The Performance Appraisal Sourcebook* (Amherst, MA: Human Resource Development Press, 1982).

D. Bryne, *The Attraction Paradigm* (New York: Academic Press, 1971).

R. B. Cialdini, *Influence: Science and Practice, Third Edition* (New York: Harper Collins, 1993), p. 136.

C. P. Fleenor and M. P. Scontrino, *Performance Appraisal: A Manager's Guide* (Dubuque, IA: Kendall/Hunt Publishers, 1982).

10 E. Aronson, *The Social Animal, Third Edition* (San Francisco: W. H. Freeman & Company, 1980).

11 D. Davis, "Implications for Interaction Versus Effectance as Mediators of the Similarity-Attraction Relationship," *Journal of Experimental Social Psychology*, vol. 17, no. 1 (1981), pp. 96–116.

12 L. Baird, R. W. Beatty, and C. E. Schneier, *The Performance Appraisal Sourcebook* (Amherst, MA: Human Resource Development Press, 1982).

R. B. Cialdini, *Influence: Science and Practice, Third Edition* (New York: Harper Collins, 1993),

C. P. Fleenor and M. P. Scontrino, *Performance Appraisal: A Manager's Guide* (Dubuque, IA: Kendall/Hunt Publishers, 1982).

W. C. Hamner, J. S. Kim, L. Baird, and N. J. Bigoness, "Race and Sex as Determinants of Ratings by Potential Employers in a Simulated Work Sampling Task," *Journal of Applied Psychology*, vol. 59, no. 6 (1974), pp. 705–711.

T. M. Rand and K. N. Wexley, "Demonstration of the Effect 'Similar to Me,' in Simulated Employment Interviews," *Psychological Reports*, vol. 36, no. 2 (1975), pp. 535–544.

13 J. Pfeffer, *Managing With Power: Politics and Influence in Organizations* (Cambridge, MA: Harvard Business School Press, 1992).

14 J. Pfeffer, *Managing With Power: Politics and Influence in Organizations* (Cambridge, MA: Harvard Business School Press, 1992), p. 218.

15 J. Pfeffer, *Managing With Power: Politics and Influence in Organizations* (Cambridge, MA: Harvard Business School Press, 1992), p. 216.

16 R. B. Cialdini, *Influence: Science and Practice, Third Edition* (New York: Harper Collins, 1993).

17 L. Festinger, S. Schachter, and K. Back, *Social Pressures on Informal Groups: A Study of a Housing Community* (New York: Harper, 1950).

R. L. Moreland and R. B. Zajonc, "Exposure Effects in Person Perception: Familiarity, Similarity, and Attraction," *Journal of Experimental Social Psychology*, vol. 18 (1982), pp. 395–415.

18 E. Aronson, *The Social Animal, Third Edition* (San Francisco: W. H. Freeman & Company, 1980).

A. J. Lott and B. E. Lott, "Group Cohesiveness as Interpersonal Attraction: A Review of Relationships With Antecedent and Consequent Variables," *Psychological Bulletin*, vol. 64, no. 4 (1965), pp. 259–309.

19 J. A. C. Brown. *Techniques of Persuasion*. Baltimore: Penguin Books, 1963.

20 A. J. Lott and B. E. Lott, "Group Cohesiveness as Interpersonal Attraction: A Review of Relationships With Antecedent and Consequent Variables," *Psychological Bulletin*, vol. 64, no. 4 (1965), pp. 259–309.

21 R. B. Cialdini, *Influence: Science and Practice, Third Edition* (New York: Harper Collins, 1993).

M. Manis, S. D. Cornell, and J. C. Moore, "Transmission of Attitude Relevant Information Through a Communication Chain," *Journal of Personality and Social Psychology*, vol. 30, no. 1 (1974), pp. 81–94.

22 A. Tesser, and S. Rosen, "The Reluctance to Transmit Bad News," In L. Berkowitz (Ed.), *Advances in Experimental Social Psychology, Volume 8* (pp. 193–232) (New York: Academic Press, 1975).

23 J. J. Gabarro, "The Development of Working Relationships." In J. Galegher and R. E. Kraut (Eds.), *Intellectual Teamwork: Social and Technological Foundations of Cooperative Work*, pp. 79–110 (Hillsdale, NJ: Lawrence Erlbaum Associates Publishers, 1990).

24 G. F. Farris and F. G. Lim, Jr., "Effects of Performance on Leadership, Cohesiveness, Influence, Satisfaction, and Subsequent Performance," *Journal of Applied Psychology*, vol. 53, pp. 490–497.

J. J. Gabarro, "The Development of Working Relationships." In J. Galegher and R. E. Kraut (Eds.), *Intellectual Teamwork: Social and Technological Foundations of Cooperative Work*, pp. 79–110 (Hillsdale, NJ: Lawrence Erlbaum Associates Publishers, 1990).

C. B. Wortman and J. A. W. Linsenmeier, "Interpersonal Attraction and Techniques of Ingratiation in Organizational Settings." In G. Salancik and B. M. Staw (Eds.), *New Directions in Organizational Behavior*, pp. 133–178 (Chicago: St. Clair Press, 1977).

25 J. Van Maanen, *Organizational Careers: Some New Perspectives* (New York: John Wiley and Sons, 1977).

26 B. R. Schlenker, *Impression Management* (Belmont, CA: Wadsworth Publishers, Inc., 1980).

27 D. Mechanic, "Sources of Power of Lower Participants in Complex Organizations," *Administrative Science Quarterly*, vol. 7, no. 3 (1962), pp. 349–364.

28 G. Morgan, *Images of Organizations* (Thousand Oaks, CA: Sage Publications, 1997).

29 R. B. Shaw, *Trust in the Balance: Building Successful Organizations on Results, Integrity, and Concern* (San Francisco: Jossey–Bass, 1997).

30 T. Teal, "The Human Side of Management," *Harvard Business Review,* vol. 74, no. 6 (1996), pp. 35–42.

31 Harvard Ethics Teaching Group. *Integrity and Management*. Harvard Business School Publishing product 9-392-005. Accessed at <http://www.hbsp.harvard.edu March 8, 1999>.

32 R. C. Mayer, J. H. Davis, and F. D. Schoorman, "An Integration Model of Organizational Trust," *Academy of Management Review*, vol. 29, no. 3 (1995), pp. 709–734.

L. McFall, "Integrity," *Ethics*, vol. 98, no. 1 (1987), pp. 5–20.

33 C. L. Adkins, E. C. Ravlin, and B. Meglino, "Value Congruence Between Co-Workers and its Relationship to Work Outcomes," *Group and Organizational Management*, vol. 21, no. 4 (1996), pp. 439–460.

N. M. Ashkanasy and C. O'Connor, "Value Congruence in Leader-Member Exchange," *The Journal of Social Psychology*, vol. 137, no. 5 (1997), pp. 647–662.

E. C. Ravlin and B. M. Meglino, "Effect of Values on Perception and Decision Making: A Study of Alternative Work Values Measures," *Journal of Applied Psychology,* vol. 72, no. 4 (1987), pp. 666–673.

34 C. Kluckhohn, "Values and Value-Orientations in the Theory of Action: An Exploration in Definition and Classification." In T. Parsons and E. Shils (Eds.), *Toward a General Theory of Action*, pp. 388–435 (Cambridge, MA: Harvard University Press, 1951).

35 T. K. Das and B. Teng, "Between Trust and Control: Developing Confidence in Partner Cooperation in Alliances," *Academy of Management Review*, vol. 23, no. 3 (1998), pp. 491–512.

36 W. Bennis and B. Nanus, *Leaders: The Strategies of Taking Charge* (New York: Harper, 1985).

D. McClelland, *Power: The Inner Experience* (New York: Irvington Publishers, 1975).

37 D. Mechanic, "Sources of Power of Lower Participants in Complex Organizations," *Administrative Science Quarterly*, vol. 7, no. 3 (1962) pp. 349–364.

38 J. Pfeffer, *Managing With Power: Politics and Influence in Organizations* (Cambridge, MA: Harvard Business School Press, 1992), p. 168.

39 C. I. Barnard, *The Functions of the Executive* (Cambridge, MA: Harvard University Press, 1938).

D. Katz and R. L. Kahn, *The Social Psychology of Organizations*, 2nd Edition (New York: Wiley, 1978).

D. W. Organ, "The Motivational Basis of Organizational Citizenship Behavior," in B. Staw and L. Cummings (Eds.), *Research in Organizational Behavior*, Volume 12 (pp. 43–72) (Greenwich, CT: JAI Press, 1990).

40 P. M. Podsakoff, S. B. MacKenzie, and C. Hui, "Organizational Citizenship Behaviors and Managerial Evaluations of Employee Performance: A Review and Suggestions for Future Research," In G. R. Ferris (Ed.), *Research in Personnel and Human Resources Management*, Volume 11 (pp. 1–40) (Greenwich, CT: JAI Press, 1993).

41 T. D. Allen and M. C. Rush, "The Effects of Organizational Citizenship Behavior on Performance Judgments: A Field Study and a Laboratory Experiment," *Journal of Applied Psychology*, vol. 83, no. 2 (1998), pp. 247–260.

42 D. W. Organ, "The Motivational Basis of Organizational Citizenship Behavior," in B. Staw and L. Cummings (Eds.), *Research in Organizational Behavior, Volume 12* (pp. 43–72) (Greenwich, CT: JAI Press, 1990).

P. M. Podsakoff and S. B. MacKenzie, "The Impact of Organizational Citizenship Behavior on Organizational Performance: A Review and Suggestions for Future Research," *Human Performance*, vol. 10, pp. 133–152.

43 K. R. Murphy and J. N. Cleveland, *Performance Appraisal: An Organizational Perspective* (Boston: Allyn & Bacon, 1991).

44 J. Pfeffer, *Managing With Power: Politics and Influence in Organizations* (Cambridge, MA: Harvard Business School Press, 1992), p. 172.

45 Tom Bird offers some interesting observations on this in "Mutual Adaptation and Mutual Accomplishment: Images of Change in a Field Experiment." In A. Lieberman (Ed.), *Rethinking School Improvement*. New York: Teachers College Press 1986. There's also an excellent discussion of the impact of age and other considerations on teachers' attitudes and perspectives to be found in Robert Evans's *The Human Side of School Change,* San Francisco: Jossey-Bass, 2001.

46 Also very useful are:

P. J. Sikes, L. Measor, and P. Woods, *Teacher Careers: Crises and Continuities* (London: The Falmer Press, 1985).

M. Huberman, "Teacher Careers and School Improvement," *Journal of Curriculum Studies,* vol. 20, no. 2 (1988), pp. 119–132.

47 Several of these questions were drawn from conversations with Dr. Samuel A. Culbert in the Anderson School of Management at UCLA. Professor Culbert teaches classes in organizational behavior, power and motivation, and management. He is the author of *The Organization Trap and How to Get Out of It* (New York: Basic Books, Inc., 1974), co-author with John J. McDonough of *The Invisible War: Pursuing Self-Interests at Work* (New York: John Wiley & Sons, 1980), which was named the best business and management book of 1980 by the Association of American Publishers, and *Radical Management: Power Politics and The Pursuit of Trust* (New York: Free Press, 1985). All three are recommended for additional reading.

Chapter 4

Influence Draws on Heuristic Thinking

As important as your personal attributes are in promoting workplace influence, they're not the whole of it. There are some general tools—some call them weapons—of influence that you can put to work to increase your influence potential. This chapter outlines six of them. Of course, if these ideas capture your interest, there's rich research literature available to you and you can always track down more information about them and others.

Before you begin, however, stop for a moment and consider the statements that appear in Figure 4.1. Which of them are true all of the time, most of the time, some of the time, rarely, or never? As you rate these statements, you may wonder what in the world they have to do with a school librarian's ability to influence events at work. You'll see the connections as you read the chapter, but it's enough for the moment to say that your evaluations will create a useful mind set for what follows.

Figure 4.1: How True Are These Statements?

1 = Always   4 = Once in a while
2 = Most of the time   5 = Never
3 = About half of the time

---

1 2 3 4 5   You get what you pay for.

1 2 3 4 5   There is safety in numbers.

1 2 3 4 5   Never trust an old enemy or a new friend.

1 2 3 4 5   Birds of a feather flock together.

1 2 3 4 5   Cheap goods are inferior goods.

1 2 3 4 5   Experts know what they are talking about.

1 2 3 4 5   Politicians cannot be trusted.

1 2 3 4 5   Statistics don't lie.

1 2 3 4 5   You should give as good as you get.

1 2 3 4 5   Once you make up your mind, you should stick with your decision.

1 2 3 4 5   Something you earn is more valuable to you than something given to you.

These statements are examples of what researchers call "judgmental heuristic assumptions." *The American Heritage Dictionary* defines "heuristic" as meaning "helping to discover or learn."[1] In operation, heuristics are rules of thumb, a sort of unconscious wisdom. Largely unstated and untested, but deeply imbedded, heuristic assumptions offer simple decision rules as the world presents us with choices. If you're like most people, you probably rated at least half of these ideas as true at least half of the time, some number of them as true most of the time, and at least one of them as true every time.

Social psychologists and persuasion researchers contend that most people, most of the time, unconsciously use heuristic thinking to assess what they encounter in their worlds.[2] Heuristics allow us to act as "cognitive misers" and to avoid having to exert great mental effort to explain to ourselves why something is happening, or if something is acceptable or unacceptable.[3]

This isn't necessarily bad. Social psychologists argue that heuristic thinking is necessary.[4] We live in very complicated and fluid environments, and heuristics allow us to take mental shortcuts by providing ready-made evaluation frameworks. The speed and complexity of modern society is such that we need to take advantage of them. Employing cognitive heuristics means we don't have to identify, analyze, interpret, and evaluate every aspect of every situation and person we confront in order to feel we understand. Judgmental heuristics provide us with rules of thumb that save time and effort in deciding whether we should believe what we see or hear.

Presented with a situation or person that requires us to take an action, these thinking and judgment rules unconsciously come into play and shape of our responses. Heuristic assumptions help us make sense of the world. Our individually crafted sets of heuristics accurately frame what each of us perceives as reality most of the time, though not always. Take the "You get what you pay for" assumption for example. It's one of the most common heuristics and tells us that "expensive" equates to quality and "cheap" to inferior. Think about the last time you were in the market for some electronic or clothing item or were looking to buy jewelry, a refrigerator, or a car. Price is a quality guide—not always because we sometimes can find real bargains—but the heuristic holds true for most items most of the time. Because these simple guides are true the vast majority of the time, we use them in an automatic and non-reflective manner as we process situational data. They not only inform our decisions about quality and trustworthiness, but they also guide how we should act in a particular circumstance.

Heuristics are powerful and help explain why personal attributes are important components in influence building. Heuristics like "experts know what they are talking about" and "likeable people are more trustworthy" are part of what gives strength to expertise and personal attractiveness as factors in interpersonal influence.[5]

As much as heuristics may be shortcuts, they can also be short circuits. It appears that when faced with a social situation that needs to be evaluated, we are most likely to give priority attention to the characteristics that are most readily available. Certain characteristics or attributes of a person, an event, or a situation trigger heuristic responses. If that happens, we may very well base our decisions or conclusions on heuristic assumptions and may not go on to examine any further evidence to ascertain the truth. Studies in persuasion research show that unless we are deeply involved in the subject at hand and highly motivated to know more, it is likely that some heuristic will influence our judgments of what is true or right.[6]

This, of course, points to the dangers of cognitive and judgmental heuristics. They lead us toward unthinking, even automatic, responses. Ethnic and gender heuristics, for example, frequently provide inaccurate assumptive understandings of why people behave a certain way. If we don't take time to reflect and examine, we might well find ourselves accepting and doing things that we otherwise would not. It is because these mechanical response patterns are so common that a basic understanding of heuristics has power for influence building.

Heuristics as Tools of Influence

Researchers have identified many heuristics that affect how people think and react every day in all kinds of situations. Robert Cialdini put seven of them together in a wonderful little book called *Influence: Science and Practice,* which provides a useful overview for anyone interested in influence building.[7] In addition to liking, which has already been discussed as the personal "likability" attribute, these judgmental heuristics are:

- Reciprocity
- Contrast
- Commitment and consistency
- Social proof
- Scarcity
- Authority

Knowing about these heuristics can help you become more influential in two ways: (1) in helping you devise and evaluate ways of interacting with others, and (2) in detecting when you are the target of someone else's influence attempt.

Reciprocity

The Concept

Probably the strongest judgmental heuristic is reciprocity. Think back to the statements you evaluated at the beginning of the chapter. Do you like to be in other people's debt? Do you feel uncomfortable when people do things for you and you can't respond in kind? Do you believe you should give as good as you get?

Reciprocity is the universal belief that people should be paid back for the things they do.[8] The concept of reciprocity appears in every society everywhere in the world and all across time. Through referred to as a norm by social psychology researchers, it operates more as a rule or law. Cialdini argues, in fact, that once put into operation, the rule of reciprocity is too powerful to resist. A person's best defense is to prevent its activation.[9]

The reciprocity rule is simple: whenever we accept an object or favor from someone, we incur a feeling of obligation that will not be satisfied until something of at least equal value has been repaid. Reciprocity is a powerful tool in exercising influence because our sense of debt increases the odds that we will comply with a future request made by virtually anyone who does a favor for us.

The universality of the reciprocity norm appears to have derived from its role in early human survival. Anthropologists and social historians argue that reciprocity supports the social structures that made possible the practices of cooperation and exchange, which in turn insured the growth of human society. In the dim past of human history, it was suicidal to part with resources without believing that they would be returned in kind or in some alternative form that was at least equally valuable in helping meet the challenges of the world. For example, if I gave you food, you might reciprocate with some other kind of food, but more likely you would respond by extending me shelter, protection, or assistance. In the modern workplace, if, for example, I were your principal, I might tell you about a particularly interesting upcoming librarian conference and then pay all or part of your costs to go. I would not expect you to repay me by identifying and sending me to an administrative conference. I'd probably want payback in the form of service on some committee or help in developing some new public relations program.

It's very important to understand that reciprocity is not the same as exchange. First, exchanges are initially desired by both parties. Reciprocity doesn't require mutual desire, and this adds to its power. The item that initiates the relationship may not have been requested, maybe not even wanted, by the person who receives it. But, solicited or not, accepting an item, invitation, or favor puts the receiver into the giver's debt and the law of reciprocity into operation. Using the conference example again, you might not even have known about the conference and so never would have asked me to help you attend, but reciprocity would still be invoked once I made you aware and you accepted my assistance.

Second, unlike reciprocity, exchanges require that the terms of responsibility or the scope of the obligation be specified at the time the favor is done or the gift is made. Without specification of the debt, the recipient is left with a much more non-particularized, generalized obligation than would ever be part of any formal exchange or cooperative effort. This open-endedness is very important in influence situations because it can produce unequal exchanges. It provides the person who began the action with the ability to choose both the nature of the initiating favor and the nature of the return favor.[10] Drawing on the conference example once more, I might ask you to chair a particular committee, not just serve on it. In the long run, you would return much more in time and effort than I ever expended to get you to the conference in the first place.

The power of the reciprocity rule is visible all around us. Cialdini lists other examples that range from minimal to substantial:

- The free samples in the supermarket that really are aimed at making you feel like you should buy the product;

- The feeling we get that we should invite a couple over for dinner at our house just because they had us to theirs, even if we didn't have a very good time;

- The Christmas cards or birthday cards you feel you ought to send to people just because they sent you one, maybe as long ago as last year;

- The greeting cards or return address labels that come as a "gift" in mailed solicitations from charities; and

- The gathering of favors and the stockpiling of obligations that are a way of life for politicians.

Another interesting feature of the reciprocity rule for influence consideration is that it also operates in negotiating situations. If one side begins with an extreme demand and then backs off to a more modest position, the appearance is that something has been given up. The idea is to make the adversaries feel the obligation to reciprocate with a concession of their own.

Implications for Librarians

The reciprocity rule can be among the strongest influence tools you have. The richness of the resources at your disposal and the flexibility of your time schedule put you in a position to supply all kinds of services and materials to teachers and administrators, including things for which they have not yet thought of asking. In an educational environment, ideas and services are resources as much as media or equipment. Something that appears small to you in the giving, may result in a larger sense of debt in the receiver. This is a key point: don't limit your definition of resources. A resource is *anything* you have that someone else can use, wants, or can be made to want. It may be something as central to schooling as books, computers, instruction, or expertise, but it might also be something as peripheral as use of your telephone, a small meeting room, or an hour's worth of help stuffing envelopes by one of your library aides or volunteers.

To maximize the benefits of the reciprocity principle in your school, you need to do three things. First, make a conscious effort to increase the resources you control so you have more things to choose from as you present gifts to and do favors for others. Campaign for every dollar, every staff member, every inch of space you can get. Pursue grants, solicit donations, and recruit volunteers from the ranks of parents and retired teachers.

Second, fashion a reputation for expertise that will attach value to any intellectual gifts you can provide, such as curriculum and instructional approaches. This is another instance where heuristics and personal attributes intersect and complement each other. Expertise is essential in building workplace influence.

Third, build communication networks and develop a sensitivity to the needs of others so you know better what they can use and are more likely to appreciate. Appreciation isn't necessary for the invocation of reciprocity, but it does intensify the pressure on the recipient to respond. Sensitivity is not only an attribute of influential persons, as discussed in Chapter 3; it's also an important tool in identifying reciprocity opportunities.

Armed with resources, a strong reputation, and a sense of people's needs, you can create great opportunities to use and benefit from the workings of the reciprocity rule.

The importance of the reciprocity principle will be further illustrated later in the book, but you can get a quick sense of its pervasiveness just by thumbing through the chapters on building influence with your principal and the teachers in your school. Many of the tactical ideas outlined in Section III of the book involve invoking reciprocity as well.

Contrast

The Concept

Contrast is a distortion of judgment that results from the human tendency to perceive things from a particular reference point. When we do that, we make comparisons that can be misleading. As Cialdini explains it, this tendency affects our perception of two things—particularly two similar things—when they are presented to us in a certain way or in a short time span.[11] We almost automatically, heuristically, compare the first and second items against each other instead of comparing both to an objective standard. The effect is to exaggerate any substantial differences between the first item and the second.

Cialdini describes a delightful demonstration you can try at home or in your library to illustrate the principle. Get three pails of water. One should be cold, one room temperature, and one hot. Place one hand in the cold water and the other in the hot. Leave them submerged for a minute or two, then plunge both hands into the tepid water pail simultaneously. Even though they are in the same water, the temperature will feel differently to each hand. Sensations from the hand that was in the cold water will tell you that the water is much warmer than it really is, while the sensations from the hand that was in the hot water will tell you that it's colder. For purposes of influencing things, the lessons of the demonstration are clear. Almost anything can be made to appear different depending on what accompanies it. The same thinking is part of why a batter in baseball warms up with a weighted bat. The principle works in the intellectual and emotional world just as powerfully as it does in the physical.

The contrast principle abounds in the sales world where the best practice is always to present an expensive item first. For example, $500 may seem like a lot of money to spend on an automobile option if it is viewed by itself. But if you spend thousands of dollars on a new car before you ever consider any extra features, the $500 the car dealer asks for for an additional option will seem small. The same process occurs when people evaluate ideas and social situations. There is even a management approach suggesting that if employees fear you are going to take their heads, they will be grateful when you only take an arm.

This principle also undergirds much of the behavior in contract negotiations and in damage suit settlements. The cost of an initial proposal can be so high that a later proposal, still higher than would ever be acceptable on its own merits, appears to be reasonable. In situations like these, however, there is a need to be careful. If the extreme position advanced first is patently unreasonable, the effect is destroyed because no one will accept it as a reference point from which to judge the second proposal.

Both the first and second proposals have to be within the realm of the possible. If they are, there can be a combining of the contrast principle and the reciprocity rule since the second proposal looks like a concession following the rejection of the first. Then the odds increase again that the second proposal will be acceptable.

Implications for Librarians

The contrast heuristic can be useful in building school influence. It says that the odds of getting support or approval for your budget request, your program proposal, or any other idea you might advance can be affected by how what you want appears in relation to similar items and where it appears in the order of things considered— whether in a simple conversation or on a formal meeting agenda. It argues again for active participation in work and social groups so you have a voice in how issues are arranged and presented. It also argues for very carefully assessing your proposal in light of competing proposals. If your proposal looks outclassed, you may want to withdraw it with the intention of bringing it forward again at a later time.

The manner in which issues are framed and presented can be of the utmost importance. A good example is found in the old story of the parishioner who asked if it was all right to smoke while praying. The priest answered, "Absolutely not; such an action is an effrontery to God." Later, the parishioner asked if it was all right to pray while smoking. "Of course, my child," the priest answered, "prayer is always appropriate." The way we ask a question can predispose its answer.

Successfully framing issues in organizations seems to work best when what will be gained or saved is emphasized, rather than emphasizing what will be damaged, diminished, or lost. Influence is also stronger when the framing of an issue appears to be free of self-interest. The gains or savings must be organizational in nature and tied to the organization's mission and goals. In schools, any proposal framed as something that will maintain or positively affect student achievement, student attendance, or public image is likely to have a better chance of adoption. This is ideal for school library media specialists. Virtually every proposal you can make to expand the role of the library can be framed as simultaneously helping teachers and students. Material requests should always be presented as items to fulfill student, teacher, or programmatic needs—not the library's. Rarely, if ever, ask for anything for the library itself. Ask for things to support the science program. We'll just house them in the library.

Another important element in issue framing, especially in institutions like schools, is the emotional element. People like to think they are rational, and organizations go to great lengths to appear as though they have made rational decisions by gathering all types of quantitative evidence to support their decisions. There is a strong argument to be made that appealing to emotions can help to shape issues along a different dimension, one every bit as powerful as the numerical. Research indicates that vivid stories, the evocation of powerful feelings, and case studies may well be more persuasive than any set of statistics.[12] These techniques will be explored in more depth in a later chapter.

As Jeff Pfeffer points out, the framing of an issue can often decide its outcome, so it is important to be a part of the process of framing issues in your school.[13] The opportunity to frame issues requires that you be present when the issues surface. This means seeking access to the places where decisions are made: board meetings, the principal's cabinet, the department chairs' council, ongoing committees, ad-hoc committees, and task forces.

Attending more meetings is not usually an attractive proposition for school people. Yet, the research suggests that presence and persistence are two of the cardinal rules in being able to influence the way issues take shape and how they are decided. The further advantage is the increase in your visibility.

Attention to the contrast heuristic is also useful in deciding where to place issues on meeting agendas. If a proposal can benefit from the effects of contrast with what came before it, its chances of being adopted are increased. If the proposal can be framed as a concession to an objection, the odds of getting support through a reciprocal concession are again increased.

It is obviously beneficial to be able to control the agenda of any group you wish to influence. The value of controlling the agenda lies not only in being able to select the placement of items, but also—in some situations—to determine whether or not a particular item even gets on the agenda. The price of agenda control is usually paid through a willingness to serve as the group's chair, or at least as secretary (or a willingness to be the chair's or secretary's very good friend).

Consistency and Commitment

The Concept

Once we take a position on a particular idea or situation, it's our human nature to try to remain consistent in that position. Review again your rating of the statements at the beginning of the chapter. Do you want to be seen as "wishy-washy"? Do you like people who continually change their minds? Do you respect people who are consistent in the positions they take?

Consistency is a powerful force in shaping our behavior for two reasons. First, it's a heuristic practice that allows us another cognitive shortcut. Just as taking time to examine each facet of everything we encounter would paralyze us, so would re-examination. Additionally, reviewing mistakes, lost opportunities, and wrongful acts can be both energy consuming and painful, especially when they cannot be called back or corrected.[14]

Second, we value consistency in other people and in ourselves. Consequently, we want to look and feel consistent in our actions and beliefs. Leon Festinger's cognitive dissonance theory helps to explain why. Dissonance theory contends that most of us feel uncomfortable when we have to deal with information inconsistent with what we believe, and that we have similar difficulty accommodating differences between our attitudes and our behaviors.[15] We want to have harmony and balance in our interactions with the outside world.

This helps to explain why it's often difficult to get people to change their opinions or to accept new information as accurate. When we have very strongly held views, the discomfort associated with processing information that challenges what we believe leads us to avoid such information. If we can't avoid it, we tend to reject its validity, either outright or by impugning the credibility of the source. Made to deal with it, we have a tendency to distort it in our memories or to quickly forget it.[16] Good examples of this surface all the time in anti-smoking campaigns.

At the professional level, this kind of thinking helps explain why school librarians have not frequently and aggressively challenged the perceptions many other educators have of them. It is simply more comfortable to deny being thought of as peripheral, to reject the fact that others don't attach the same value to the library, or to suggest that others simply are closed minded and recalcitrant. No engagement means no conflict—and, hence, no need to reassess our own positions.

When we do engage our feelings and assess our own positions, we have to deal with any incongruency we find between our actions and our beliefs. Most people feel uncomfortable when their behavior is inconsistent with their attitudes and try to restore some sort of balance by changing one or the other. Since behaviors are more public and visible than attitudes, and once performed they cannot be changed, it is frequently easier to change an attitude.[17]

For example, we appear foolish if we work very hard to be admitted to a social group that really has no worth, just as we do if we work very hard to complete a task that is essentially meaningless. In order to avoid such feelings, we distort information and change our attitudes to convince ourselves that what we are doing is worthwhile. It is easier to convince ourselves that something we're working on is valuable than it is to acknowledge that we're working like crazy on something worthless.

We almost always distort information and perceptions when we see ourselves as acting stupidly or immorally.[18] This happens because, just as we do in making judgments of other people, we use our own behaviors to judge what we are really like.[19]

An important condition affecting this process is whether the behavior is engaged in freely or is coerced. We have no problem in rejecting responsibility for the effects of behavior for which we had no choice. Forced compliance undermines all the power of cognitive dissonance because we did not choose to behave in a particular fashion. Absent that choice, the behavior doesn't really open a gulf between our attitudes and our activity.

Assume for a moment that you have a very strong work ethic and believe that no one should ever be absent from the job because an educator's work is so important. Then you miss work. If you missed because you decided to go to the beach or the movies, or to extend a romantic weekend one more day, you probably will have to wrestle with your attitudes about work. Erving Goffman, a scholar in these things, argues that we only escape the negative implications of an act by offering excuses or justifications for our behavior that we truly believe.[20]

An excuse, Goffman says, frees us of responsibility because it demonstrates the impossibility of choice: I couldn't come to work today because I was injured in an auto accident and was taken to the hospital. A justification, on the other hand, admits that we were in control of our choices when the behavior was performed, but circumstances dictated that we make the choice we did: My daughter broke her arm and I took her to the hospital. This is a justification because it argues that while I had a choice, anyone in my place would have done the same thing. Only behavior that is out of line with our attitudes and for which we have no excuse or justification causes dissonance.

Implications for Librarians

The importance of all this in exercising influence at work rests in the fact that once people make a decision, make a commitment, or take a position, they are more likely to agree to things they perceive as consistent with those decisions, commitments, or positions. This is especially true when the initial action is voluntary, irrevocable, and public.[21] The key is in getting someone to take the initial step.

Research suggests three reasons why getting an initial commitment from someone can have a real impact on later efforts to influence that person's behavior. First, if a person can be made to comply on a minor issue, he or she is more likely to conform to larger requests later on.[22] This is known as the foot-in-the door technique, and each escalating commitment tightens the links between behavior and attitude. It helps to explain, for example, why it is easier to get someone to come into work on a Saturday morning six months from now if you can get him or her to come in a half hour early every once in a while now.

This speaks to getting people initially involved in library activities in a small way if you can't get them involved in a larger way at the outset. The groundwork you lay now can make all the difference in whether a problem or an opportunity that you have no way of foreseeing is successfully handled in the future. An iron rule of influence—as of administration—is that your ability to solve problems and take advantage of opportunities in the present depends upon the relationships you have established with others in the past.

Second, getting a commitment in writing increases its intensity. Think about why psychologists encourage you to write down your New Year's resolutions, your annual goals, and your life plans. Think about why, if it's typical, your school district asks you to write your own professional development goals as a part of your evaluation instead of just handing you a list of things to accomplish.

Writing is an action; it carries more of an impact than just verbal agreement. It also renders support of a position permanent. The document can be shown to other people.[23] Encourage people inside the school and out to give you written proposals for library involvement. Encourage them to write—not just speak—to a business, a parent group, a department head, an administrator, or a board member in support of some grant proposal, acquisition, schedule change, program, service, or other idea you have. Ask your principal, superintendent, parent group president, union leader, or business partner liaison to write something about the library for your library newsletter, the principal's newsletter, or the district newsletter. Get them or others to make statements that you can post on your Web site. Even if a particular thing doesn't come to fruition, a public statement in support of the library has been made. The person is committed to maintaining that position.

Third, the more effort invested in a commitment, the more that commitment will influence later actions.[24] This is what gives fraternities, military academies, the clergy, and certain professions the hold they have on their members. You can't hope to match the intensity of those experiences, but inducing someone to work hard for the library either intellectually, as in writing a grant proposal, or physically, as in painting a room, is a step in the right direction.

Social Proof

The Concept

The social proof heuristic assumes that the group knows best—that collective judgment is better than individual judgment. It isn't just children who defend their actions by saying, "but everybody else's parents let them do it" or "everyone else has one." How did you rate the statements relating to this at the beginning of the chapter? Is there safety in numbers? Can 50 million Frenchmen be wrong? Do you want to be fashionably dressed? Are popular movies good?

Put another way, social proof is the tendency to look at the way others behave in order to determine if the way we are behaving is appropriate.[25] We all do it. Think of the last time you couldn't remember which fork to use at a certain stage of a formal dinner, or of the last time you drove faster or slower than the posted speed limits. Think of the last time you sat in a tense faculty meeting, someone made a joke, and there was that terrible silent moment before laughter erupted. In the tension of the situation, people looked around to see whether others were going to laugh, moan, or ignore it.

Social proof is the thinking behind recording the laughter of live audiences when taping television situation comedies. Do you remember the opening of each *Cheers* episode? "*Cheers* is filmed before a live studio audience." If you're older, or if you watch any of the television nostalgia stations, you'll remember laugh tracks were added to programs recorded without an audience. In both cases, the immediately sequential presentation of an actor's line and the laughter invokes the social proof heuristic, providing simple decision rules for what to perceive as funny and when you are supposed to laugh.

We've had recent examples of this in education. One has to ask why so many schools all at once moved toward block scheduling and so many districts toward site-based management in the late 1980s to mid-1990s. Research suggests that it was because so many others were doing it.

Social proof, or social influence as many social psychologists refer to it, supports heuristic thinking because it frees us again from having to make a close examination of every situation. It provides a simple decision rule: if others are doing it, it must be acceptable.

Coupled with the notions of commitment and consistency, social proof powerfully influences both our behaviors and attitudes. Once we do something because others are doing it, we tell ourselves that it is the right thing to do. That helps us avoid the cognitive dissonance we would experience if the behavior were otherwise out of line with our thinking.

Implications for Librarians

The power of social proof is strongest in three particular situations. First, it is strong in situations where people are like ourselves. In that sense, social proof ties back to the personal attribute of similarity as a component of likability. Both provide social validation.

Second, social proof is strong in cases where there is a high level of individual uncertainty, such as when someone is just starting a new job or is working where very little performance feedback is provided.

Third, social proof is strong when the environment itself is uncertain, such as when there are a lot of organizational changes taking place in a short amount of time.

These three conditions are common in schools. As a result, social proof can be an especially useful influence tool for you. First, most of the adults around us in schools are very much like ourselves. Certificated employees—teachers, administrators, counselors, and the like—share similar educations because of credentialing laws, have similar working lifestyles and experiences, and share an interest in and a commitment to young people. While members of the classified staff may have varying educational backgrounds, they too share the same environment and many interactions with young people.

Second, individual levels of uncertainty can run high in schools. Student and employee turnover occurs every year, and newcomers are always uncertain. A change of principal, a new department head, or a shift in the board's majority can all raise questions about how the school will function. The pressures of a curriculum change, the implementation of an untried bell schedule, the imposition of standards and standardized testing, or the mandating of a new teaching technique all engender uncertainty. Even in the most stable of schools, teachers most often work in isolation, spending their days in separate classrooms apart from other adults. It is very difficult for them to acquire a very complete or accurate understanding of all that is going on in a building at any given time.[26]

Third, the overall goals and objectives of work in schools are frequently unclear. There are subjective and varying definitions of what constitutes quality education, and the shifting demands and limitations society places on schools further cloud the issue. With the current emphasis on shifting paradigms, restructuring, and new governance systems, schools can be very uncertain environments.

You can develop the influence potential of social proof two ways. The first is by demonstrating linkages between your ideas and the approval of others: "When I showed this to Mr. Johnson's students ..." or "There are 55 schools in the state enthusiastically supporting this system ..." Even if your idea is completely original, it can pay dividends to search the research literature for evidence supporting ideas that approximate it.

Social proof's power can be multiplied when the "others" speak from positions of individual or collective authority: "I heard the superintendent say ..."; "This notion of library services is supported by the NASSP, the NEA, the AFT, the ASCD, and the National Council on Staff Development."[27]

The second way to use social proof is by applying your skills and knowledge to help reduce uncertainty: "Sure, lots of people are doing this, and I know how to find just what you need;" "Let me teach your students how to do this;" "I heard you were just beginning to work with this approach and I wanted you to know that I have some things which may be helpful;" "Research shows ..."

Whatever you elect to do, it's important to initiate it as early as you can. Getting involved in decision-making and causing your influence to be felt early are powerful tactics. As soon as people decide to confront a certain issue, they begin to shape their attitudes and beliefs in regard to it and begin to look for allies who support their positions. Given the nature of social proof, once things begin to move in a particular direction, they are hard to stop. Visualize a ball rolling down a hill toward a division in the path. If you just touch the ball, just give it a little nudge *before* it gets to the division point, it will slip into the right or left fork as you desire. But if you let it get past the division point before putting your finger on it and it goes down the wrong path, you're faced with the task of stopping it and then of either rolling it back up to the division point or portaging it over the divider between the paths. It's best to get involved early.

The rub here, of course, is that you must position yourself uphill of the division point, meaning that you must be at the committee meeting, faculty meeting, department meeting, board meeting, or other gathering where the issue ball is launched and directed toward a certain path. The cost of influence is involvement.

Scarcity

The Concept

Unavailability enhances desirability, and abundance or scarcity serves as a heuristic cue to any item's value.[28] We tend to place a higher value on things that are harder to come by than on things that are easily available. Look back at how you rated the statements associated with this principle at the beginning of the chapter. What did your father tell you about earning your own money to buy your first car? About paying your own way through school? How do Marines feel about the Corps? What are the differences in status between a medical school education, a law school education, a liberal arts degree, and a teaching certificate? Are cheap goods inferior? Is the last cookie tastier than the first?

Difficulty in obtaining something usually involves one or more of three conditions: (1) the item itself is in limited supply; (2) the item is very expensive and available only to a limited portion of the population; or (3) access to the item is limited in some way, such as admission to Harvard or access to a censored book.

School librarians are as familiar with the scarcity principle as anyone could be. A sure way to draw attention to and increase the efforts of readers to obtain a copy of a book is to refuse to buy it, to censor it, to ban it, or to otherwise make it unavailable. Restricting access increases demand.

The scarcity principle is invoked around us all the time. It is, for example, a mainstay of advertising. When an item is difficult to obtain, people are motivated to find positive attributes in it that justify its scarcity and the fact that they don't have it.[29] Trading on this, advertisers fill newspapers and television with announcements of products and services available "for a limited time only" and admonitions to "Hurry! Only a few left."

The scarcity principle also applies to information. What was your reaction the last time someone said to you: "I can't tell you that" or "I'm not at liberty to say"? The odds are that your interest in the information increased. Think of a meeting where everyone but you received a particular memo. If you had received it, you might have thrown it away with all the other memos. But, as a result of not receiving it, its value jumped. As the Roman poet Ovid put it 2,000 years ago: "Easy things nobody wants, but what is forbidden is tempting."[30]

Researchers have identified several reasons why scarcity is such a powerful motivator. First, like most heuristic assumptions, there is a lot of truth in the association of value and scarcity. It's not true all the time, but it certainly is true as often as it is not true. Unconsciously applying the scarcity principle saves immense mental effort.

Second, possessing things unavailable to most people provides an opportunity for self-enhancement. People with such possessions see themselves as unique and worthy.[31] Tied to this is a third reason: Others see the possession of something scarce as special, which enhances the status of the possessor.[32]

Fourth, unavailability or diminishing availability is interpreted by many people as a narrowing of their choices in life. Social psychologist Jack Brehm termed this as "reactance," noting that when something becomes more difficult to acquire than it was previously, people will react against this narrowing of their choices and struggle all the harder to obtain whatever the thing might be.[33] Of particular interest secondary to school librarians is the fact that the reactance effect is especially strong among teenagers. Adolescence is a period in which the youngster is developing a sense of individuality and is very sensitive to issues of freedom, rights, restrictions, and control.[34]

Implications for Librarians

As a potential source of influence, it is important to note that the scarcity principle is strongest when people are in a situation where they need to compete for whatever it is that is limited. Whether the item that is restricted or in short supply is tangible, intangible, or just an opportunity to get or do something, its value is increased by actual or threatened scarcity.

This suggests that you might consider approaches like these:

• Make it known that you have a limited budget for purchasing new materials.

• Consider establishing valuable services and then let it be known that not all requests can be accommodated: audiovisual or technology support services; the number of books which can be put on reserve; display space; research services.

- Make it known that you are available to teach a class on subject X (which may or may not necessarily be a library topic), but only until the end of the quarter.

- Announce that there is a short window of opportunity to file a grant proposal that could bring significant resources to the library and selected teachers—if they are willing to work hard on it right now.

It may be that you are doing things like these now, but there doesn't seem to be much competition for them. The lack of competition may not stem from a lack of interest. Rather, it may be the result of a lack of widespread knowledge of their existence. If they are not well known, you may want to do two or three things: Get time at a faculty meeting or visit department meetings to describe and discuss them (only their availability and usefulness, not their limitations); put out a flyer; or get the information included in the faculty handbook.

If these services are well known and you are receiving no benefit from them, you may want to consider other examples of services and materials—or you may want to consider restricting or discontinuing one or more of those you have in place and see what reaction you get.

The key is that the service or item must be of value to others. The more integral they perceive it to be to *their* success, the greater the value it will possess, and the greater the reaction to its limitation, restriction, or loss.

Authority

The Concept

The recognition of authority is another powerful source of heuristic decision rules. We are socialized from early childhood to respect and defer to authority, and most of us take the lessons to heart. Review your ratings at the beginning of the chapter. Do you listen to what experts say? How do you react to someone with a badge? in a uniform? with the title of Director or Professor? Do you carry out the principal's and superintendent's wishes just because of the offices they hold? Shakespeare summed it up when he had King Lear observe the power of a watchdog in Act IV:

> Thou hast seen a farmer's dog bark at a beggar? And the creature run from the cur? There thou mightst behold the great image of authority; a dog's obey'd in office.

We live with a bias to give appointed leaders the benefit of the doubt, especially whenever we're not sure of the rationale for what we're being asked to do. This provides people with formal authority or outstanding reputations a great measure of influence over our behavior.

Need for Authority Structures: Appropriate recognition of authority is a positive in society. Without it, vital systems of production, coordination, and distribution cannot be constructed, let alone function effectively. Moral authority is a similar necessity. Alexander Hamilton once observed that the reason governments exist at all is because our passions will not conform to the dictates of reason and justice without restraint.[35] A society without recognized and institutionalized authority systems is an anarchy.

Consequently, we are taught at home, in school, and through religion to respect and defer to authority. In most instances, this is appropriate. As Pfeffer points out, we learn early in life that people in authority typically *do* know more about things than we do. If we accept at all the idea that promotions and appointments are based on merit, then we must accept the likelihood that a person vested with formal organizational authority possesses knowledge, skill, and experience exceeding those of the average employee.[36]

The Dangers of Authority: The danger in complete deference to authority, of course, is that mindless obedience can lead us into disaster. Proof of this doesn't require large-scale evidence, such as the Nazi experience. There are plenty of examples that strike much closer to home. Stanley Milgram's classic 1965 study is a clear demonstration.[37]

Milgram wanted to test how much pain one person would inflict on another simply because someone in authority ordered it. He set up an experiment in which he told participants that he was researching the effects of punishment on learning. Subjects were asked to give a "learner" an electric shock each time an incorrect answer was delivered. The shocks would range from slight to moderate, strong, very strong, intense, extremely intense, and dangerous and would be administered solely at Milgram's direction. As a recognized world-class expert in psychology and the director of the Yale University based project, Milgram possessed a great deal of authority in this context.

The "learner" was a confederate. Not actually in any danger at all, the learner was paid to give an incorrect answer and then to jump, complain, and protest when the increasingly potent "shocks" were delivered. At some point, the learner would demand to be set free.

Milgram consulted with psychiatrists before beginning his experiments. They predicted that most subjects would never administer shocks above the moderate level, that less than 5% would ever give very strong shocks, and that only one in 1,000 would ever deliver dangerous shocks. The frightening result was that almost two-thirds of the subjects punished the "learners" with dangerous shocks. The power of Milgram's authority was overwhelming.

The most frightening thing about this study and the results of similar studies done since is that the subjects were not evil people. They were deliberately chosen because they were "ordinary" people. It is just that evil and immoral behavior doesn't alone belong to the pathological. Given the right circumstances, virtually all of us are vulnerable to the power of authority. In fact, as Pfeffer observes, the power of authority is so accepted that it makes news when someone breaks the chain of command and defies the structure of the hierarchy.[38]

Implications for Librarians

School librarians rarely possess organizational authority. That doesn't necessarily keep you from tapping into its influence potential, however, because there are alternatives to formal authority. "Authority" as an influence force is not limited to formal position. Research shows that we also react and defer to reputations of power and symbols of authority very much like we do to actual formal authority. Titles affect the way we think about people, as do the way people dress and the trappings with which they surround themselves.

Reputation: Reputation is a powerful force for influence. Reputations affect how others respond to us. People perceived as powerful and competent are less likely to be resisted or challenged. The result is they get more things accomplished with less effort, an effect that adds to their reputation for power and begins the cycle again.[39]

Reputations are built on a number of factors. Among these are the ways people perceive your performance record, your expertise, your personal attributes, and your association with successful endeavors and people. This means that you need to avoid being associated with losing causes except by design.

A reputation for success or failure is not usually built on one particular incident. Rather, it comes from others' perception of a pattern in your associations and behavior. Building a reputation as an effective contributor depends on being successful with several projects over time. It is best, of course, to begin with a string of successes and build on that foundation rather than beginning with failures and having to pull yourself out of a reputational hole.[40]

The lesson here is to avoid being associated with losing causes with any regularity. Losing causes help to create a reputation of either being a "loser" or of being what Stephen Robbins refers to as a "tainted" member.[41] A tainted member is one whose performance, loyalty, or status is questionable. Tainted members are the people at the fringes of the organization. A tainted image is no more productive in terms of influence than is a loser's image. Both the image and the people who carry it are to be kept at a distance.

On occasion, there may be an issue of such moral clarity that you feel you have no choice but to maintain your position even into defeat. If that occurs, only your conscience can be your guide. What influence research suggests, though, is that you will do well to make a couple of judgments before finalizing your commitment.

First, you need to ask yourself if there is anything that can be gained from defeat on this issue. Sometimes a public and open stand on what many perceive as a moral point will increase influence potential, even if the point is lost. Issues such as these surface frequently in schools because schools are such intensely human enterprises and advocates have so many different interpretations of what is right and needful for young people. If the answer to the question is yes, it may be worth losing for reasons beyond moral purity if the public exposure will attract people who will later support you on other issues. If the answer is no, commitment to the end leads only to martyrdom, the value of which only you can assess.

This leads to the second judgment to be made: is this really the final battle on this is issue? Issues in organizations, especially in schools, have a way of coming around again. It's what J. Victor Baldridge of UCLA calls the "issue carousel."[42] It may be that you can see when there will be an opportunity to deal with this issue again, and you will have the time between now and then to marshal your resources.

Titles and Appearance: Titles and clothes provide other types of heuristic clues that substitute for judgment.[43] Con artists frequently give themselves titles like doctor, judge, director, or colonel to convey an impression of certain attributes.

Titles can be tricky for school library media specialists. A four word title is simply too long, and school people, in most locations anyway, are very much accustomed to referring to the person who does the work you do as a librarian. Without a simultaneous change in the perceptions they hold, a change in the value they place on the school library media center, and a clear distinction between the activities in which you now engage and those of the traditional librarian, it may be very difficult to get school staff members to use a new title. They may, in fact, regard the demand to be called by a new title as presumptive, which will have the effect of reducing your influence potential.

You have to judge the value of pushing for a particular title. If you decide that it is important to you, you might begin in small ways and let them build. For example, make sure that all your correspondence says media center on it, that every time you sign a document it carries that title, and that the title appears in all faculty and student handbooks. It will take time to catch on.

Dress decisions for librarians can also be complicated. On the one hand, there is an argument to dress as the teachers do in order to enhance similarity. On the other, there is the question of the impression delivered by dressing more formally. Police and military uniforms, even security guard uniforms with a badge, white lab coats, clerical garb, and formal business attire all carry messages of authority to which people respond. The research literature, not to mention the advertising and criminal literature, is full of examples of people who were more able to persuade others when dressed in a certain way.

This thinking exists in schools as well as in other organizations and in society at large. Why do administrators wear much more formal dress than teachers wear? Teacher dress patterns in school settings also raise another interesting question: how, if at all, did the change from formal to informal dress for teachers in the latter 1960s and 1970s affect the way students saw their instructors? Your dress decisions will have to be made based on the merits of your individual school culture, your particular needs, and those with whom you most wish to appear similar.

Trappings and Surroundings: Authority is communicated through symbols as well as through appearances and interactions. Cialdini cites a study done in San Francisco that demonstrated that owners of luxury cars receive deference in traffic that others don't.[44] But there are more subtle and important symbols of authority than automobiles, especially in organizations like schools.

Research in office decor and arrangement has offered some interesting insights into how visitors read the physical environment in which others work. For example, prominently displayed diplomas, certificates, and licenses have a positive effect on a visitor's first impression of an office occupant's authority and expertise.[45] Professionally related objects such as plaques, books, and journals add to the impression of occupant authoritativeness.[46] It is a common experience to be exposed to such things when waiting to see physicians, dentists, and attorneys. Perhaps you could provide the same opportunity to those who visit you.

Aesthetic objects can also serve as status symbols, marking rank in the hierarchy and levels of special service. The ability to personalize a space is a mark of authority in an organization.[47] Consider how much more a school administrator can personalize an office compared to a teacher in the classroom, where subjects taught and student accomplishments are given paramount attention. Consider how much more you can personalize your office.

Conclusion

Heuristic assumptions pervade our interactions with other people. As much as others are vulnerable to their effects, so too are we. From the perspective of someone trying to influence another, heuristic-thinking patterns can be made useful in the presentation of ideas and arguments. On the other hand, from the target's perspective, heuristic thinking can be dangerous.

Heuristic thinking is easily triggered as a part of argumentation. When an honest case is presented in ways that enlist social proof, authority, and other heuristic forces, everyone benefits. But it is a moral violation when a case is grounded on false information and heuristic responses are triggered with the specific intention of masking the deficiencies of an item or idea.

The context of a conversation often gives the key clue in deciding whether to trust our decisions to our heuristic preferences. It's a fairly safe bet that it's better not to take cognitive or judgmental shortcuts in discussions of policy change or innovation approval. The price of misjudgment can be very high.

References

1 *The American Heritage Desk Dictionary* (Boston: Houghton Mifflin Company, 1981), p. 461.

2 A. H. Eagly and S. Chaiken, "Cognitive Theories of Persuasion," In L. Berkowitz (Ed.), *Advances in Experimental Social Psychology, Volume 17* (pp. 267–359) (New York: Academic Press, 1984).

S. Chaiken, "Heuristic Versus Systematic Information Processing and the Use of Source Versus Message Cues in Persuasion," *Journal of Personality and Social Psychology*, vol. 39, no. 5 (1980), pp. 752–766.

3 S. Taylor, "The Interface of Cognitive and Social Psychology," In J. H. Harvey (Ed.), *Cognition, Social Behavior, and the Environment* (pp. 189–211) (Hillsdale, NJ: Lawrence Erlbaum Associates Publishers, 1981).

4 R. B. Cialdini, *Influence: Science and Practice, Third Edition* (New York: Harper Collins, 1993), p. 6.

J. Sabini, *Social Psychology* (New York: W. K. Norton and Company, 1992).

W. Stroebe and K. Jonas, "Strategies Of Attitude Change," In M. Hewstone, W. Stroebe, J. Codol, and G. M. Stephenson (Eds.), *Introduction to Social Psychology: A European Perspective* (pp. 167–195) (Oxford, England: Basil Blackwell Ltd., 1988).

5 D. Kahneman, P. Slovic, and A. Tversky (Eds.), *Judgment Under Uncertainty: Heuristics and Biases* (New York: Cambridge University Press, 1982).

6 A. H. Eagly and S. Chaiken, "Cognitive Theories of Persuasion," In L. Berkowitz (Ed.), *Advances in Experimental Social Psychology, Volume 17* (pp. 267–359) (New York: Academic Press, 1984).

S. Chaiken, "The Heuristic Model of Persuasion," In M. P. Zanna, J. M. Olso, and C. P. Herman (Eds.), *Social Influence: The Ontario Symposium, Volume 5* (pp. 3–39) (Hillsdale, NJ: Lawrence Erlbaum Associates Publishers, 1987).

S. Chaiken, "Heuristic Versus Systematic Information Processing and the Use of Source Versus Message Cues in Persuasion," *Journal of Personality and Social Psychology*, vol. 39, no. 5 (1980), pp. 752–766.

7 R. B. Cialdini, *Influence: Science and Practice, Third Edition* (New York: Harper Collins, 1993).

8 A. W. Gouldner, "The Norm of Reciprocity: A Preliminary Statement," *American Sociological Review*, vol. 25, no. 2 (1960), pp. 161–178.

H. C. Triandis, "Some Universals of Social Behavior," *Personality and Social Psychology Bulletin*, vol. 4, no. 1 (1978), pp. 1–16.

9 R. B. Cialdini, *Influence: Science and Practice, Third Edition* (New York: Harper Collins, 1993), p. 45.

10 R. B. Cialdini, *Influence: Science and Practice, Third Edition* (New York: Harper Collins, 1993), pp. 31–32.

11 R. B. Cialdini, *Influence: Science and Practice, Third Edition* (New York: Harper Collins, 1993), p. 12.

12 D. C. Kazoleas, "A Comparison of the Persuasive Effectiveness of Qualitative versus Quantitative Evidence: A Test of Explanatory Hypotheses," *Communication Quarterly*, vol. 41, no. 2 (Winter 1993), pp. 40–50.

R. M. Perloff, *The Dynamics of Persuasion* (Hillsdale, NJ: Lawerence Erlbaum Associates, Publishers, 1993).

K. K. Reardon, *Persuasion in Practice* (Newbury Park, CA: Sage Publishers, 1991).

13 J. Pfeffer, *Managing With Power: Politics and Influence in Organizations* (Cambridge, MA: Harvard Business School Press, 1992), p. 205.

14 R. B. Cialdini, *Influence: Science and Practice, Third Edition* (New York: Harper Collins, 1993), p 53.

J. Pfeffer, *Managing With Power: Politics and Influence in Organizations* (Cambridge, MA: Harvard Business School Press, 1992), p. 194.

15 L. Festinger, *A Theory of Cognitive Dissonance* (Stanford, CA: Stanford University Press, 1957).

16 E. Aronson, *The Social Animal, Third Edition* (San Francisco: W. H. Freeman Publishers, 1980).

D. Frey and M. Rosch, "Information Seeking After Decisions: The Roles of Novelty of Information and Decision Reversibility," *Personality and Social Psychology Bulletin*, vol. 10, no. 1 (1984), pp. 91–98.

G. Strauss and L. R. Sayles, *Behavioral Strategies for Managers* (Englewood Cliffs, NJ: Prentice-Hall, 1980).

17 E. Aronson, "The Theory of Cognitive Dissonance: A Current Perspective," In L. Berkowitz (Ed.), *Advances in Experimental Social Psychology*, Volume Four (pp. 1–34) (New York: Academic Press, 1969).

L. Festinger, *A Theory of Cognitive Dissonance* (Stanford, CA: Stanford University Press, 1957).

18 E. Aronson, T. Chase, R. Helmreich, and R. Ruhnke, "Feeling Stupid and Feeling Guilty— Two Aspects of the Self-concept Which Mediate Dissonance Arousal in a Communication Situation," In E. Aronson (Ed.), *Readings About the Social Animal* (San Francisco: Freeman Publishers, 1981).

19 D. J. Bem, "Self-perception Theory," In L. Berkowitz (Ed.), *Advances in Experimental Social Psychology, Volume 6* (pp. 2–62) (New York: Academic Press, 1972).

20 E. Goffman, *Relations in Public* (New York: Harper and Row, 1971).

21 R. B. Cialdini, *Influence: Science and Practice, Third Edition* (New York: Harper Collins, 1993), p. 92.

22 C. A. Kiesler and S. B. Kiesler, *Conformity* (Reading, MA: Addison-Wesley Publishers, 1969).

23 R. B. Cialdini, *Influence: Science and Practice, Third Edition* (New York: Harper Collins, 1993), pp 64–69.

24 E. Aronson and J. Mills, "The Effect of Severity of Initiation on Liking for a Group," *Journal of Abnormal and Social Psychology*, vol. 59, no. 9 (1959), pp. 177–181.

25 R. B. Cialdini, *Influence: Science and Practice, Third Edition* (New York: Harper Collins, 1993), p. 95.

26 M. W. McLaughlin, J. E. Talbert, and N. Bascia (Eds.), *The Contexts of Teaching in Secondary Schools: Teachers' Realities* (New York: Teachers College Press, 1990).

27 National Association of Secondary School Principals (NASSP)

National Education Association (NEA)

American Federation of Teachers (AFT)

Association for Supervision and Curriculum Development (ASCD)

28 T. C. Brock, "Implications of Commodity Theory for Value Change," In A. G. Greenwald, T. C. Brock, and T. M. Ostrom (Eds.), *Psychological Foundations of Attitudes* (pp. 243–275) (New York: Academic Press, 1968).

R. Folger, "On Wanting What We Do Not Have," *Basic and Applied Social Psychology*, vol. 13, no. 1 (1992), pp. 123–133.

M. Lynn, "Scarcity's Enhancement of Desirability: The Role of Naive Economic Theories," *Basic and Applied Social Psychology*, vol. 13, no. 1 (1992), pp. 67–78.

29 J. J. Seta and C. E. Seta, "Personal Equity-Comparison Theory: An Analysis of Value and the Generation of Compensatory and Noncompensatory Expectancies," *Basic and Applied Social Psychology*, vol. 13, no. 1 (1992), pp. 47–66.

30 Ovid, *The Art of Love* (R. Humphries, translator) (Bloomington, IN: Indiana University Press, 1957).

31 C. R. Snyder and H. L. Fromkin, *Uniqueness: The Human Pursuit of Difference* (New York: Plenum Publishers, 1980).

T. A. Wills, "Downward Comparison Principles in Social Psychology," *Psychological Bulletin*, vol. 90, no. 2 (1981), pp. 245–271.

32 T. Veblen, *The Theory of the Leisure Class* (New York: Kelly Publishers, 1965).

33 J. W. Brehm, *A Theory of Psychological Reactance* (New York: Academic Press, 1966).

34 R. B. Cialdini, *Influence: Science and Practice, Third Edition* (New York: Harper Collins, 1993), p. 220.

35 A. Hamilton, J. Madison, and J. Jay, *The Federalist Papers*, Edited by Clinton Rossiter (New York: New American Library of World Literature, Inc., 1964).

36 J. Pfeffer, *Managing With Power: Politics and Influence in Organizations* (Cambridge, MA: Harvard Business School Press, 1992), p. 132.

37 S. Milgram. *Obedience to Authority*. New York: Harper and Row Publishers, 1974.

38 J. Pfeffer, *Managing With Power: Politics and Influence in Organizations* (Cambridge, MA: Harvard Business School Press, 1992), p. 133.

39 J. Pfeffer, *Managing With Power: Politics and Influence in Organizations* (Cambridge, MA: Harvard Business School Press, 1992), p. 136.

40 G. M. Bellman, *Getting Things Done When You Are Not in Charge: How to Succeed From a Support Position* (San Francisco: Berrett-Koehler Publishers, 1992), p. 201.

J. Pfeffer, *Managing With Power: Politics and Influence in Organizations* (Cambridge, MA: Harvard Business School Press, 1992), p. 140.

41 S. P. Robbins. *Training in Interpersonal Skills: TIPS for Managing People at Work*. Englewood Cliffs, NJ: Prentice-Hall Publishers, 1989, p. 174.

42 J. V. Baldridge, "Rules for a Machiavellian Change Agent: Transforming the Entrenched Professional Organization," In J. V. Baldridge and T. Deal (Eds.), *The Dynamics of Organizational Change in Education* (pp. 191–208) (Berkeley, CA: McCutchan Publishing Corporation, 1983).

43 R. B. Cialdini, *Influence: Science and Practice, Third Edition* (New York: Harper Collins, 1993), pp. 181–186.

44 A. N. Doob and A. E. Gross, "Status of Frustrator as an Inhibitor of Horn-Honking Response," *Journal of Social Psychology*, vol. 76, no. 2 (1968), pp. 213–218.

45 T. R. V. Davis, "The Influence of the Physical Environment in Offices," *Academy of Management Review*, vol. 9, no. 2 (1984), pp. 281–283.

P. Heppner and S. Pew, "Effects of Diplomas, Awards and Counselor Sex on Perceived Expertness," *Journal of Counseling Psychology*, vol. 24, no. 2 (1977), pp. 147–149.

J. C. Siegel and J. Sell, "The Effects of Objective Evidence of Expertness and Nonverbal Behavior on Client-Perceived Expertness," *Journal of Counseling Psychology*, vol. 25, no. 3 (1978), pp. 188–192.

46 E. W. Miles and D. G. Leathers, "The Impact of Aesthetic and Professionally-Related Objects on Credibility in the Office Setting," *Southern Speech Communication Journal*, vol. 49, no. 3, pp. 361–379.

P. C. Morrow, and J. C. McElroy, "Interior Office Design and Visitor Response: A Constructive Replication," *Journal of Applied Psychology*, vol. 66, no. 5 (1981), pp. 646–650.

47 E. Konar, E. Sundstrom, C. Brady, D. Mandel, and R. W. Rice, "Status Demarcation in the Office," *Environment and Behavior*, vol. 14, no. 5 (1982), pp. 561–580.

M. Korda, *Power: How to Get it, How to Use it* (New York: Random House Publishers, 1975).

Chapter 5
Some Positions Facilitate Influence Building

As much as another's personal attributes or our own heuristic thinking may predispose us to react to other people in certain ways, these interactions never take place in a vacuum. Work environments, especially work environments like schools, are social settings where we constantly interact with supervisors, colleagues, and clients. Many things influence the ways in which we approach and treat each other. Not least among these are the relative positions we hold in the organizational structure.

Before you begin this chapter, stop for a moment and think about the operation of your media center and your job as the school librarian. How do you answer each of the questions in Figure 5.1?

1 = To a high degree   4 = A little
2 = Generally   5 = Not at all
3 = Somewhat

1 2 3 4 5   My library media center collection conforms to established quality standards for my school level (elementary, middle, high school).

1 2 3 4 5   Teachers depend on me to provide research skill instruction to students.

1 2 3 4 5   The library media center operation visibly supports the stated mission of our school.

1 2 3 4 5   Over the course of a typical school week, I can determine which tasks I will perform and when I will perform them.

1 2 3 4 5   The library is near the physical center of the school building.

1 2 3 4 5   Teachers and administrators consult me when any new curriculum is being developed.

1 2 3 4 5   I have control of the library budget for new material and equipment purchases.

1 2 3 4 5   I can determine the rules regarding acceptable student behavior in the library.

1 2 3 4 5   I can determine the policies for teacher use of equipment and materials.

1 2 3 4 5   The principal and I regularly interact.

1 2 3 4 5   I am regarded by the other adults in the building as an educator in the same way teachers and administrators are regarded as educators.

1 2 3 4 5   Teachers feel free to come to the library to socialize with the library staff and with other teachers.

1 2 3 4 5   Over the course of the school year, I will interact with virtually every other faculty member in the school.

1 2 3 4 5   The quality of the library collection and the range of library operations are well understood by parents.

1 2 3 4 5   My professional friendships are spread across all the departments and programs in the school.

1 2 3 4 5   I participate in many of the same school activities that the teachers in the building participate in.

Research has identified half a dozen positional characteristics that foster influence opportunities for the people who hold them. The questions you just answered illustrate these characteristics. Without saying so, they asked you to think about what resources you control, how much autonomy you have, whether people depend on you for elements of their own success, how visible and how closely identified your library is with the school's mission, and what access you have to information.

To a greater or lesser extent, these characteristics exist in all organizational positions, including school library media centers. The potentialities are obviously more developed in higher level positions, but lower level positions are not without their advantages and opportunities.[1]

The ability to make a difference in what goes on at work increases as you rise in the organization and gain formal authority. In fact, how high a position sits in the hierarchy is probably the first thing people think of—and rightly so—when considering any job's potential for influence. It is important to remember, however, that while elevation in the organizational structure is an important consideration, it's not the only one. There are other important elements to think about in assessing the potential your job holds for helping you build influence.

Any position's influence potential rests in its relationship to the positions that horizontally and vertically surround it. In those relationships are the seeds of opportunities to promote the growth of influence with peers and superiors. The elements of a job that can contribute to building influence for its occupants include:

- Control of resources that others want

- Performance of tasks critical to the success of others

- Work clearly aligned with major organizational goals

- High organizational visibility

- Internal autonomy of action

- Central location in the communication system

Let's take a look at each of these in relation to your library and your influence building potential.

Control of Resources that Others Want

The Concept
Nothing is more fundamental in exercising power and influence than controlling resources.[2] Resources are essential for getting things done, they denote status, and they represent opportunities to invoke the reciprocity heuristic. Consequently, the people who need certain resources in order to do their jobs are dependent upon the people who control them. From an influence building perspective, resources are defined in the broadest of terms. A resource is *anything* you control that someone else wants: a necessary object; a physical location; a specialized service; money; time; people; energy; expertise.

Note that the keyword is "control" and not "possess." Influence potential rests in control, not in custody. The supply warehouse in your school district has possession of all kinds of materials, but the disbursement of those materials is controlled from somewhere else. People who want something in the warehouse must have approvals from people in other locations. Those are the people who have the influence and power.

Organizational researchers Jeff Pfeffer and Gerald Salancik have defined "control" of resources as a combination of two elements beyond possession.[3] The first is access; it is possible to control the access to something without owning it. Power is in the hands of the person who controls access. The second is the ability to make the rules regarding how the resources may be used and who may use, possess, or reallocate them.

The basic skill in developing resource-based influence lies in being able to recognize the things others need and want in a particular situation. This is one of the reasons why sensitivity to others is an important personal attribute among influential people.

Influential people not only control access to resources, but they watch for opportunities to increase the value and importance of their resources to others. The greater the perceived value of what you control, the more people will be willing to do to gain access to it.

Implications for Librarians

Resources are among the strongest of influence building tools that are available to you. In most divisions of a bureaucracy, power and resources are deliberately limited to a division's particular functions. But you have control of materials that cut across bureaucratic divisions. Somewhere in your collection are things useful to virtually everyone in the building. Additionally, you have the power to decide what new materials will be added, which sections of the collection will be broadened and deepened, and how these resources will be made available to those who might want them.

This kind of resource control puts you in a position to do favors for people, to augment their resources, and to materially assist them in their endeavors. Resources of the magnitude the typical school librarian governs allow the mounting of a major campaign to invoke the reciprocity principle and to create dependencies in the operations of others.

Two conditions must be met to turn resource control potential into influence. First, others must know what you have. Teachers and administrators cannot attach value to things they don't know about. This argues for aggressively publicizing what your library contains and what services you provide. Second, others must see the value of your resource collection in terms of its potential to contribute to their own success. It is not enough to know what the library has; they must know what those things can do for them.

Technology provides an excellent example. Assume that your library is fortunate enough to have a technological system linked to databases and other schools across the country or across the world. The real influence potential of these resources lies dormant until teachers and administrators understand how those links can be put to work to make teachers and administrators personally more effective and successful.

There is a lot of attention paid to technology in the school library media center today, but the vast majority of that attention is focused on how technology represents a wonderful study and research resource for students. Technology surely is a boon to students, but the likelihood of getting additional terminals, subscriptions to additional services, upgrades of equipment, and additional maintenance and support service rests more with linking the value of the system to the critical needs of the adults in the building than it does to those of students.

The idealist view of schools says that people will commit funds to improve things for students above all else. The political realist's view of schools says people will more quickly commit those funds if the systems in question also improve their own capacity for effectiveness, success, and recognition.

The more resources you control, of course, the greater your potential for influence. This fact encourages you to actively work on gathering material support for the library: an ever-increasing budget; more technology; a greater collection; and a larger staff.

The extent to which you can be successful in acquiring resources from existing budgets and programs depends upon multiple factors. Not the least of these is the funding foundation for your district. If your situation is such that funds are limited (the constant condition of schools), you may need to find or create new ones.

One way to create additional resources is to go outside the organization to get them. Think beyond writing grant proposals. Do write grant proposals, but do other things as well. For example, develop a strong and active "friends of the library" group, or get a local business to "adopt" the library media center. By identifying and coordinating the kinds of things bought with funds from grants or donations, or by specifying the kinds of media and equipment you want to have donated, you can shape the resources to be particularly attractive to the individuals or groups you wish to target for influence.

A second way to create new resources is to find current resources that are not being used, gain control of them, and find ways to develop them into something valuable to someone else. Developing services is a particularly important resource creation. When people find a service helpful and are not charged for it, they use it often. Over time, they become accustomed to its benefits. They assume its presence and integrate it into their activity plans. In other words, they become dependent upon it and will work to ensure its continuance. In turn, they will work to see you have the resources you need to continue providing the service.

Need and scarcity contribute to the power potential of resources. Power rarely organizes around abundant resources. Rather, the greatest power accrues to those control resources that are critical and in short supply.[4] Only you can identify the exact kinds of services you might create or develop because only you know your school, but it shouldn't take much to identify some rich possibilities.

Even if you can't secure additional resources, research shows that you can still increase your influence potential if you work to increase the value of your existing resources. If you are successful, you will correspondingly increase your potential for being influential. With increased value comes increased demand and increased influence.[5]

There are at least three ways existing resource values can be enhanced. The first is by exposure. The people most effective in developing influence from the use of resources are those who clearly understand what resources they possess and those who actively and visibly promote and showcase these resources in pursuit of their goals. The more people know about the resources you control, the more there will be who will perceive them as useful; the more people who perceive them as useful, the more there will be who want access.

Second, the value of resources is enhanced when resources are used to provide a critical addition to someone else's existing resources. The integration of the things you possess can sometimes make the indispensable difference in the effective application of another person's resources. When that happens, the value of your resources is multiplied beyond what it is when resources are used independently. Systematically supporting some curriculum element or specific classroom project is a good example of such application.

Finally, the value of resources also can be enhanced by reducing the alternative ways people can satisfy their needs. This is not something in which you will want to engage, nor should you. The goal of the school enterprise is the provision of the best possible program to the students, and that means sharing ways to solve problems. Still, the results of budget cutbacks in other areas may have the effect of reducing the number of ways people in those areas can get the materials they need to do their jobs. It's an ill wind and all that.

Performance of Tasks Critical to the Success of Others

The Concept
The kind of work done in a given job has an effect on the influence potential of the person who occupies it. Any position holds potential for influence to the extent that it makes the functions of surrounding units easier, faster, or more effective. The position has an even greater influence-generating capacity value if surrounding units are in some way dependent upon this particular unit's productivity.

In essence, this is what makes administration valuable. The function of administration is to create the conditions in which other units in the school can maximize their productivity and effectiveness. Classroom teaching is dependent upon administration's effective processing, scheduling, transportation, assigning, and monitoring of students, as well as on the provision of heat, light, furniture, books, and equipment. When administration is done well, employees praise and support the administrators. When poorly done, when not done at all, or when conformity to administrative authority becomes more of a priority than the operation of the classroom, office, or maintenance center, employees condemn administration as a burden and an obstacle.

People in work situations value that which they need, that which helps them succeed, and that which makes them look good. In effect, the products of the work done in virtually any position become resources others need or want in order to do their own jobs better.

Implications for Librarians
Many school librarians have been trying for years to demonstrate that the media center is a critical element in student and teacher success. The question is, "What will it take to convince teachers and administrators that this is true?"

Just acquainting them with the research will not do the job. The schools described in the research are too abstract and distant. The focus has to be brought down to the immediate level. Because of the resources you control, you're in an excellent position not only to make things easier for classroom and office personnel, but also to help them be more effective and efficient in their jobs. But it cannot be done quietly or behind the scenes. It has to be made visible to be appreciated. To become a critical element in the success of other units requires the active promotion of the library, the careful tailoring of its resources and services to the needs of targeted individuals, and the nurturing of specific dependencies.

Appearing indispensable to superiors and peers is key when trying to influence them. People protect what they perceive they need. If co-workers believe that the particular knowledge, skills, techniques, contacts, or coordinating capabilities you possess will make the difference between failure and success, or between mediocrity and excellence, the odds are high that they will do whatever they can to support your activities. If there is no other way to get what they require than to deal with you, your influence will be increased.

From a purely political point of view, it is sometimes helpful to build the impression that you remain in your present position because you enjoy it, not because it is your only option. If it is clear that you could move to another program or to another school, and your departure would discontinue access to many of the things they value, your co-workers are more likely to seriously address your needs. This is a delicate ploy, however, and cannot be ever spoken of or allowed to be seen as a threat. People react poorly to strong arm and blackmail tactics.

Work Clearly Aligned with Major Organizational Goals

The Concept
As you increase the numbers and types of functions you perform that are critical to the success of others, your work becomes increasingly associated with the accomplishment of major organizational goals in its own right.

People with influence are most often found in positions perceived as dealing directly with the organization's central goals and objectives.[6] Jobs perceived as peripheral are never accorded the respect of jobs regarded as "line" positions. The "important" work in an organization is that which most contributes to accomplishing its fundamental mission. The people who do important work are important people.

Implications for Librarians
This presents a challenge to you because libraries and librarians don't usually occupy a central position in most people's perceptions of schools. Think about the responses you might get if you did a quick people-on-the-street interview and asked passers-by to play a word-association game with you. You would say "school" and ask for the first word that pops into their minds. You'd surely get "school—student" and "school—teacher." It could be a long time before they got to "library." The sad part of this is that you'd be unlikely to get to "library" much more quickly when playing the same game with most educators.

The odds of being generally perceived as central to the school's mission go up with each person who perceives you as critical to his or her own success. But just helping teachers and administrators do better is not sufficient in itself. The development of your image as a "line" performer requires, first, that other line performers (teachers and administrators) think of you as one of their own, and second, that you receive independent recognition as a line performer from those who really define what line performance is (students). This means that you need to fashion an image of instructional centrality with students and parents as well as with other educators. If parents are going to regard you as part of the teaching staff, students first have to perceive you that way. Students define who "teaches" by the content of their conversations at home. This perception cannot be constructed if you and the library remain a unit wholly separate from the classroom and from teaching. Visible linkages have to be forged with all kinds of programs. You have to become involved in programs in a manner that allows you to have a voice in student evaluation.

The importance of a visible linkage to the core of the school operation can hardly be overstated. In addition to its power in identifying you as holding a line position, it is a specific and crucial representation of the general value of high visibility in the organization.

High Organizational Visibility

The Concept

A position's influence potential is directly related to its visibility. People cannot become aware of accomplishments, expertise, resources, or services if they are not exposed to them. Visibility makes the achievements, the effective use of resources, and the central goal alignment of the position's tasks more evident, especially to the people who make decisions. This helps to explain why positions where the jobholder is regularly engaged with fellow workers tend to develop more powerful people than do positions where the work is technical and done independently.

Visibility, however, carries the price of scrutiny. People at all levels of the organization are aware of successes and failures. Good performance without visibility will not significantly advance potential influence, but poor performance coupled with visibility will destroy it. Performance must be both good and visible.

There are two simple measures of how visible a position is in an organization. The first is in the numbers of people with whom the position's occupant interacts; the second is in the types of people with whom the position's occupant interacts. Numbers are important, particularly in service positions like libraries, because they indicate levels of activity and may represent the breadth of engagement within the organization. But numbers by themselves are not accurate indicators of influence potential.

Contacts with some members of an organization are more important than contact with others. For a position to offer influence-building opportunities, it's essential to have contacts with both peers and formal leaders. They are the people who will determine the amounts and kinds of support that will be forthcoming.

The importance of contacts with superiors is obvious. The importance of contacts with peers goes beyond simple support at the same hierarchical level. Peer influence can translate to influence with superiors because of contacts and relationships peers may independently have with people in upper levels of the hierarchy. Consider the probability, for example, that some peers share personal friendships with your principal or other upper-level administrators, or that they serve on the same civic boards, belong to the same gym, or are members of the same congregation, political, recreation or social group.

Implications for Librarians

You must take every opportunity to develop media center visibility. Given the other characteristics of the job, this usually can be accomplished with a concerted effort.

Visibility is attained in two ways. The first is personal visibility. Becoming personally visible is a result of interactions. This means engaging in things as simple as having lunch in the faculty lunchroom instead of in the library, showing up at student activities and staff social functions, serving on committees, pressing for a spot on student and employee orientation programs, and attending board meetings. Building personal visibility is time consuming, but there is no substitute for the benefits it affords.

The second method of attaining visibility is to build the interactive dimensions of your job. It is imperative that people perceive you as making a significant and critical contribution to the accomplishment of organizational goals. For school librarians, this contributory perception can be constructed along three avenues. The first is service as a critical informational support for administration. If decisions cannot be made, or if people cannot feel comfortable making them without the information you can supply, your work takes on a semi-line quality. The second avenue is service as an essential cog in the gears of public relations through direct contact with parents and community groups. The third, and most important, avenue is the provision of a critical element in the process of teaching and learning. The positions most perceived as "line" positions in schools are teaching positions. To be identified with teaching is to acquire line responsibility.

Internal Autonomy of Action

The Concept
Internal autonomy is simply the ability of the position holder to determine the nature of the position's tasks, to make decisions about work priority and flow, and to control a budget and decide where money will be spent. People whose jobs offer internal autonomy can use their time and financial resources to facilitate the growth of alliances and to encourage others to support their activities.

One of internal autonomy's major benefits is that it allows the jobholder to arrange interactions with people from other parts of the organization. This is important because it enhances the jobholder's operational visibility. With this kind of discretion, position holders can adjust their schedules to fit those of people who can make a difference in the organization.

Implications for Librarians
You have a real advantage in the autonomy of your position. As you are able to determine the use of certain funds, able to control at least some of your own time, and able to reach every part of the school operation, you have the ability to gather information, establish contacts, and provide the individualized attention upon which most influence is based.

Central Location in the Communication System

The Concept
The amount of information coming into a position is a very important component in influence building. Information is valuable because the ability to discover opportunities for action and influence is directly proportional to the amount of information available. The more central the position in the structure, both physically and operationally, the more information will come through it.

Daniel Brass' study of non-supervisory personnel offers some very useful insights regarding organizational information flow.[7] His results described three sources of information coming into any position. First, official information comes through what Brass calls the "work flow network," formal communications relevant to work activities. This is information to which anyone holding the same job is entitled. The broader the position's activities, the broader the information stream; the more critical the activities, the deeper the stream. The more any unit is involved with other work units at its own and other levels, the more it will receive officially sanctioned information about what is going on in other parts of the organization.

Second is the "informal communication network." How much and what kind of information come to the jobholder is influenced by the extent and nature of that person's informal associations and by the physical location of the job site. A unit housed in a central site will receive more information simply as a function of its location than will the same unit housed at the end of a long hallway or in a separate wing. As Jeff Pfeffer points out, out-of-the-way locations leave people out of the flow of events. Moreover, they create an image that the work done there is peripheral and not central to the organization's mission.[8]

Where you sit can influence whom you know, what you know, and the types of networks you can establish. Thomas Allen at M.I.T. illustrated this with research showing that the probability of communication between any two people in any organization severely decays with distance. As though that were not enough by itself, building circumstances can make it worse. The negative effect of distance is increased by each corner that must be turned and each indirect pathway that must be followed in order to reach other people's offices and rooms. Worst of all for most school people, Allen did all of his research on single floors within single buildings.[9] Many schools have multi-floor or multi-building facilities—and teachers mostly work in closed-door rooms that reduce the likelihood of effective sustained communication.

Physical locations and narrow job descriptions can be compensated for, however, by the third information source, what Brass calls the "friendship network." The amount of information that comes into any jobholder's hands is significantly influenced by the personal networks the individual has established with other workers. Brass found evidence that the friendship network, especially when it involves supervisors and upper level management, can be very important in influence development. This is information that a jobholder receives just because a friend somewhere else in the organization felt that the jobholder ought to know about it.

Implications for Librarians

Formal communications are a function of how wide you can spread your activity net. Informal communications are a function of both your activities and your personal relationships, both as a colleague and as a friend.

It is unlikely, unless you are deeply involved in the original design or remodeling of a school, that you can assure the library will be centrally located in a physical sense. If your library isn't centrally located physically, then you need work at making it centrally located conceptually. To the extent that you increase the centrality of the library facility in the work lives of teachers and students, to that extent you increase the likelihood of collecting information informally. You increase centrality by using your resources to make dependency connections with people, by linking your operations to the core mission of the school, by promoting your visibility, and by taking advantage of the internal autonomy of your position to interact with others on a variety of levels.

Another way to increase centrality is to carry the library's presence outside the library walls. You can do this by using library resources to help solve problems in other areas of the school, by increasing your participation in collaborative projects, and, lastly, simply by going out into the hallways and coffee rooms.

Developing a friendship network carries more benefits than just information collection. Power and influence researchers continually document the importance of having friends and allies throughout the organization.[10] The fact is that bureaucratic organizations, including schools, are complex systems, marked by people and groups with varying agendas, divided into separate and sometimes competing units. Unless you are officially in charge, and often even then, it is very difficult to make things happen by yourself. If you further accept the notion that bureaucracies create dependent relationships, then it becomes all the more clear why you need allies sprinkled throughout the organization. There are potential allies at every level in the organization, and all should be cultivated.

The benefits of developing supportive and positive relationships with those on the upper rungs of the hierarchy are obvious, but similar relationships with peers and lower level participants are also very important. Peers and lower level participants have specific spheres of influence in which they operate, both collectively and as individuals. Many of those reach to the elevated levels of the hierarchy. Sensing an alliance with you may well mean the protection of your interests when you are not around.

There are multiple ways of building alliances with others. Which methods you may be able to utilize best will depend upon your personality and the conditions in your school, but research suggests that the following guidelines are very often helpful:

1. Build alliances with powerful people. The most important alliances are with those who control resources and have formal authority. To be successful in this, you have to become visible to and supportive of the people in control. You need to be perceived as someone who renders a service that will make them successful. Whenever possible, it is in your best interest to make the principal and assistant principal(s) look good, help them succeed, protect them from surprises, and support them publicly.

2. Build allies among peers by mentoring newcomers. All newcomers, whether they are brand new to the field or veteran newcomers who come to your school from another, experience periods of uncertainty.[11] It is the nature of job transition.[12] The effort put into helping them develop the knowledge and skills they need to become comfortable and successful will be repaid to you in future support.

There is another side to mentoring that should be mentioned. If you can obtain a mentor for yourself from the ranks of your superiors or from among the most influential of peers, you can reap additional benefits. A mentor means access to information and opportunities you might not otherwise have, and a mentor provides a signal to observers that you have the support, and perhaps the resources, of others available to you.[13]

Mentors can be difficult to come by. Research on mentorship suggests that the best mentoring relationships are those that naturally evolve as a result of the shared values attraction between two people.[14] Finding a mentor can be a matter of odds.

You can increase the odds of encountering someone who will serve as a mentor for you by increasing the number of contacts you have, particularly with powerful people. This suggests that it may be a good idea to participate in organizational events, accept invitations to go for lunch or a cup of coffee even if you are busy, socialize with selected colleagues outside of work, and take on visible projects. Making presentations, for example, to the board, the faculty, the administrative group, or to parent groups when board members or administrators are present is a good way to come to the attention of potential mentors.

3. Build allies in the support staff. Schools are like most other organizations in that the attitude and commitment of the support staff can make a real difference in someone's ability to get things done. Secretaries, clerks, custodians, and transportation, operations personnel can either supply or withhold information. They can immediately deliver or agonizingly delay answers, materials, services, and support. They can greatly enhance or seriously damage the success potential of almost any project or person.

Alliances among support staff members are important in developing resources and establishing relationships with more powerful people. It is worth noting, for example, that initial access to the principal's or assistant principal's ear is often acquired through positive relationships with the secretary.

4. Build allies across the board by doing favors for people. Doing favors for people activates the reciprocity rule.

5. Build allies across the board through hiring, promotions, and appointments. Most school librarians are not in a position to decide who is or is not hired in a school, but it will be to your advantage to be as much a part of the selection process as you possibly can. People rarely forget who was on the interview committee they saw when they applied. Involvement in employment decisions opens the door to building relationships from the beginning of each new person's tenure.

The same is true about promotions. You can't control them, but you can exert some influence by sitting on committees, having relationships with powerful people that allow you to make informal recommendations, writing recommendation letters, or otherwise providing support for promotion candidates. You must be careful in deciding whom you support, however. Research documents that association with people who do not live up to expectations is counterproductive to influence building.

You may be able to develop your own small measure of selection power in regard to internal opportunities for individual recognition. Appointment power can come to you when you serve as a committee or task force chair. Appointing people to visible positions offers them opportunities for recognition, which is almost always positive, and they owe you for the opportunity.

6. Build allies across the board by sharing credit and recognition. Giving recognition to people at every opportunity helps to bind them to you. As you know from teaching—and it is every bit as true with adults as with children and adolescents—compliments need to be sincere, individualized, specific, and timely. Even when they meet all those criteria, however, the bureaucratic context still has an effect on them. Unlike classroom compliments to students, you will find your compliments spread across three directions in the hierarchy—your peers, your subordinate co-workers, and your supervisors. Compliments, credit, and recognition are less suspect, of course, when they are given to peers and to co-workers below you in the hierarchy.

Even then, however, you cannot allow them to be perceived as ringing false. In order to insure that such remarks are taken seriously and add to instead of detracting from your status, organizational researchers suggest that you emphasize complimenting concrete accomplishments and individualizing your statements.

Research has clearly shown that people are more likely to believe praise that is specific and tagged to identifiable actions. They would rather hear about the specifics of their good work than generalized statements that they are good people.[15] Further, the value of recognition is in proportion to its focus and individualization. If you use the same phrases or send the same memos, notes, or letters to everyone you would praise, the impact will be considerably lessened. Alliances are built on relationships; relationships are individual.

Conclusion

Frequently, much of the potential power of an organizational position goes unnoticed and undeveloped. School librarians have positions with wonderful potential for influence building. Taking the time to examine the extent to which you have maximized the benefits of your job characteristics and looking for ways to enhance them further can pay great dividends in influence generation. Given the trends and conditions in schools today, school librarianship is a position rich with influence opportunity.

In summation, the important thing to keep in mind is that the potential for building influence in any kind of organization, including a school, doesn't flow from any one source. Rather, the potential for becoming influential exists as a result of the interaction of factors.

The first factor, personal attributes, is probably the one that has received the most attention over the years as the focus of leadership, self-help, and "how to succeed at work" books. There is no question that personal attributes are critical elements in the ability to influence other people, but they alone are not sufficient. Organizations are really comprised of interdependent parts and people. If you can't effectively communicate with others because of your own skill deficiency, your place in the organizational structure, or your failure to take advantage of heuristic thinking, your influence is not likely to grow very much.

It is important to understand the kinds of pressures that weigh on all of us and the kinds of heuristic shortcuts we all need to take in order to cope with what the world continually confronts us. But if your personal attributes are perceived as limited and your job is at the fringes of the organization, the opportunities to employ that knowledge will be minimal.

The characteristics of the job you have may provide you with the materials you need for developing influential relationships. But if you don't capitalize on your personal attributes, invest time in applying the principles and practices of influence, and neglect the opportunities for persuasion that result from heuristic thinking, you won't maximize the benefits of the position you hold.

The potential to build influence in an organization is based on and affected by the interaction of all these factors. If you want to become more influential in your school, you need to work to develop the strongest of personal attributes, to use them and your knowledge of heuristics to strengthen your job position, and to allow that strengthened position to in turn enhance the way you are perceived personally.

References

1. D. Mechanic, "Sources of Power of Lower Participants in Complex Organizations," *Administrative Science Quarterly*, vol. 7, no. 3 (1962), pp. 349–364.

2. D. J. Hickson, C. R. Hinings, C. A. Lee, R. E. Schneck, and J. M. Pennings, "Strategic Contingencies Theory of Intraorganizational Power," *Administrative Science Quarterly*, vol. 16, no. 2 (1971), pp. 216–229.

   J. Pfeffer, *Managing With Power: Politics and Influence in Organizations* (Cambridge, MA: Harvard Business School Press, 1992).

   J. Pfeffer and G. R. Salancik, *The External Control of Organizations: A Resource Dependence Perspective* (New York: Harper and Row, 1978).

   S. P. Robbins, *Essentials of Organizational Behavior, Third Edition* (Englewood Cliffs,NJ: Prentice-Hall, 1992).

3. J. Pfeffer and G. R. Salancik, *The External Control of Organizations: A Resource Dependence Perspective* (New York: Harper and Row, 1978).

4. G. R. Salancik and J. Pfeffer, "Who Gets Power—And How They Hold on to it: A Strategic-Contingency Model of Power," *Organizational Dynamics*, vol. 5, no. 3 (1977), pp. 3–21.

5. J. Pfeffer, *Managing With Power: Politics and Influence in Organizations* (Cambridge, MA: Harvard Business School Press, 1992).

6. G. R. Salancik and J. Pfeffer, "Who Gets Power—And How They Hold on to it: A Strategic-Contingency Model of Power," *Organizational Dynamics*, vol. 5, no. 3 (1977), pp. 3–21.

7. D. J. Brass, "Being in the Right Place: A Structural Analysis of Individual Influence in an Organization," *Administrative Science Quarterly*, vol. 29, no. 4 (1984), pp. 518–519.

8. J. Pfeffer, *Managing With Power: Politics and Influence in Organizations* (Cambridge, MA: Harvard Business School Press, 1992), p. 121.

9. T. J. Allen, "Communication Networks in R&D Laboratories," In R. Katz (Ed.), *Managing Professionals in Innovative Organizations: A Collection of Readings* (pp. 391–402) (New York: Ballinger Publishing Company, a Subsidiary of Harper and Row, 1988).

10. A. R. Cohen and D. L. Bradford, *Influence Without Authority* (New York: John Wiley & Sons, 1990).

    A. DuBrin, *Winning Office Politics* (Englewood Cliffs, NJ: Prentice-Hall Publishers, 1990).

    J. P. Kotter, *Power and Influence* (New York: Free Press, 1985).

    J. Pfeffer, *Managing With Power: Politics and Influence in Organizations* (Cambridge, MA: Harvard Business School Press, 1992).

    S. P. Robbins, *Training in Interpersonal Skills: TIPS for Managing People at Work* (Englewood Cliffs, NJ: Prentice-Hall Publishers, 1989).

11. D.C. Feldman, "The Multiple Socialization of Organization Members," *Academy of Management Review*, vol. 6, no. 2 (1981), pp. 309–318.

12. N. Nicholson, "A Theory of Work Role Transitions," *Administrative Science Quarterly*, vol. 29, no. 2 (1984), pp. 172–191.

    N. Nicholson, "The Transition Cycle: A Conceptual Framework for the Analysis of Change and Human Resources Management," In K. M. Rowland and G. R. Ferris (Eds.), *Research in Personnel and Human Resources, Volume Five* (pp. 167–222) (Grenwich, CT: JAI Press, 1987).

13. S. P. Robbins, *Training in Interpersonal Skills: TIPS for Managing People at Work* (Englewood Cliffs, NJ: Prentice-Hall Publishers, 1989).

14. G. T. Chao and others, *A Comparison of Informal Mentoring Relationships and Formal Mentor Programs*, Michigan State University, 1991. ERIC Document 333 784.

    D. M. Dunlap, *Formal and Informal Mentorships for Aspiring and Practicing*

Administrators, Paper presented at the Annual Meeting of the American Educational Research Association (Boston, MA, 1990). ERIC Document 325 935.

B. R. Ragins, J. L. Cotton, J. S. Miller, "Marginal Mentoring: The Effects of Type of Mentoring, Quality of the Relationship, and Program Design on Work and Career Attitudes," *Academy of Management Journal*, vol. 43, no. 6 (December, 2000), pp. 1177–1194.

15 P. King, "How to Prepare for a Performance Appraisal Interview," *Training and Development Journal*, vol. 38, no. 2 (1984), pp. 66–69.

A. Laird, and P. G. Clampitt, "Effective Performance Appraisals: Viewpoints from Managers," *Journal of Business Communication,* vol. 22, no. 3 (1985), pp. 49–57.

K. Tracy, D. Van Dusen, and S. Robinson, "'Good' and 'Bad' Criticism: A Descriptive Analysis," *Journal of Communication*, vol. 3, no. 2 (1987), pp. 46–59.

Section II
Targets

Building influence is an exercise in interpersonal relations. Understanding that your job structure promises a potential for influence building, comprehending the power of heuristics as influence tools, and even possessing influence-supportive personal attributes count for little outside the context of your workplace relationships. In short, influence results from activating and applying these elements in particular relationships.

The school setting's nature specifies administrators and teachers as your first-level targets. Parents and students are secondary targets because they don't have direct control of school resources. Their value to you is in their ability to affect the behavior of those who do control the human and material resources you need.

Who then are your specific influence targets at each level?

Level 1

Unquestionably, your primary and immediate target is your building principal. If you are going to influence what goes on in your school, gaining the principal's support has to be an early and continuing objective in your strategy. To whatever extent you have the active support of your principal, you increase the odds that you will be successful in your other influence attempts. Conversely, a principal's indifference or, worse, resistance toward you and your ideas greatly reduces those odds.

Successfully influencing the principal to behave in ways that support your goals is done both directly and indirectly. Direct influence results from your own efforts within the context of the relationship you and the principal share. Indirect influence, which in some instances may be the preferred or the more effective method, is also the product of your efforts, but it is mediated by intervening parties. The success of your indirect influence depends on how successful you are in building relationships and influence with those who, in turn, have the ability to influence or direct the principal.

Teachers also are targets because principals listen to them and because of their own value and virtue. As you read in several parts of Section I, peer relationships are essential to influence building. You must capture teachers by appealing to their own self-interest as well as to the good of their students. Getting teachers to collaborate with you is vital to developing school-wide influence.

Level 2

There's a wonderful line from the 1940 Errol Flynn movie *The Sea Hawk* where a character observes that "we serve others best when at the same time we serve ourselves." It speaks, I think, to the role of students in librarian influence. The bottom line, as the American Association of School Librarians has recently termed it, is student achievement. We have growing research evidence that quality school library programs significantly contribute to that bottom line. If we are to give students the best schooling experience, we need to draw library support from all quarters. Unless librarians have their own professional and programmatic needs met, they cannot best serve their students.

Influence is built on our ability to persuade resource-controlling decision-makers to behave in ways that support the goals we want to accomplish. Students don't make philosophical and operational decisions in schools. In order to do the very best job we can for students, we need to be able to convince non-students to give us needed resources and opportunities. Consequently, the influence value of students rests not in what they themselves can do for the library, but in their ability to influence the behavior of those people whose cooperation and support we do require.

Much like students, parents and community members are indirect influencers. Their influence is not as constantly applied as student influence because they do not spend every day in school nor are they constantly engaged in school business. But when they do act, their influence is generally more powerful than students'. As adults, they have leverage and access to legal, political, and financial channels that students simply don't have.

This section contains eight chapters. Chapter 6 examines why it is important to build a strong relationship with the principal and why such a relationship doesn't seem to occur naturally. It outlines the kinds of things you need to know about the principalship as an office and about the principal with whom you work in order to be able to begin building an effective relationship.

Chapter 7 explores how to gain your principal's trust. There is no influence without trust. Chapter 8 offers specific suggestions on how to develop a relationship with your principal that will motivate him or her to pay closer attention to the role of the library and to you in the pursuit of school improvement.

Chapter 9 examines some ideas about effective communication with your principal. Sooner or later, the quality of every relationship comes down to communication. You want your principal to understand what you and your library truly are about.

Chapter 10 might not be useful to you for years—or it might be useful to you next week. It deals with that rare opportunity you might get to be part of a principal selection committee. The largest generation ever to go into education is approaching retirement. More than half of the current school administrators in the United States will reach retirement age in the next decade. If you're young enough that you'll be working in the schools for the foreseeable future, you may well have an opportunity to help select a principal for your school. This chapter offers some suggestions both on how to discern a candidate's initial perceptions and how to take the first shot at shaping his or her perceptions of you and your library.

Chapter 11 looks at how you can build influence with your teaching colleagues. No library or librarian exists apart from curriculum and instruction. Faculty members are one of the primary sources of opportunity and influence for you. Their perceptions not only guide their behavior toward you, but they influence how the principal sees you.

Attention then turns to the second level, where Chapter 12 suggests some things you can do to enhance your relationship with students, and Chapter 13 does the same regarding parents.

Chapter 6

The Principal I: Why It Is Important to Build a Strong Relationship

Power in any organization is grounded in the ability to control resources.[1] Because the governance of school resources is the principal's specific responsibility, the presence or absence of the principal's support is pivotal in your influence building attempts.

The principal can provide you with the budget support and additional personnel needed to build your own resource base and to free you from the plaguing clerical tasks that consume your time. Research shows that association with and support from people at upper levels in the hierarchy enhance a person's credibility and leverage with co-workers; a strong relationship with the principal can help you become more visible while it aids in the development of alliances.[2] The principal can help you reach influential people in the building, in the central office, and in the community. He or she can encourage others to work with you through the informal power of leadership, through the provision of incentives, or even by direct order. The absence of this kind of support can make your attempts at building influence much more difficult.

Conceptualizing Your Relationship with the Principal

Imagine a line representing your professional relationship with the principal. At the left end is an adversarial relationship. At the right end is a close alliance. In the middle is indifference.

Adversary————————————Indifference————————————Ally

The odds are that most school library media specialists trying to locate the professional relationship they have with their principals on such a line will find themselves somewhere to the right of center—but probably not as far to the right as they would like to be. Research on the relationship between the typical principal and the typical library media specialist indicates that the principal and librarian have differing perceptions of the roles of the library and the librarian. Principals do not usually perceive the librarian as a teacher, an instructional or curriculum consultant, a staff developer, or a program advisor.[3]

The attitudes and perceptions principals hold are the products of four event combinations in their individual histories: their experiences, their training, the nature of librarianship, and the way principals interact with the librarians with whom they currently work. The first two you can do nothing about because they are legacies of the past. The third is unchangeable. The fourth offers you your opportunity.

The first has to do with the time in which many of us grew up. Most school administrators are not former school librarians, and most probably went through their own K–12 education in schools where the librarian was not a major player.[4] They did not grow into their educational philosophies and positions in environments that fostered appreciation for the library as a major instructional resource. More likely, the images they have of libraries and of librarians are the stereotypical images many people still hold: fussy, difficult to get along with, more interested in things than in people, isolated from the staff, and given to shushing you at every chance.[5]

The average age of school administrators today hovers around 50, and nearly 40% are well over that age.[6] This means that they were themselves K–12 students in the late 1950s and through the '60s—before most school libraries became media centers, and certainly before most school librarians reached beyond their traditional roles. I am of that generation, and I have no memory of ever seeing one of my teachers working in any kind of partnership role with the school librarian. The librarian was someone who came to our classroom with a cartload of books now and again and was the woman we saw when we were sent to the library. "Sent" is the keyword. We were sent to the library to "check out a book," and which book was largely immaterial. Of course, we were also expected to be quiet while we were there. I remember the library as the only carpeted room in the school—not because of status, but because it would muffle the sounds of chairs moved in and out. One of the interesting things about stereotypes is that stereotypes sometimes are anchored in a grain of truth, and many librarians of the 1950s—certainly ours—really were interested in "shushing" you.

Outside of school, these impressions were reinforced in the stage, film, and other media images of their time. Think of Marian the librarian in *The Music Man* and the alternative destiny of Mary in *It's a Wonderful Life*. Marian was an old maid who loved her books and wanted a quiet library (except, of course, for all that singing and dancing), and she was only pulled from that life by a flamboyant con man. In *It's a Wonderful Life*, Jimmy Stewart's character was granted his wish to see the world as it would have been had he never been born. In that alternate life, absent him to rescue her, the bright and beautiful woman who would have become his wife found that her dark and lonely fate was to become a librarian. There was a message there: librarianship was a job from which one should be rescued.

And these images haven't yet altogether disappeared. Just look at the representations of librarians in many of today's television shows and commercials. The Saturn automobile company not too long ago aired a commercial aimed at impressing viewers with a new model's quiet ride. To do this, they showed a gray-haired woman riding in the back seat while two engineers rode up front. The voice-over told us that the car was incredibly quiet and that it passed the most stringent of tests: "Margaret's." "Margaret knows quiet," he said, "Margaret's a librarian."

These were the images of libraries and librarians, real and celluloid, that we took to college with us, leading to the second factor shaping our teachers' and administrators' views of libraries and our ignorance of what they have to offer. Ironically enough, it was our own professional training as educators. One would hope that such misleading impressions of school librarians would have been corrected in the course of teacher training—and, if not there, in the training we received to become administrators. Unfortunately, it didn't happen, partly because the images were not completely inaccurate in the late '50s and the '60s and partly because the people training teachers and administrators then—as now—had no alternative visions to offer us. In fact, the greater likelihood was that the perception of librarians as different from teachers was more reinforced than modified. It was that basic notion that we carried through teaching and then into the administrative office because, by law in most states, school administrators must have been teachers at one time.

Even now, few teacher-training programs contain any systematic instruction in how the library media center and media specialists might improve instruction, serve in staff development projects, assist with special student populations, or provide administrative support. There is some glimmer of hope that this is changing. Wisconsin provides an encouraging exception. Administrative rule PI 4.09(12) requires that teaching license candidates receive instruction about school library media programs and become adept in using a variety of resources and technologies. But, in the main, the predominant model in schooling is still anchored in the same basic notion it has always been: one adult in one room working with one group of students for one period of time.[7]

Teacher training emphasizes the individual classroom interactions between teacher and student. Teachers are predominantly trained as independent operators simultaneously in charge of and responsible for what goes on in their classrooms.[8] They usually are not trained in the collaborative and consultative models found in law, medicine, and the other professions. The result is that aspiring teachers are not provided with any model or expectation that school library media specialists should be regarded as partners in curriculum and instruction.

Robert Louis Stevenson once remarked that the cruelest lies are often told in silence.[9] In effect, that's the impact of administrator training programs. Any review of administrator training curricula, and the textbooks used in those programs, reveals a stunning lack of attention to the library media center and its potential.[10] The net result is that administrative training does little or nothing to enhance administrators' awareness, let alone understanding, of the library media center and the media specialist. Aspiring administrators are not made aware of the media center's potential and don't come to see themselves as important players in maximizing the specialist's contributions to school quality.

It's not too difficult to see why this happens. Most professors of educational administration are former school administrators themselves. Their perceptions of school library media programs and media specialists were shaped by the same factors shaping those of the next generation of administrators. They simply bring those perceptions with them to the university setting, and nothing there challenges them. Veltze's research shows the effect.[11] While 91% of the professors of administration across the country responding to her survey thought that media specialists could be of more help to teachers if teachers and specialists had more time to plan together, 90% didn't see the principal as an important influence in teacher/librarian collaboration—a notion that runs counter to the lessons of research.[12]

When administrative preparation programs do address library media programs, the tendency is to focus on potential problems rather than on demonstrated or possible benefits. A couple of graduate assistants and I did an informal review of about 80 administrator preparation programs in the United States and found that library media topics surface most often in school law classes where they involve discussions of copyright violation or censorship fights. This leaves many administrative students with the impression that school libraries are legal time bombs instead of the impression that the library and librarian can make significant contributions to a new principal's success. It fosters what I'll call a favorable view of negativity. The "good" isn't defined by a positive act; it's defined by the absence of a negative one. The "good" librarian is one who doesn't get me into trouble. This can have a chilling effect on any new principal's willingness to invest great trust in a school librarian—and, once in office, the demands of the principalship preclude much chance of an administrator learning the truth about libraries and librarians on the job. Without exposure to the merits of library media programs during their training, administrators in the field generally have neither the inclination nor the time to learn about them on their own. Media specialists who conform to administrators' impressions of what they should be, and who stay out of legal trouble, are likely to remain unnoticed and undervalued.

We might expect that administrators would learn about the library while on the job. The simple fact is that they just don't have the time to do this. There's no end of research confirming what one vice principal in California told me: "Being an administrator today," he said, "is like living in an Indiana Jones movie."[13]

The third reason many administrators haven't tumbled to the value of libraries and librarians also is laced with irony. It is because of the very nature of the librarian's work. Library media specialists deliver services that empower others to be successful in their jobs, and their contributions get swallowed up in the activities of those people. Teachers and students take what media specialists give them and fold it into their own thinking patterns, work products, and performances. The integration is so complete that it's very difficult to distinguish the extent of the specialist's contribution in the finished work. Ultimately, the student sees the research project, examination success, or performance quality as something he or she put together as an individual. Teachers empowered by library media materials and assistance ultimately see as their own the teaching act in which they employed the specialist's contributions.

Most teachers view librarians more as support resources than as colleagues, let alone partners.[14] Certainly there are those who have learned the value of media centers and media specialists, but the research shows that real specialist/teacher partnerships exist only for a minority.[15]

The absorbability of library media work is one of the most powerful forces clouding administrators' visions of library services. A principal can recognize a successful teacher, but it is very difficult to assess how much of that success might be a result of the media specialist's ideas, resources, services, and support. No matter how significant those contributions might be to the instructional program, they most likely are overshadowed by the public success of the teachers and administrators who are perceived as responsible for individual and collective student accomplishments and for the programs of the school as a whole.

Administrators' inability to see these contributions sometimes causes them to withhold recognition and makes them more ready to interfere with library operation when pursuing other goals. The library and its staff are often early casualties in budget cuts, in scheduling changes, and in the assignment of extra duties. There is irony in this, and sometimes tragedy. In rightly doing everything possible to protect the classroom in tight financial times, administrators may support cuts in library services, and in doing so unwittingly cut away one of the essentials of classroom quality.

And lastly, the fourth reason that many administrators don't know about the kind of research and the kinds of library programs that can make a positive difference in schools is because librarians themselves haven't told administrators much about them. A good deal of librarian invisibility flows from how they disseminate information about themselves, their programs, and their contributions. Like other educators, they publish and present. The content of their work is wonderful—it just isn't taken in by administrators.

School library media specialists impressively write and present for each other. Worthwhile international, national, regional, and local school library media publications are marvelous resources filled with articles persuasively arguing the importance of school libraries. Rich with wonderful ideas for practice, they offer suggestions on all kinds of ways media specialists might improve their operational efficiency and effectiveness and enhance the positions of their media centers—and themselves—in their schools.

The same thing can be said of the presentations librarians make at school library media conferences. Regional, state, national, and international conferences offer wonderful sessions on what school libraries can and ought to be, what the future holds, how terrible problems have been overcome, the latest research on the positive effects of library media support on students and teachers, and descriptions of model programs from all over the country, if not the world.

The problem is that administrators almost never see these journals or hear these presentations. Very few are regularly exposed to information about the myriad ways school library media specialists can contribute to improving curriculum and instruction, public relations, staff development, and a variety of other essential school activities. Administrators read administrative journals and attend administrative conferences. They don't read library media publications, and they don't attend library media conferences.

Some administrators do appear at library media conferences when invited by media specialists from their schools. But their attendance is usually short-lived. They will come for an awards ceremony or a luncheon or perhaps to hear a keynote address, but they don't usually attend the break-out sessions where they would be exposed to the realities of library media contribution. They really have no great motivation to attend such sessions. They've not been led to think about library media and media specialists in that way. Administrators in their field, like media specialists in theirs, stay attuned to problems and possibilities through their own journals and meetings—and library media and media specialists have been conspicuously absent from those information sources.

Unless you are dealing with the rare administrator who had an overwhelmingly positive experience as a teacher working with the school librarian, or the even more rare former librarian, the odds are that he or she gives little consistent thought to the library. It's even less likely that the principal thinks of you in the multiple roles outlined for you in *Information Power.*[16]

Principals Can Learn from the Librarians with Whom They Work

From an influence point of view, the good news is that research shows that the most important and lasting source of information the majority of school principals have about the operation and value of the library comes from the specialists with whom they work.[17] This provides you with a foundation for your activities and explains the need to concentrate on building an effective and positive relationship with the principal.

What You Need to Know to Begin Building a Strong Relationship with Your Principal

Influence and power are relationship entities. That is, they exist as a result of the relationship between two people, and they ebb and flow with changes in that relationship.

Every relationship has two sides. Your principal represents only half of the whole. The quality of your relationship with your principal does not depend alone on how your principal acts. Relationship quality is equally, some would argue more, dependent upon how you act. To build a strong relationship with your principal, you need to have a pretty clear idea of what each of you wants, the strengths and weaknesses you both have, and the characteristics of your personal styles. In short, you need to understand yourself and you need to understand your principal.

Management and personnel researchers John Gabarro and John Kotter point out that you and your boss have individual personality structures, values, and ways of working that have been built over time, and you are not going to change either yours or your principal's.[18] What you can do, however, is try to identify elements in those structures and systems that either facilitate or impede your ability to work together. Once you are aware of these, you can take actions to enhance or mitigate their effects.

Understanding Yourself

Before you begin investigating your principal's characteristics, it's appropriate to look at your own. After all, it's your half of the relationship over which you have the most control. It's important to understand at the outset, however, that you probably cannot get a comprehensive, clear, and completely accurate picture of what you are like either personally or professionally. There are too many variables, too many things that are situationally determined, and too many ingrained psychological defenses for any of us to really see ourselves clearly.

The effort to try is worthwhile, however. Some level of self-understanding is necessary before you can make a comparison of your own characteristics with those of your principal. But a more important value is that self-understanding helps you to identify the patterns of behavior in which you tend to either habitually or instinctively engage.

If you automatically initiate or react to situations in a particular fashion, you limit the range of behavior choices you might have. It is what psychologist Robert Cialdini calls the "click, whirr" response of "fixed-action patterns," the heuristics discussed in Chapter 4.[19] The danger is that sometimes the fixed-action pattern in which we respond is not best, or even appropriate, for that particular context. When that occurs, we make silly and costly mistakes. When we do it in interpersonal situations, we can jeopardize relationships—and relationships are the foundation of influence.

Understanding Your Principal

In thinking about how to better understand your principal, the same fundamental concept has to be kept in mind: you will never be able to fully understand him or her. There are just too many variables for you to see, comprehend, and interpret in the principal's personal and professional behavior. What you can do, however, is be observant enough to get a handle on his or her motivations and style. Your goal is to see things from the principal's perspective and to help the principal see things from yours.

Keep in mind that the principal is a target for inquiry and influence, not an adversary. It is an easy mistake to think of the principal as an adversary if he or she seems to consistently give attention, priority, resources, and recognition to school functions and needs other than your own.

A fundamental tenet of psychology is that we react to our perceptions, and self-fulfilling prophesies do exist.[20] If you perceive the principal as an adversary you will behave differently than if you perceive the principal as a potential partner in helping you achieve your objectives. Adversaries are to be defeated. Partners are to be courted and supported. When in doubt about your feelings regarding the principal, keep this guideline in mind: The principal, like all other school personnel, if not already an ally is to be converted into one.

If you adopt this philosophy, your task then becomes one of targeted education for the both of you. The need for educating your principal about the resources and potential you hold has already been discussed. Without that understanding, he or she has little motivation to listen to you or to support your activities. On the other side of the coin, you have an equal need to educate yourself about your principal and the context in which he or she works.

The Advantages of Viewing the Principalship from the Perspective of the Librarianship

In educating yourself about the principalship, you have an advantage over teachers trying to do the same thing. Even if you're like most school library media specialists and haven't studied school administration any more than administrators have studied libraries and librarians, the nature of your work builds a lot of contact points. In many respects, much of the work you do in administering the media center parallels what the principal does in administering the school, though most often on a much smaller scale. It's one of the reasons why more and more people are beginning to look at the librarianship as a viable route to the principalship.[21]

That is not to say that the principalship and the librarianship are two versions of the same job. It is only to say that there are enough operational contact points to allow librarians to understand the principalship at a level beyond that which most other school personnel can attain. It also means that the specialist position offers librarians greater opportunities than the positions teachers or classified staff members hold to build influence with the administration through the similarity principle.

Most people in a school are not aware of the similarities between administrative work and the librarianship. Again, this is a function of the fact that the administration is so much more visible than the library in most school people's lives. A look under the surface, though, demonstrates that fully committed and involved librarians share a lot of common ground with administrators.

At the most basic level, principals and librarians both administer varieties of programs and services that contribute to teacher and student success. Both make student-advancement contributions, which are translated and delivered through the actions of other adults. Both plan and execute budgets, oversee the acquisition, use, and inventory of materials and equipment, and assign priorities to the use of a facility. Both are engaged with others across the whole spectrum of the school, and both are charged with maintaining an environment conducive to learning.

In those cases where librarians are involved in collaborative curriculum and instructional projects with teachers, they often are called upon to act in an administrative and quasi-administrative fashion. For example, librarians assess (albeit informally) and accommodate teachers' instructional styles and capabilities in order to develop working relationships. They must engage in team building, coordinate activities, and negotiate for time, space, and content priority. In many ways, helping teachers understand the latest in information retrieval techniques, find materials they want, and design research projects for students constitutes experience in staff development.

Principals and librarians are both boundary spanners. The activities of principals cut across all departments and programs and take principal's outside the confines of their own institutions to represent the school to the community. They serve as liaison, spokesperson, negotiator, figurehead, and information processor, buffering the organization from intrusions and building bridges to external constituencies.[22]

The library media specialist's role also involves boundary spanning, but usually in a narrower context and within a contained realm. That is to say, the librarian's activities potentially reach beyond the boundaries of the library into every discipline, department, program, and division within the school but are usually limited to inside the building. Working collaboratively with teachers takes the librarian out of the library in the same way that community interactions take the principal out of the building. It's not too much of a stretch to say that the teaching staff represents the librarian's community. Of course, aggressively active librarians often span the larger organizational boundaries when dealing with vendors, interacting with other school and public libraries, and reaching out into the community for additional resources and support.

Using these similarities as a foundation, it should not be too difficult to see the school from your principal's point of view. To accomplish this, or at least to approximate the principal's vantage point, it helps to broaden and sharpen your perspective on at least three things: (1) the nature of the principal's work; (2) the substance of the principal's personal motivation in responding to the challenges and relationships of the job; and (3) the nature of the superordinate/subordinate relationship the two of you have. When you have a handle on these, you'll be in a better position to observe how your principal operationalizes his or her personalized conception of administration through an individual working style.

1. The Nature of the Principal's Work

The work context of every principal is different, and these differences are compounded by the unique personality each individual brings to the principalship. Still, there are enough common features shared by all schools that some general observations can be drawn. These may serve as a starting place from which to build understanding of your particular principal.

The Principal's Realm

Douglas Mitchell and William Spady offer a conception of schools which helps to clarify the nature of the principal's role.[23] They suggest that administrators and teachers, including librarians, work in separate, but connected realms in the secondary school setting. The residents in each realm perform their own specific roles. Mitchell and Spady identify these realms and role sets as (a) "transformational" and (b) "stabilizing." While the activities of both groups are necessary to school functioning, and the two groups are bound together through the interplay of their roles, they differ in important ways.

Teachers and others who work directly, individually, and continually with students generally are responsible for the execution of transformational activities. Transformational activities are behaviors aimed at changing or transforming individual students through learning. This is in line with the fundamental definition of learning as change we were all exposed to in our educational psychology classes.

Through instruction and interaction, students are "transformed" from unaware to aware, from ignorant to knowledgeable, and from unskilled to skilled. The classroom is the central location for this changing or transforming of students, but students are also exposed to transforming experiences through activity programs, counseling programs, and other school endeavors. In schools where the library and librarian are properly recognized as integral to student success, the library is a powerful arena for transformation.

Stabilizing activities, on the other hand, are activities oriented toward stabilizing the school as an organization; that is, the promotion and maintenance of consistent and acceptable behavior patterns by members of the organization, including both adults and students. The purpose of this behavior regulation is to maintain a stable and supportive environment in which teachers and others can work their transformations with students. The principal has the primary responsibility for defining and maintaining the integrity of this environment.

The need for stabilizing activities with students is obvious. Truancy, disrespect, recalcitrance, theft, violence, unwarranted noise, and other forms of misbehavior disrupt the transformational activities of the classroom, media center, and counseling offices.

The need for stabilizing activities with adults, while not quite as obvious, is still significant. A couple of examples will illustrate. The smooth functioning of support services is necessary for school effectiveness, including secretarial, clerical, maintenance and operation, transportation, and food service activities. The adults carrying out these functions must be provided with resources, support, and direction.

Probably one of the best, and most important, examples can be seen in curriculum and instruction implementation. The principal, as the appointed leader, has two important roles to play in this area. The first role involves the concept of instructional leadership: creating and communicating a vision of what the school is about; and working with the staff to define the goals, objectives, and quality standards of the curriculum and the instructional processes. Ethical and legal considerations must be observed in everything from equal access to grading consistency.

Second, the principal has the task of overseeing the alignment and coordination of the various activities undertaken in the pursuit of these goals, objectives, and standards. This coordination requires a monitoring of the environment across all its segments. The skills and knowledge that constitute the content of most secondary school classes are sequential and cumulative. The teacher who instructs students in Subject A must teach what students will need to succeed in Subject B. Problems develop if this doesn't occur.

Consider, for example, if there are multiple teachers of Subject A, and one of them elects to teach a different skill or knowledge set than the one expected by the teachers who will receive the students for Subject B. The students who had that teacher will be at a disadvantage in Subject B and it will retard their transformation. The problem is compounded by the fact that the students from all the teachers of Subject A are mixed and resorted as they are assigned to the teachers of Subject B. Because students cannot be academically abandoned, the teachers of Subject B have to remediate those students who are behind. That process requires the diversion of time, attention, and resources from the group at large. This, in turn, causes a slowing of the transformational progress of the entire group, including the students whose Subject A teachers fulfilled their responsibilities.

Tensions Between Activities

There is a constant tension between administrative organizational stabilization activities and teacher/student transformational activities. The pressures of the transformational function encourage teachers to experiment and innovate in order to lead students to individually explore new and different belief systems and master new and different skills. Simultaneously, the pressures of the environmental stability function encourage administrators to get consistency and coordination of content from teachers and compliance to behavior standards from students as a group.

At some point, the activities of those involved in individual transformation and those involved in organizational stability will clash. This happens because teachers and administrators view the same organization from different perspectives. Teachers most often think in terms of an individual student: a student's grades; a student's attendance; a student's achievement; a student's behavior; a student's graduation. Administrators most often think in terms of the aggregate: grade distributions; attendance rates; mean achievement scores; referral rates; graduation/dropout ratios. In the administrative view, curriculum alignment, sequential learning, and discipline codes require convergent behavior from teachers and students, not divergent behavior and accommodations of individual preference.

Locked into the same building over time, individual expression and individualistic behavior clash with organizational norms of group behavior. How these conflicts are perceived and resolved, especially by the administration that controls authority and responsibility in the school setting, is important to both teachers and administrators.[24] It is of particular importance to the principal, however. Ultimately, as the chief executive in the building, the principal bears responsibility for the achievements and effectiveness of both realms and must account for both to the superintendent, the board of trustees, and the community.

Probably the most distinctive part of the principalship is the fact that the core elements of the job center on the construction of a culture. The ways in which the tensions and conflicts between the transformational and stabilizing realms will be defined and resolved are conditioned by the cultural norms of the building. Widely divergent outcomes result from differing cultural approaches to problem solving. This is one of the things that makes the principal's job as important as it is. The principal is instrumental in defining what is valued, and in so doing, becomes instrumental in defining the culture. In fact, Edgar Schein of M.I.T. has argued that the creation of an organization's culture through the definition and inculcation of broad-based beliefs may be the only really important thing leaders do.[25]

Implications for the Librarian

This conception of schools implies at least four things to consider as you try to understand your principal's perspective. First, the principal's perspective on what goes on in the school, and on what should go on in the school, is likely to be different in many respects from most of the faculty's. Your conception of how the school should ideally operate is probably closer to the principal's than the typical classroom teacher's, but it can't be identical.

Second, it is likely that the principal will always want to know what is going on in the school and within its component parts. The search for information is constant and wide ranging. The principal needs this information for reasons that follow. The important point here is that you are in an excellent position to be a purveyor of useful information.

Third, the principal's spheres of authority and responsibility are much larger than yours. The principal has to be alert not only to potential disruptions of the transformational process, but also to the direction and quality of the transformations attempted and achieved. This means that the principal must both plan, provide for, and protect what is currently in place and must also be thinking of the ramifications of each event and decision in relation to the outside society and to the potential for future accomplishment.

To at once monitor the present and project into the future requires a simultaneous attention to long-range needs and short-term results. On a different scale, you're involved in much the same process in planning the future of the library.

Fourth, the large sphere of responsibility and authority inevitably means that the principal has to struggle with competing and conflicting demands. In fact, as Stanford University's Larry Cuban has observed when talking about school superintendents, conflict is the DNA of school administration.[26] There are two fundamental reasons for this.

First, the nature of the school organization presents principals with the challenge of balancing the competing values of excellence, equity, and efficiency. These are ever in tension, and each has its vocal advocates both within and outside the school organization.[27] The decision to give priority to any one of these three values has great impact not only on budgets, schedules, curriculum, and student and employee work conditions, but also on how community members perceive the school.

Two good examples of this tension are common features in secondary schools: (1) Principals have to evaluate excellence and equity issues in deciding which classes and programs should be funded and made available to different types of students. Is it right to spend more money and personnel on one type of student than on another? Should we promote excellence with special education classes, honors programs, and advanced placement, or should we provide a core of classes funded at the highest possible level to everyone? (2) Principals have to try to balance excellence and efficiency in making scheduling and instructional quality decisions. Should a teacher be assigned outside his or her area of expertise because we need a fourth period history class and the master schedule will not work any other way, or should that particular class not be offered because a teacher trained for it is not available? Do we hire the best English teacher we can possibly find, or do we hire the best English teacher we can find who can also coach a sport?

Second, the nature of the principalship itself contains conflicting role demands. *Information Power* calls for librarians to be information specialists, teachers, and instructional partners. These are all compatible and complementing roles. The principalship, on the other hand, is a bundle of multiple and often conflicting roles. For example, an academic and social conflict is apparent when trying to spread too few dollars among too many worthy programs: do you support chemistry or chemical dependence prevention?

Another inherent conflict is found in serving as both employee facilitator and evaluator, trying to be a sounding board or confidant for staff members and simultaneously being responsible for their evaluation. Student discipline provides another example: How do you always support teachers and be just in discipline application if the student is in the right?

Other conflicts emerge from demands of those outside the building that are incompatible with the needs of those inside: how do you reconcile the need to satisfy the people in the central office or the community who want rapid change in the school with the need to allow time for planning, implementation, adjustment, reflection and evaluation among members of the school staff?

Role theorists suggest that people's behavior can be shaped by their perceptions of how other people want them to behave.[28] This creates a terrible pressure on principals who are immediately subject to the expectations of a large number of people, among them:

- Certificated staff members, who will sometimes act as a unit, expecting the principal to buffer them from outsiders, and other times will be competing and in conflict themselves and expect the principal to solve the problem.

- Classified staff members, who also will sometimes act as a unit, expecting the principal to buffer them from outsiders, and other times will be competing and in conflict themselves and expect the principal to solve the problem.

- Their own assistant principals

- Their peers in other schools

- The union

- The students

- The parents

- Community members

The communication of the expectations these people hold is sometimes subtle and sometimes very direct. Inevitably, the principal gets caught between two or more conflicting expectations.

You experience some of this kind of pressure in trying to balance the demands of the various individuals and groups who expect the library to meet their needs. As you relate to the principal's situation, it helps to remember that he or she has the same problems you do but across a broader horizon. The principal has to deal with many more people than you do and is consequently under more pressure. Not only does the principal carry responsibility for what you do as a library media specialist, but there is also responsibility for all library activities in relation to all other parts of the school enterprise. While you may see the library as the center of the universe, the principal may see it as a body orbiting larger issues.

All of this indicates a point of major importance to school librarians: because the principal is charged with meeting multiple demands in a context of finite and limited resources, virtually all of the requests anyone makes of the principal will be in competition, if not in conflict, with requests or demands made by others, both inside and outside the school organization. Competition is pervasive and relentless. The implication is clear that you must present your needs and desires in the most compelling light if you expect to receive support.

2. The Substance of Motivation

Understanding the school from the principal's perspective also involves understanding what personally motivates him or her to respond to the opportunities and pressures of the office in certain ways. Again, you will never fully understand what motivates your principal, but you can detect some traits and trends if you are willing to observe and assess.

The Need for Achievement, Power, and Affiliation

One way of trying to understand your principal's working style is to see what he or she seems to value most in the context of work. Noted psychologist David McClelland has developed the argument that everyone has needs for achievement, for power, and for affiliation.[29] The manner in which these needs are mixed in an individual, and which dominates the other two, affects the way that person behaves in working relationships.

Certainly, no two people experience the needs for achievement, power, and affiliation in exactly the same way. Each of us has our own proportion and balance. Where the need for achievement is dominant, McClelland's work has shown that individuals tend to want to structure only moderate risk situations and develop mechanisms whereby they can get rapid and concrete feedback about their performance.

People with high achievement needs set challenges to make themselves stretch a little but only in situations where they can influence the result by personally performing the work. They prefer to labor on a problem themselves rather than trust it to others or leave the outcome to chance. They don't like to gamble. They are concerned with personal accomplishment more than with the rewards of success, and they like to have up-to-date information on how they are progressing.

Where the need for power is dominant, people tend to seek situations in which they can arrange things or events the way they want them, where they can influence or direct people to do what they want to have done. They want to get recognition. They want to command attention, and they want to have control. They are political in their activities and are particularly interested in controlling communication channels, both up from them to their superiors and down from them to their subordinates, so they can feel more in charge of situations.

Where the need for affiliation is dominant, people tend to want close friendships and maintain friendly relations with others. They are more concerned with how well they are liked or accepted than with achievement. These people have a greater need for fellowship than for achievement or power.

All three of these needs are present in each of us. The question is, in what proportions? The stereotypical view of school administrators is that administrators probably have a greater need for power than for either achievement or affiliation. There's a logic to this, given the nature of the work the principalship calls for. But it would be a mistake to assume it is true about your principal without thinking it through and testing it against the ways in which you have seen him or her handle opportunities, challenges, and problems.

If you are interested in how you might be mixing your own needs for achievement, power, and affiliation, you can complete the short "Needs" questionnaire at the end of this chapter. Keep in mind that inventories like this provide only the slightest glimpse into what really exists, but they do have the twin values of surfacing your thoughts on the subject and asking you to confront your feelings.

The Importance of Understanding Your Principal

It is important to understand how your principal's need mix shapes an approach to the challenges of the job because it helps to clarify the situation for you. When the principal's actions cannot be understood, it is very easy to make incorrect assumptions. The danger to you comes from acting on assumptions that are erroneous. To whatever extent you can demystify the principal, you improve the odds of accurately assessing situations, adjusting to his or her reality, and being able to effectively work with him or her. You can't change the principal, but any insights you gain can help you to better manage your half of the relationship.

The difficulty with attempting to gain insights about another person is that such insights have a shelf life. That is, people and situations change over time, and people often change as situations change. Your ability to predict the direction of the changes would be better if you had full information about all the pressures, personal and professional, that your principal is subject to, but you never will. You will always be making judgments based on incomplete and changing data. This means that you must continually observe and never assume that you have learned all you need to know.

3. The Superordinate/Subordinate Relationship

The third element in understanding your principal's perspective is to understand how you are perceived as a subordinate. John Gabarro and John Kotter of the Harvard Business School argue that many people misread the boss-subordinate relationship.[30] They contend that people do not often enough recognize the relationship between the boss and subordinate as one of mutual dependence. Wrongly feeling themselves to be impotent to affect the relationship, subordinates don't try as they might to improve it or to make it more effective.

Further, argues Kotter, many subordinates do not recognize the power they have or can build in the superior/subordinate relationship. For example, he contends, subordinates have power to the extent that:

- The skills they have are difficult to replace easily or quickly;

- They possess important specialized knowledge that others don't have;

- They have strong and positive personal relationships across the hierarchy that make it difficult to discipline or remove them without incurring the wrath of others;

- The jobs they have are central to the accomplishment of the boss's goals and agenda, and, therefore, they have a large impact on the boss's ability to be successful;

- The jobs they do are interrelated with other important jobs and to jobs that are important to other people.[31]

It doesn't take much to see that these are all consistent with the descriptions of influential job characteristics discussed in Chapter 5 and that they could describe the position and status of any active librarian.

The simple truth is that the principal cannot individually make the school successful as an institution nor make the students successful as individuals. Research clearly shows that one of the characteristics that distinguishes managerial positions from other jobs is continual dependence on the activities of other people.[32]

This is a fact too little examined in schools. Personal success in organizations, even the success of the most visible and highest placed individual, is most often a result of working with and through other people. The overall success of the organization is determined not by how well one person performs but by how well the activities of individuals all across the system can be coordinated.[33] In the main, those activities must in and of themselves be successful. In order for the principal to be successful, people in the school must be successful in their own spheres of operation.

The principal needs the help and cooperation of employees in order to do his or her job effectively. It is not possible to just order things done correctly. The nature of schools makes this very clear. Unlike many companies in the private sector, the security of tenure provides teachers with a large measure of autonomy. Teaching has no system for vertical advancement except in the rarest of cases. Unless teachers leave the classroom for administration, the possibility of promotion is virtually nil. As Sharon Feiman-Nemser and Robert Floden of Michigan State University point out, the typical teaching career is marked by a few years' work to establish competence and secure tenure followed by decades of performing the same work over and over with different students.[34]

The consequence is that there is no threat of being denied promotion that can motivate teachers. While they cannot be directly insubordinate, teachers can effectively minimize their commitment and service if they wish to. The isolation of the classroom offers teachers the opportunity to have a large portion of self-determination.[35]

Classified employees are not quite as secure as teachers in their positions, but once past a probationary period, they also can choose to maintain a minimally active work life if they wish. Given that schools are perennially understaffed for clerical and operational needs, a refusal to work at a level above the minimum can be crippling.

There is some broadening recognition of this conception of the leader/follower relationship showing up in the educational literature. The whole idea of empowerment suggests a realization that followers are central rather than tangential to the success of an organization. If leaders are to have good followers, they must offer them opportunities to shape and participate in the progress of the organization.[36] Your opportunity to influence what goes on in your school grows out of this reality.

It's not self-serving to try to improve working associations or to increase your influence. Improved relationships serve the organization as well as the individual participants. As John Kotter points out, the managing of the relationship with the boss is a necessary and legitimate part of your job, especially in a period or situation where leadership is particularly difficult—as it is in schools today.[37] There are two reasons for this, he argues.

First, the superior/subordinate relationship is one of mutual dependence between people with different skills, perspectives, backgrounds, and pressures who must work together. If the relationship is not well managed, neither person can be maximally effective. Second, unless you are willing to accept the idea that the boss/subordinate relationship is like the one between parent and child, you have to take some responsibility for managing it. The principal is not always more wise, mature, well informed, or knowledgeable than others in the school. The counsel, support, and quality performance of the subordinate are essential, and they should be shared.

In short, you and the principal need each other. You have the potential to make each other successful, and the success of the organization is grounded in your doing so. "Good leadership," as Trudy Heller and Jon Van Til put it, "enhances followers, just as good followership enhances leaders."[38]

Figure 6.1: The Needs Questionnaire

Please respond to the statements that follow by assigning the appropriate number:

1 = Always   4 = Rarely
2 = Most of the time   5 = Never
3 = About half of the time

1. 1 2 3 4 5   I socialize with co-workers off the job.

2. 1 2 3 4 5   I am deeply bothered when someone else gets the credit for something I did.

3. 1 2 3 4 5   I like difficult, challenging work rather than routine assignments.

4. 1 2 3 4 5   I have my diplomas, certificates, and licenses displayed in my work area.

5. 1 2 3 4 5   I enjoy working on a team.

6. 1 2 3 4 5   I work better when I'm facing a deadline.

7. 1 2 3 4 5   I like to give orders.

8. 1 2 3 4 5   I avoid confrontation.

9. 1 2 3 4 5   I like to be left alone when I work.

10. 1 2 3 4 5   I feel uncomfortable when co-workers are critical of my approach.

11. 1 2 3 4 5   I set high standards for myself and others.

12. 1 2 3 4 5   I truly enjoy winning awards.

13. 1 2 3 4 5   When I begin a task, I like to keep working on it until I have completed it.

1 = Always	4 = Rarely
2 = Most of the time	5 = Never
3 = About half of the time	

14. 1 2 3 4 5   I like to have communications routed through me.

15. 1 2 3 4 5   I want to know what my subordinates are doing

16. 1 2 3 4 5   I try to know my co-workers on a personal level

17. 1 2 3 4 5   I try to meet newcomers as soon as I can and establish a relationship with them

18. 1 2 3 4 5   I enjoy debating issues with co-workers.

19. 1 2 3 4 5   I continually seek greater responsibility.

20. 1 2 3 4 5   I think it is important to be liked by your co-workers.

21. 1 2 3 4 5   I regularly ask my supervisor to give me assessments of my performance

22. 1 2 3 4 5   I attend the ceremonies when my co-workers receive an award, get promoted, or retire.

23. 1 2 3 4 5   A team needs a strong leader to assign responsibilities and evaluate progress.

24. 1 2 3 4 5   I believe that if you want something done well, you pretty much have to do it yourself.

Statements 3, 6, 9, 11, 13, 19, 21, and 24 relate to your need for achievement. If you marked ones or twos for most of these, it may indicate that you have a fairly strong need for achievement. People who have an achievement need are more concerned with accomplishment than they are with recognition for their accomplishments. They have a need for feedback. They like challenging tasks, but they like work that doesn't involve particularly high risk. They prefer to have a major role in the work themselves and are not given to investing a great deal of trust in others to do it.

Statements 2, 4, 7, 12, 14, 15, 18, and 23 relate to the need for power. If you marked ones and twos for most of these, it may indicate a fairly strong power need. People who have a need for power tend to want to influence or direct people and situations. They want to command attention and recognition, and they want to have control. They like to know who is doing what and to control communications.

Statements 1, 5, 8, 10, 16, 17, 20, and 22 relate to the need for affiliation. People with strong affiliation needs want to maintain friendly relations with their co-workers, want to be liked, and want to build personal relationships. They have a greater need for acceptance than for power or achievement.

All three of these needs are present in each of us. The question is, in what proportions? Review how you responded to the statements in each category, and see the ranking. In which set did you list the greatest number of ones and twos? Please remember that there is no right or wrong, better or worse, result here. It just helps to have a glimpse of which needs drive most of our own actions, and it helps to use the concepts as evaluative frameworks on those with whom we work.

References

1 J. Pfeffer, *Managing With Power: Politics and Influence in Organizations* (Boston: Harvard Business School Press, 1992).

2 It's good to keep in mind, of course, that this relationship is recursive. That is, a strong and close relationship with teachers—one where they say good things about you when you're not around—is also a tactic in building influence with the principal.

3 W. C. Buchanan, "The Principal and Role Expectations of the Library Media Specialist," *The Clearing House*, vol. 55, no. 6 (February 1982), pp. 253–255.

J. M. Campbell, *Principal-School Library Media Relations as Perceived by Selected North Carolina Elementary Principals and School Library Media Specialists* (Doctoral Dissertation, University of North Carolina, 1991).

P. A. B. Cruzeiro, *Role and Function Attitudes of Public School Principals Regarding the Library Media Program* (Media Center) (Doctoral Dissertation, University of South Dakota, 1991).

K. K. Edwards, "Principals' Perceptions of Librarians: A Survey," *School Library Journal*, vol. 35, no. 5 (January 1989), pp. 28–31.

N. E. Gast, *The Role of the High School Library Media Specialist as Perceived by High School Library Media Specialists, Principals, and Teachers in the State of Oregon* (Doctoral Dissertation, Portland State University, 1989).

W. A. Scott, *A Comparison of Role Perceptions of the School Library Media Educators, School Library Media Specialists, Principals, and Classroom Teachers* (Doctoral Dissertation, Vanderbilt University, 1987)

4 D. B. Austin and H. Brown, Jr., *Report of the Assistant Principalship, Vol. 3: The Study of the Secondary School Principalship* (Washington, D.C.: National Association of Secondary School Principals, 1970).

W. C. Buchanan, "The Principal and Role Expectations of the Library Media Specialist," *The Clearing House*, vol. 55, no. 6 (February 1982), pp. 253–255.

D. R. Chamberlain, *Career Pathways to the Middle Grade Principalship in Georgia* (Doctoral Dissertation, University of Georgia, 1993).

C. Marshall, *The Assistant Principal: Leadership Choices and Challenges* (Newbury Park, CA: Corwin Press, 1992.

E. Miklos, "Administrator Selection, Career Patterns, Succession, and Socialization," In N. J. Boyan (Ed.), *Handbook of Research on Educational Administration* (pp. 53–76) (New York: Longman Publishers, 1988).

L. O. Pellicer, L. W. Anderson, J. W. Keefe, E. A. Kelley, and L. E. McCleary, *High School Leaders and Their Schools, Volume 1: A National Profile* (Reston, VA: National Association of Secondary School Principals, 1988).

5 P. Cavill, "Saying Farewell to 'Miss Prune Face'; or, Marketing School Library Services," *Emergency Librarian*, vol. 14, no. 5 (May–June 1987), pp. 9–13.

B. Herrin, L. R. Pointon, and S. Russell, "Personality and Communications Behaviors of Model School Library Media Specialists," In D. V. Loertscher (Ed.), *Measures of Excellence for School Library Media Centers*, pp. 69–90 (Englewood, CO: Libraries Unlimited, 1988).

M. Land, "Librarians' Image and Users Attitudes to Reference Interviews," *Canadian Library Journal*, vol. 45, no. 1 (February 1988), pp. 15–20.

L. R. Silver, "Deference to Authority in the Feminized Professions," *School Library Journal*, vol. 34, no 5 (January 1988), pp. 21–27.

6 Educational Research Service (ERS), National Association of Elementary School Principals (NAESP), and National Association of Secondary School Principals (NASSP), *Is There a Shortage of Qualified Candidates for Openings in the Principalship? An Exploratory Study* (Arlington, VA: Educational Research Service, 1998).

C. E. Feistritzer, *Profile of School Administrators in the U.S.* (Washington, D.C.: National Center for Education Information, 1988).

National Center for Education Statistics (NCES), S*chools and Staffing in the United States: A Statistical Profile 1993–1994* (NCES 96-124) (Washington, D.C.: U.S. Department of Education, Center for Education Statistics, 1996).

7 S. Feiman-Nemser and R. E. Floden, "The Cultures of Teaching." In M. C. Wittrock (Ed.), *Handbook of Research On Teaching, Third Edition* (pp. 505–526) (New York: Macmillan Publishing Company, 1986).

J. T. Greer and P. M. Short, "Restructuring Schools," In L. W. Hughes (Ed.), *The Principal as Leader* (pp. 143–160) (New York: Merrill, 1993).

A. Lieberman, "Why We Must End Our Isolation," *American Teacher,* vol. 70, no. 1 (1985), pp. 9–10.

J. B. Shedd and S. B. Bacharach, *Tangled Hierarchies: Teachers as Professionals and the Management of Schools* (San Francisco: Jossey-Bass, 1991).

L. A. Shulman, "Teaching Alone, Learning Together: Needed Agendas and the New Reforms," in T. J. Sergiovanni and J. H. Moore (Eds.), *Schooling for Tomorrow: Directing Reforms to Issues That Count* (pp. 156–187) (Boston: Allyn & Bacon, 1989).

8 M. Friend and L. Cook, *Interactions: Collaboration skills for school professionals* (New York: Longman Publishers, 1992).

9 R. L. Stevenson, "Truth of Intercourse," in *Virginibus Puerisque and Other Papers* (1879). Available online at <http://www.bartleby.com/28/11.html> and <http://www.world-wideschool.org/library/books/phil/modernwesternphilosophy/VirginibusPuerisqueandOtherPapers/toc.html>.

10 L. Veltze, L. "School Library Media Program Information in the Principalship Preparation Program," In J. B. Smith and J. G. Coleman, Jr. (Eds.), *School Library Media Annual*, 1992, Volume Ten (pp. 129–134) (Englewood, CO: Libraries Unlimited, 1992).

P. J. Wilson and M. Blake, "The Missing Piece: A School Library Media Center Component in Principal-Preparation Programs," *Record in Educational Leadership*, vol. 12, no. 2 (Spring/Summer 1993), pp. 65–68.

11 L. Veltze, L. "School Library Media Program Information in the Principalship Preparation Program," In J. B. Smith and J. G. Coleman, Jr. (Eds.), *School Library Media Annual, 1992, Volume Ten* (pp. 129–134) (Englewood, CO: Libraries Unlimited, 1992).

12 For insight into the importance of principal support, see such works as "The Role of the Principal is the Key Factor in the Development of an Effective School Library Program," *Emergency Librarian* (January–February, 1989), p. 31.

K. Bishop and N. Larimer, "Literacy Through Collaboration," *Teacher Librarian*, vol. 27, no. 1 (October, 1999), pp. 15–20.

R. Blazek, *Influencing Students Toward Media Center Use: An Experimental Investigation In Mathematics* (Chicago: American Library Association, 1975).

B. S. Campbell and P. A. Cordiero, *High School Principal Roles and Implementation Themes for Mainstreaming Information Literacy Instruction. Paper presented at the annual meeting of the American Educational Research Association* (New York, April 8–12, 1996). ERIC Document Number ED 399 667.

J. B. Charter, *Case Study Profiles of Six Exemplary Public High School Library Media Programs* (Doctoral dissertation, Florida State University, 1982).

Executive Summary: Findings from the Evaluation of the National Library Power Program (Madison, WI: University of Wisconsin at Madison School of Library and Information Studies and School of Education, 1999).

V. S. Gehlken, *The Role of the High School Library Media Program in Three Nationally Recognized South Carolina Blue Ribbon Secondary Schools* (Doctoral dissertation, University of South Carolina, 1994).

A. E. Hambleton and J. P. Wilkinson, *The Role of the Library in Resource-Based Learning. SSTA Research Center Report #94-11*. Available at <http://www.ssta.sk.ca/research/instruction/94-11.htm> 2001.

D. Hamilton, "The Principal and the School Library," *Education Canada*, vol. 23, no. 3 (Fall, 1983), pp. 31–35, 38.

L. Hay, J. Henri, and D. Oberg, "The Role of the Principal in an Information Literate School Community: Think Global, Act Local," In J. Henri and K. Bonanno (Eds.), *The Information Literate School Community: Best Practice* (Wagga Wagga, Australia: Centre for Information Studies, Charles Sturt University, 1999), pp. 121–147.

K. Haycock, "Fostering Collaboration, Leadership, and Information Literacy: Common Behaviors of Uncommon Principals and Faculties," *NASSP Bulletin*, vol. 83, no. 605 (March, 1999), pp. 82–87.

D. L. Hellene, *The Relationship of the Behaviors of Principals in the State of Washington to the Development of School Library Media Programs* (Doctoral dissertation, University of Washington, 1973).

A. M. Lumley, *The Change Process and the Change Outcomes in the Development of an Innovative Elementary School Library Media Program* (Doctoral dissertation, Kansas State University, 1994).

L. Master and N. L. Master, *A 1988 Statewide Survey of Nevada School Librarians' Self-Perceptions as Instructional Leaders in Their Schools*. ERIC Document No. 300 016.

D. Oberg, *Principal Support: What Does It Mean to Teacher-Librarians? Paper presented at the annual conference of the International Association of School Librarianship* (Worcester, England, July 17–21, 1995) ERIC Document ED 400 851.

D. Oberg, "The School Library Program and the Culture of the School," *Emergency Librarian*, vol. 18, no. 1 (1991), pp. 9–16.

R. C. Pearson, *A Critical Relationship: Rural and Small School Principals and Librarians* (1989). ERIC Document Number ED 390 589.

J. I. Tallman and J. D. van Deusen, "Collaborative Unit Planning—Schedule, Time, and Participants, Part Three," *School Library Media Quarterly*, vol. 23, no. 1 (1994), pp. 33–37

C. M. Townsend, *The Principal's Role in Implementing "Information Power": The New National Guidelines for School Library Media Centers* (1988) ERIC Document Number ED 338 250.

P. M. Turner, "The Relationship Between the Principal's Attitude and the Amount and Type of Instructional Development Performed by the Media Professional," *International Journal of Instructional Media*, vol. 7 (1979–1980), pp. 127–138.

J. F. Watkins and A. H. Craft, "Library Media Specialists in a Staff Development Role: Teaming With the Principal for Instructional Leadership," *School Library Media Quarterly*, vol. 16 (Winter, 1988), pp. 110–114.

P. P. Wilson and J. A. Lyders, *Leadership for Today's School Library: A Handbook for The Library Media Specialist and the School Principal* (Westport, CT: Greenwood Press, 2001).

13 For insight into the administrator's world, see such works as

D. B. Austin and H. Brown, Jr., *Report of the Assistant Principalship, Vol. 3: The Study of the Secondary School Principalship* (Washington, D.C.: National Association of Secondary School Principals, 1970).

N. J. Boyan, *Handbook of Research in Educational Administration* (New York: Longman Publishers, 1988).

E. L. Boyer, *High School: A Report on Secondary Education in America* (New York: Harper and Row, 1983).

W. D. Greenfield, *Instructional Leadership: Concepts, Issues, and Controversies* (Boston: Allyn and Bacon, 1987).

G. N. Hartzell, R. C. Williams, K. T. Nelson, *New Voices in the Field: The Work Lives of First-Year Assistant Principals* (Thousand Oaks, CA: Corwin Press, 1995).

C. Marshall, *The Assistant Principal: Leadership Choices and Challenges* (Newbury Park, CA: Corwin Press, 1992).

W. J. Martin and D. J. Willower, "The Managerial Behavior of High School Principals," *Educational Administration Quarterly*, vol. 17, no. 1 (Winter 1981), pp. 69–90.

V. C. Morris, R. L. Crowson, C. Porter-Gehrie, and E. Hurwitz, Jr., *Principals in Action: The Reality of Managing Schools* (Columbus, OH: Charles E. Merrill Publishing, 1984).

F. W. Parkay and G. E. Hall, *Becoming a Principal: The Challenges of Beginning Leadership* (Boston: Allyn and Bacon, 1992).

L. O. Pellicer, L. W. Anderson, J. W. Keefe, E. A. Kelley, and L. E. McCleary, *High School Leaders and Their Schools, Volume 1: A National Profile* (Reston, VA: National Association of Secondary School Principals, 1988).

K. Peterson, "The Principal's Tasks." *Administrator's Notebook*, vol. 26, no. 8 (1977–1978), pp. 1–4.

14 W. C. Buchanan, "The Principal and Role Expectations of the School Library Media Specialist," *The Clearing House*, vol. 55, no. 6 (February 1982), pp. 253–255.

F. C. Pfister, "Library Media Specialists: What Role Should They Play?" In D. Loertscher (Ed.), *School Library Media Centers: Research Studies and the State-of-the-Art* (pp. 31–40) (Syracuse, NY: ERIC Clearinghouse on Information Resources, 1980).

15 M. Bell and H. L. Totten, "Cooperation in Instruction Between Classroom Teachers and School Library Media Specialists: A Look at Teacher Characteristics In Texas Elementary Schools," *School Library Media Quarterly*, vol. 20, no. 2 (Winter-1992), pp. 31–38.

J. M. Campbell, *Principal-School Library Media Relations as Perceived by Selected North Carolina Elementary Principals and School Library Media Specialists* (Doctoral Dissertation, University of North Carolina, 1991).

E. Getz, *Inservice and Preservice Teachers' Attitudes Towards Working Cooperatively With School Librarians* (Doctoral Dissertation, University of Pittsburgh, 1992).

K. Haycock, "Research in Teacher-Librarianship and the Institutionalization of Change," *School Library Media Quarterly*, vol. 23, no. 4 (Summer 1995), pp. 227–233.

16 American Association of School Librarians and the Association for Educational Communications and Technology, *Information Power: Guidelines for School Media Programs* (Chicago: American Library Association, 1988).

American Library Association and the Association for Educational Communications and Technology, *Information Power: Building Partnerships for Learning* (Chicago: American Library Association and the Association for Educational Communications, 1998).

L. D. Dorrell and V. L. Lawson, "What Are Principals' Perceptions of the School Library Media Specialist?" *NASSP Bulletin*, vol. 79, no. 573 (October 1995), pp. 72–80.

17 J. M. Campbell, *Principal-School Library Media Relations as Perceived by Selected North Carolina Elementary Principals and School Library Media Specialists* (Doctoral Dissertation, University of North Carolina, 1991).

18 J. J. Gabarro and J. P. Kotter, "Managing Your Boss," *Harvard Business Review*, vol. 71, no. 3 (May–June 1993), pp. 150–157.

19 R. B. Cialdini, *Influence: Science and Practice, Third Edition* (New York: HarperCollins Publishers, 1993).

20 D. Eden, "Self-fulfilling Prophesy as a Management Tool: Harnessing Pygmalion," *Academy of Management Review*, vol. 9, no. 1 (1984), pp. 64–73.

21 K. Haycock, "The Teacher-Librarian as School Principal: A Natural Progression," *The Emergency Librarian*, vol. 19, no. 2 (May–June 1992), pp. 21–22.

R. Pennock, "Trading Places: A Librarian's Route to the Principal's Office," *School Library Journal*, vol. 35, no. 1 (September 1988), pp. 117–119.

22 H. E. Aldrich and D. Herker, "Boundary Spanning Roles and Organizational Structure," *Academy of Management Review*, vol. 2, no. 2 (1977), pp. 217–230.

R. Leifer and G. P. Huber, "Relations Among Perceived Environmental Uncertainty, Organizational Structure, and Boundary Spanning Behaviour," *Administrative Science Quarterly*, vol. 22, no. 2 (1977), pp. 235–247.

23 D. E. Mitchell and W. G. Spady, *Authority, Power, and Expectations as Determinants of Action and Tension In School Organizations*. Paper presented at the annual meeting of the American Educational Research Association, New York City, April, 1977.

D. B. Reed, *The Work of the Secondary Vice Principalship: A Field Study*. Paper presented at the annual meeting of the American Educational Research Association, New Orleans, April 23–27, 1984. ERIC Document ED 246 527;

D. B. Reed and A. Himmler, "The Work of the Secondary Vice Principal," *Education and Urban Society*, vol. 18, no. 1 (1985), pp. 59–84.

24 For discussions of this from the various perspectives of teachers, administrators, and reformers who would speak for administrators, see such works as

A. Lieberman, "Why We Must End Our Isolation," *American Teacher*, vol. 70, no. 1 (1988), pp. 9–10.

L. M. McNeil, "Contradictions of Control, Part 1: Administrators and Teachers," *Phi Delta Kappan*, vol. 69, no. 5 (January 1988), pp. 333–339.

T. Sizer, *Horace's Compromise* (Boston: Houghton Mifflin, 1984).

R. Tyler, "Education Reforms," *Phi Delta Kappan*, vol. 69, no. 4 (December 1987), pp. 277–280.

P. Woodring, "A New Approach to the Dropout problem," *Phi Delta Kappan*, vol. 70, no. 6 (February 1989), pp. 468–469.

25 E. H. Schein, *Organizational Culture and Leadership, Second Edition* (San Francisco: Jossey Bass, 1992).

26 L. Cuban, "The District Superintendent & The Restructuring of Schools: A Realistic Appraisal," In T. J. Sergiovanni and J. H. Moore (Eds.), *Schooling for Tomorrow: Directing Reforms to Issues That Count* (pp. 251–271) (Boston: Allyn and Bacon, 1989).

27 J. W. Guthrie and R. J. Reed, *Educational Administration and Policy: Effective Leadership for American Education* (Englewood Cliffs, NJ: Prentice-Hall, 1986).

28 R. L. Kahn, D. M. Wolfe, R. R. Quinn, and J. D. Snoek, *Organizational Stress: Studies in Role Conflict and Ambiguity* (New York: John Wiley & Sons, 1964).

29 D.C. McClelland, "Toward a Theory of Motive Acquisition," *American Psychologist*, vol. 20, no. 5 (May 1965), pp. 321–333.

D.C. McClelland, "The Two Faces of Power," *Journal of International Affairs,* vol. 24, no. 1 (1970), pp. 29–47.

D.C. McClelland, *Power: The Inner Experience* (New York: Irvington Publishers, 1975).

30 J. J. Gabarro and J. P. Kotter, "Managing Your Boss," *Harvard Business Review*, vol. 71, no. 3 (May–June 1993), pp. 150–157.

31 J. P. Kotter, *Power and Influence* (New York: Free Press, 1985), p. 82.

32 See, for example

J. Pfeffer, *Managing With Power: Politics and Influence in Organizations* (Boston: Harvard Business School Press, 1992).

W. E. Rosenbach and R. L. Taylor (Eds.), *Contemporary Issues in Leadership* (San Francisco: Westview Press, 1993).

L. Sayles, *Managerial Behavior: Administration in Complex Organizations* (New York: McGraw-Hill, 1964).

R. Stewart, *Managers and Their Jobs* (London: Macmillan Publishers, 1967).

33 J. Pfeffer, *Managing With Power: Politics and Influence in Organizations* (Boston: Harvard Business School Press, 1992).

34 S. Feiman-Nemser and R. F. Floden, "The Cultures of Teaching," In M. C. Wittrock (Ed.), *Handbook of Research on Teaching, Third Edition* (pp. 505–526) (New York: Macmillan, 1986).

35 J. B. Davis, "Teacher Isolation: Breaking Through," *The High School Journal*, vol. 70, no. 2 (1987), pp. 72–75.

S. Feiman-Nemser and R. F. Floden, "The Cultures of Teaching," In M. C. Wittrock (Ed.), *Handbook of Research on Teaching, Third Edition* (pp. 505–526) (New York: Macmillan, 1986).

M. W. McLaughlin, J. E. Talbert, and N. Bascia (Eds.), *The Contexts of Teaching in Secondary Schools: Teachers' Realities* (New York: Teachers College Press, 1990).

S. J. Rosenholtz, *Teachers' Workplace: The Social Organization of Schools* (New York: Longman Publishers, 1989).

36 W. E. Rosenbach and R. L. Taylor (Eds.), *Contemporary Issues in Leadership* (San Francisco: Westview Press, 1993).

37 J. P. Kotter, *Power and Influence* (New York: Free Press, 1985).

38 T. Heller and J. Van Til, "Leadership and Followership: Some Summary Propositions," *Journal of Applied Behavioral Science*, vol. 18, no. 3 (1982), pp. 405–414.

Chapter 7

The Principal II: Capturing Your Principal's Trust

Play a game with me for a moment and run through this short three-step exercise. First, think about the people you really trust at work. Then ask yourself why you trust them. See if you can list three or four specific reasons. When you've done that, turn your attention to the people you trust in your private life—family members and friends—and repeat the process. Again, see if you can list three or four specific reasons why you trust them. Third, compare the two lists you've compiled. What do you see? Clearly, the elements of trust in your work relationships and your private relationships are similar, but they're not identical. It's those differences that provide the framework for this chapter. If you are going to capture your principal's support, you first must capture your principal's trust.

Workplace and Social Relationships Differ

Let me expand on an idea introduced earlier in the book. Workplace relationships are different from private social and love relationships.[1] They exist only because the organization exists. This is not to say that interpersonal attraction doesn't have a role in working relationships. It does. It is only to say that the power of interpersonal attraction runs second to task considerations.[2]

One clear difference between social and workplace relationships rests in how interactions with the other person are defined. Social relationships are what we might call "self-defined." That is, we define our own roles as we create the relationship. You could say that we come into social relationships in something of an exploratory mode. We aren't quite sure at the outset what the dynamics will be, how we will relate to each other, what we can expect from each other, and exactly what roles each of us will play. Our initial roles are often unclear and may evolve significantly over time. Just think through the history of your marriage or a close friendship.

In clear contrast, work relationships are embedded in a hierarchical structure that has already predetermined each participant's role—in fact, the roles are determined and defined before the participants are even identified. The positions of principal and librarian were created and their fundamental relationship was established well before you and your principal were ever hired to fill them. Our roles and role expectations are sharply defined by our job descriptions in working relationships. Whether or not these roles and expectations eventually evolve into something more depends on two things: first, on how our perceptions of each other develop through interaction, and, second, on the structure, climate, and culture of our workplace.

Hierarchical positions and role expectations are powerful forces in working relationships because they influence how we interpret each other's behavior. Our expectations of our co-workers are often guided by our perceptions of the groups to which they belong—teacher, administrator, counselor, librarian, secretary, custodian.[3] If your principal sees you only as a librarian, his or her perceptions of your intentions and behavior are likely to be different from what they would be if you were seen as a fully unique individual—just as your perceptions of your principal are likely to change when and if you come to see the person inside the image.[4]

Of course, any job only really comes to life when an actual person fills it. As much as you and your principal give character to your jobs, however, the task nature and hierarchical definition of your relationship have a considerable effect on you and how you will interrelate. This effect often is manifested in a lesser willingness in each of you to disclose as much about yourselves as you would in a social relationship—and this constitutes one more important way in which workplace relationships differ from their social counterparts.

The fact that workplace relationships are grounded in task accomplishment means that we tend to make interpersonal connections on fewer levels than we would in a social relationship. That's because working relationships are narrower in scope, focusing only on certain segments of our being.[5] They are specifically targeted on the attitudes and competencies related to the tasks we face. Although aspects of our lives outside of work have a major impact on how we behave on the job,[6] the core of workplace interaction has more to do with our professional identities than with our broader natures.

This narrower scope is reflected in the information we share about ourselves at work. Self-disclosure—revealing facts about our private lives, situations, and inner thoughts, feelings, and emotions[7]—is of paramount importance in social, and particularly in intimate social, relationships. However, because working relationships are driven by the task at hand, personal disclosure becomes secondary to professional disclosure. What we are willing to reveal about our personal side is less important than what we are willing to disclose regarding what we know and how we feel about the work to be done and about our role in it.

How much we reveal about ourselves in any situation is affected by how safe we feel, and the very fact that one member of a working relationship formally evaluates the other introduces a dynamic absent in social relationships. Social relationships usually are made up of peers, but boss/subordinate relationships by definition link people from different levels of the hierarchy. Those levels determine the authority and responsibility each of us can exercise. The inherent power imbalance generally encourages us to be cautious in sharing information about ourselves, especially in the early stages of the relationship. That caution endures if the relationship fails to evolve toward a trusting association.

There can be a negative looping effect in this because low levels of self-disclosure keep us from really getting to know one another; not knowing one another keeps us from trusting each another enough to lower our guards and disclose more about ourselves. Unbalanced superior/subordinate relationships tend to perpetuate themselves because they don't encourage information exchange and self-disclosure. When we don't share as much about ourselves as we would in a friendship, it becomes considerably more difficult to get to really know each other as well. Without a rich understanding of what each other is about, we usually are dependent upon an impressionistic sense of the other person, drawn from surface knowledge—just typical "biographic" information.[8] This lack of knowledge can thwart the relationship's evolutionary growth and can truly keep it different from what it might have been in a social setting.

Workplace Trust

Given the nature of workplace relationships, what causes us to trust another person at work? Because the context of the job frames the context of the relationship, it follows that the definition and operation of trust in a working relationship are different from what they are in a social relationship. Some things remain constant, of course. Integrity is an essential ingredient in both social and working relationships. But workplace trust also demands types of commitments and levels of technical competence that are not part of even the most intimate social relationships.

Understanding the role trust plays in a working relationship is essential, but not always easy. Workplace trust is a complex concept, incorporating ideas that sometimes take a moment to assimilate. Its complexity is reflected in the fact that the word "trust" is both noun and verb. Like the word "learning," trust is what researchers call an "achievement verb."[9] It refers to both an outcome and a process. This duality, as organizational researchers Karl Weick and Frances Westly point out, "complicates understanding by giving the word a circular, tautological sense, concealing rather than revealing the dynamics of the process and the exact nature of the outcome."[10]

In achievement verbs, the entity is built through the action. That is, the verb creates the noun—which, in turn, prompts the practice of the verb. Unless principal and librarian trust (verb) each other, there can be no trust (noun) in their relationship. Unless some measure of trust (noun) exists between them, neither will be motivated to trust (verb) the other. Trust, then, is simultaneously a cause and product of your interactions.

Beyond its complexity, trust can be difficult to clearly understand because—while its benefit is to make us feel comfortable and secure in our relationship with another—trust only exists in uncertain and risky environments.[11] If we have sure and certain knowledge that the other person will not let us down, then we're not actually investing any real trust in him or her. Every act of trust really is a test of trust and must involve a willingness to be vulnerable.[12] We are vulnerable because to trust means that we must stand to lose more if the trust is broken than we'll gain if our trust is confirmed. Unless that's the case, it doesn't really matter if the other person doesn't come through.[13] Absent any risk, our arguments that trust is a virtue and a high order interpersonal value are trivialized.[14]

Sometimes this element of trust is hard to visualize and to accept because it fundamentally says that trusting others is non-rational.[15] Dale Zand provides a clarifying example in an everyday scenario.[16] We live out this definition of trust, he argues, every time we hire a babysitter so we can go out to a movie. We're vulnerable because we can't control the sitter's behavior once we leave the house. If the sitter takes advantage of our trust and fails to meet the safety needs of our children, a tragedy might ensue that could devastate our lives. If, on the other hand, the babysitter lives up to our trust and takes excellent care of our children, the only gain we can realize is the pleasure of seeing a movie. It's a classic example of the potential for damage or loss exceeding the potential for gain or benefit in a trusting situation. Given how precious children are to parents, the rational thing would be to take care of them ourselves.

Administrators face similar situations in the workplace. Letting others represent the school to the community, letting them take the lead in curriculum revision, or letting them structure and administer budgets, hire and fire, alter procedures and timelines, or actually decide policy carry a potential for damage or loss that is greater than any possible gain. It's little wonder that many principals appear untrusting of their staffs.

Workplace Trust Components

Having said all this, what does it take to get your principal to trust you? We know that workplace trust is rooted in four elements. The first three are our perceptions of the other person's integrity, commitment, and competence. The fourth is in the nature of how we manage our interactions. Shaping your principal's perceptions probably will require a concentrated effort on your part and a determination to educate him or her to what you and your library are like and really have to offer. Improving how you manage your interactions probably will require you to assume greater responsibility in orchestrating the specifics of when and how you encounter each other. Let's begin by examining what each of these means in the workplace context.

Integrity

Just as in any social relationship, the first element of trust in a working relationship is integrity. You and your principal have no hope of trust if either perceives the other as less than honest and ethical.[17] No matter how bright or competent I perceive you to be, I am not likely to give you control of any vital part of my organization or my professional life if I think you're dishonest or completely self-serving.

For a quick conceptual review of integrity, look back to the discussion in Chapter 3. The relationship between integrity and trust is not complicated. Trust requires an acceptance of vulnerability on the part of the trustor. To put yourself or a vital part of your organizational operation in the hands of someone perceived to be other than honest and morally consistent would be patently foolish.

Commitment

The second element in workplace trust is a belief that the other person is committed both to the shared quality of the relationship and to your individual interests. This element, of course, also appears in friendships and marriages. In working relationships, however, the two people in the union are not the totality. In education, the union reaches beyond the participants to the school organization, its clients, and even to the external community. Workplace trust is promoted through a sense that the other person intends to make the organization successful and is willing to put organizational goals at the forefront of his or her actions, often ahead of personal goals.[18] Research has found that caring and commitment are critical to an ethical school climate and are consistently related to faculty trust, employee job satisfaction, and school health.[19]

Trust relationships are benevolent. That is, we each assume that the other will not exploit our inherent vulnerability. Caring for the other person's welfare is an essential element in the concept of trust[20] and requires a genuine responsiveness to that person's needs.[21] In trust relationships, the center of interest and attention is in the other, not in the self. Trust is what researchers like to call "heterocentric"—its core always contains at least two people.[22]

Competence

Integrity and commitment are essential but not sufficient in workplace trust. Professional competence is equally important—and is much more important than it could ever be in friendships or love relationships. Job competence is at the heart of the difference between trust in a social relationship and trust in a working relationship. Because working relationships are both bounded and driven by task achievement concerns, there is no trust without competence. No matter what we may think of a person's intent and integrity, competence is an essential measure. I may think you are the most dedicated, honest, and true person I have ever met, but I'm not going to trust you with any significant part of my organization if I also think that you're inept.

This desire for competence cuts both ways, of course. Your principal must be competent in order to draw your trust, just as you must be competent in your responsibilities if you want him or her to trust you. It is difficult to overstate the importance of being effective in your job if you wish to be trusted in a working relationship. There is evidence that job competence accounts for more of the variance in leader/follower working relationships than any other factor.[23]

When people fail to deliver expected results, a pervasive distrust is created. In schools in particular, the radiating effects of failure and failed trust reach across a broad expanse of the organization. First, of course, students suffer. This is unacceptable because it goes to the core of the school's purpose. The school's product is student achievement.

At the same time, schools are also workplaces for adults, and adults need to feel a sense of efficacy in what they do.[24] Students in a school are assigned to specific teachers. When a failure to deliver occurs that affects those students, even when someone other than the teacher herself or himself is responsible for the letdown, the teacher still feels the weight of it. This has particular relevance for librarians. As discussed previously, much of a school librarian's contribution to instruction is absorbed by the teachers with whom he or she works. Students don't perceive themselves as being assigned to the librarian, nor does the principal perceive them that way. If the librarian lets down the teacher in any manner that affects the students, blame attaches to the teacher—and, by extension, the principal who supervises the teacher—and it becomes unlikely that the librarian will ever again enjoy a high level of trust with either of them.

Very few secrets are preserved in organizations over time. If you fail to exhibit high levels of competence in dealing with teachers and students, the principal will hear of it. If the information comes from people the principal trusts, it will be all the more damaging. Reputation is a powerful force in one person's assessment of another, ranking second only to direct experience.[25] Since research shows that successful library media programs are dependent upon the principal's support,[26] problems can follow if the principal never clearly understands the breadth and depth of your abilities or, perhaps worse, if your principal's trust is shaken in whatever he or she does perceive as your ability.

Component Interaction

Integrity, commitment, and competence interact and combine to create something holistic in workplace relationships. A person's integrity, commitment, and competence have a multiplying effect on each other, the product of which determines the overall degree of trust that one of us has in the other.[27] We develop greater trust in the other person when we perceive him or her as operating at high levels in multiple dimensions. For example, think about the degree of trust you have in your physician when you believe him or her to be both competent to deal with your affliction and concerned with your personal well being, as opposed to being competent alone.

On the other hand, if we think that the other person is operating at a low level in any one of the three areas, that sense offsets the trust generated by our perception that he or she is high in the other two. As an illustration, think about the counselor who is well intentioned but also inept or indiscrete.

The relative importance of each dimension may vary with the situation.[28] In a crisis, for example, we may place more trust in the person who can get results than in the person who is compassionate. Sometimes we will overlook shortcomings in one area if we perceive strength in the other two—within certain limits of acceptability, of course.[29] In the long run, however, the trust dimensions influence each other and affect the level of trust generated in the relationship.

Managed Interactions

Most often, we don't decide to trust someone just on the spur of the moment. A confirming belief in the other person's integrity, commitment, and competence is built through repeated interaction over time. Generally, trusting decisions are based upon shared experiences, the part and parcel of working relationships, just as they are of social relationships. These experiences provide the framework within which the various dimensions of the relationship take shape and develop. I decide whether to trust you today depending on what I saw in you last week, last month, and last year. The odds of you being trusted by your principal next year depend upon the interactions you have this year. Those interactions either will or will not convince him or her that you can indeed be relied upon to do what needs to be done in a given situation—and that you're doing it for the right reasons.

There are two reasons why both the act and the motivation are important. First, trust decisions are simultaneously cognitive and emotional.[30] With every interaction, we consciously or unconsciously consider an objective element related to behavior and a subjective element related to the personal characteristics we perceive as underlying that behavior.[31] In short, these assessments combine into our operational judgment of how well the other person's competence, integrity, and commitment are integrated.

Second, there's the sad fact that the number of high quality trusting relationships between superiors and subordinates in any organization is restricted by human limits and frailties. Leaders such as principals have limited time and resources. They have neither the physical nor emotional capacity to build close trusting relationships with every one of the people they supervise. As a result, they choose—not necessarily consciously—to develop a few high quality working relationships among their subordinates.[32] If you'll look around your school, you'll identify those few who enjoy such relationships.

Here's where we come to the main point. In all likelihood, the principal and the other person in each of these relationships discovered each other's attributes through shared experiences.[33] I'm confident that the people who most enjoy the principal's trust where you work—and who have the most influence with him or her—are not faculty members whose days are defined by the negotiated contract. They don't just come to work at the required time, disappear into their classrooms, and then go home as soon as it is permissible for them to do so. Rather, they have a track record of sharing time with the principal. It may be official time such as working on a committee together or making a presentation to the parent group, quasi-official time such as supervising an after-school activity or showing up at a retirement dinner, or patently unofficial time like sharing a cup of coffee during a break, shooting the breeze in the hallway, or sharing some recreational interest outside of school.

Shared experiences—if they're good experiences—accelerate relationship development and trust building. At the simplest level, just being around another person generally increases our favorable beliefs about him or her. This occurs partly because communication is better. Interpersonal clues are harder to misconstrue in face-to-face situations and it's easier for us to move beyond just exchanging surface information to more substantive levels of mutual understanding.[34]

Shared experiences can also affect our willingness to make ourselves vulnerable to another person in a trusting situation. People in risky situations seek ways to reduce their uncertainty. They want additional assurances that their initial beliefs regarding another person are accurate.[35] At those times, experiential evidence is especially valued because people generally consider information acquired through experience to be more reliable than information acquired indirectly.[36] If the outcomes of those experiences are positive, and if trust investments are respected and fulfilled, a stronger foundation for later interaction is laid down.

You and your principal are going to interact. You work in the same school, and your principal is your supervisor. That alone makes interaction inevitable, but it doesn't guarantee meaningful, let alone positive or mutually beneficial interaction, and it certainly doesn't ordain that trust will develop between you. In deciding whether or not to trust you, your principal draws on past experience with you to assess your competence, integrity, and commitment.[37] You have to manage your interactions; you have to think about their number and nature, their timing and their results if you want to maximize the likelihood that you will enjoy one of the limited number of truly significant relationships your principal can offer.

What Now?

The working relationship you have with your principal is interpersonal, continuing, task-based, and important.[38] It is interpersonal because organizations don't exist apart from the people who comprise them; your working relationship continues so long as the two of you hold your positions. Your relationship is task-based because it is the work that brings you and your principal into the relationship. Lastly, it is important because the quality of the relationship influences how effectively and efficiently both you and your principal are able to work, the levels of your individual job satisfaction, the amount of support that each of you enjoys, and the likelihood of how long each of you will stay.[39] Clearly, these relationships can be critical to both organizational and personal success.[40] In Chapter 8, we'll look at strategies and tactics for improving working relationships and capturing your principal's trust.

References

1 J. J. Gabarro, "The Development of Working Relationships," In J. Galegher and R. E. Kraut (Eds.), *Intellectual Teamwork: Social and Technological Foundations of Cooperative Work*, pp. 79–110 (Hillsdale, NJ: Lawrence Erlbaum Associates Publishers, 1990).

2 J. J Gabarro, "The Development of Trust, Influence, and Expectations," In A. G. Athos and J. J. Gabarro (Eds.), *Interpersonal Behavior: Communication and Understanding in Relationships* (pp. 290–303). Englewood Cliffs, NJ: Prentice-Hall, Inc., 1978.

3 E. E. Jones and D. McGillis, "Correspondent Inferences and the Attribution Cube: A Comparative Reappraisal," In J. H. Harvey, W. J. Ickes, and R. F. Kidd (Eds.), *New Directions in Attribution Research, Volume 1*, pp. 389–420 (Hillsdale, NJ: Erlbaum Publishers, 1976).

4 J. M. Guiot, "Attribution and Identity Construction: Some Comments." *American Sociological Review*, vol. 42, no. 5 (1977), pp. 692–704.

5 I. Altman and D. A. Taylor, *Social Penetration: The Development of Interpersonal Relationships* (New York: Holt, Rinehart and Winston, 1973).

6 G. L. Staines, "Spillover Versus Compensations: A Review of the Literature on the Relationship Between Work and Nonwork," *Human Relations*, vol. 33, no. 2 (1980), pp. 111–129.

K. J. Williams and G. M. Alliger, "Role Stressors, Mood Spillover, and Perceptions of Work-Family Conflict in Employed Parents," *Academy of Management Journal*, vol. 37, no. 4 (1994), pp. 837–868.

7 T. L. Morton, "Intimacy and Reciprocity of Exchange: A Comparison of Spouses and Strangers," *Journal of Personality and Social Psychology*, vol. 36, no. 1 (1978), pp. 72–81.

8 J. J. Gabarro, "The Development of Working Relationships," In J. Galegher and R. E. Kraut (Eds.), *Intellectual Teamwork: Social and Technological Foundations of Cooperative Work*, pp. 79–110 (Hillsdale, NJ: Lawrence Erlbaum Associates Publishers, 1990).

9 L. Sandelands and R. Drazin, "On the Language of Organizational Theory," *Organization Studies*, vol. 10 (1980), pp. 457–478.

10 K. E. Weick and F. Westley, "Organizational Learning: Affirming an Oxymoron," In S. R. Clegg, C. Hardy, and W. R. Nord (Eds.), *Handbook of Organizational Studies*, pp. 441–458 (Thousand Oaks, CA: Sage Publications, 1996), p. 441.

11 R. Bhattacharya, T. M. Devinney, and M. M. Pillutla, "A Formal Model of Trust Based on Outcomes," *Academy of Management Review*, vol. 23, no. 3 (1998), pp. 459–472.

12 R. C. Mayer, J. H. Davis, and F. D. Schoorman, "An Integration Model of Organizational Trust," *Academy of Management Review*, vol. 29, no. 3 (1995), pp. 709–734.

A. K. Mishra, "Organizational Responses to Crisis: The Centrality of Trust," In R. M. Kramer and T. R. Tyler (Eds.), *Trust in Organizations: Frontiers of Theory and Research* (pp. 261–287) (Thousand Oaks, CA: Sage Publications, 1996).

R. B. Shaw, *Trust in the Balance: Building Successful Organizations on Results, Integrity, and Concern* (San Francisco: Jossey-Bass, 1997).

13 N. Luhmann, "Familiarity, Confidence, Trust: Problems and Alternatives," In D. Gambetta (Ed.), *Trust: Making and Breaking Cooperative Relations* (pp. 94–107) (Oxford, England: Basil Blackwell, 1988).

14 R. Bhattacharya, T. M. Devinney, and M. M. Pillutla, "A Formal Model of Trust Based on Outcomes," *Academy of Management Review*, vol. 23, no. 3 (1998), pp. 459–472.

15 M. Deutsch, "Trust and Suspicion," J*ournal of Conflict Resolution*, vol. 2, no. 4 (1958), pp. 265–279.

16 D. E. Zand, "Trust and Managerial Problem Solving," *Administrative Science Quarterly*, vol. 17, no. 2 (June 1972), pp. 229–239.

17 J. K. Butler and R. S. Cantrell, "A Behavioral Decision Theory Approach to Modeling Dyadic Trust in Superiors and Subordinates," *Psychological Reports*, vol. 55, no. 1 (1984), pp. 19–28.

M. C. Clark and R. L. Payne, "The Nature and Structure of Workers' Trust in Management," *Journal of Organizational Behavior*, vol. 18, no. 3 (1997), pp. 205–224.

J. J. Gabarro, "The Development of Trust, Influence, and Expectations," In A. G. Athos and J. J. Gabarro (Eds.), *Interpersonal Behavior: Communication and Understanding in Relationships* (pp. 290–303). Englewood Cliffs, NJ: Prentice-Hall, Inc., 1978.

R. C. Mayer, J. H. Davis, and F. D. Schoorman, "An Integration Model of Organizational Trust," *Academy of Management Review*, vol. 29, no. 3 (1995), pp. 709–734.

P. L. Schindler and C. C. Thomas, "The Structure of Interpersonal Trust in the Workplace," *Psychological Reports,* vol. 73, no. 2 (1993), pp. 563–573.

R. B. Shaw, *Trust in the Balance: Building Successful Organizations on Results, Integrity, and Concern* (San Francisco: Jossey-Bass, 1997).

18 R. M. Kanter, *Commitment and Community* (Cambridge, MA: Harvard University Press, 1972).

R. C. Mayer, J H. Davis, and F. D. Schoorman, "An Integration Model of Organizational Trust," *Academy of Management Review*, vol. 29, no. 3 (1995), pp. 709–734.

B. Rosen and T. H. Jardee, "Influence of Subordinate Characteristics on Trust and Use of Participative Decision Strategies in a Management Situation," *Journal of Applied Psychology*, vol. 62, no. 5 (1977), pp. 628–631.

19 C. V. Khoury, *Ethical Climate of Secondary Schools: A Study of Trust, Satisfaction, and School Health* (Doctoral dissertation, Rutgers University, 1993).

20 J. K. Rempel and J. G. Holmes, "How Do I Trust Thee?" *Psychology Today*, vol. 20, no. 2 (1986), pp. 28–34.

21 N. Friedland, "Attribution of Control as a Determinant of Cooperation in Exchange Interactions," *Journal of Applied Social Psychology*, vol. 20, no. 4 (1990), pp. 303–320.

22 J. MacMurray, *Persons in Relation* (London: Humanities Press International, Inc., 1991).

23 R. J. Deluga and J. T. Perry, "The Role of Subordinate Performance and Ingratiation in Leader-Member exchanges," *Group and Organization Management*, vol. 19, no. 1 (1994), pp. 67–86.

24 A. Bandura, "Self-Efficacy Mechanism in Human Agency," *American Psychologist*, vol. 37, no. 2 (1982), pp. 122–147.

25 J. Pfeffer, *Managing With Power* (Boston: Harvard Business School Press, 1992).

26 W. C. Buchanan, "The Principal and Role Expectations of the School Library Media Specialist," *The Clearing House*, vol. 55, no. 6 (February, 1982), pp. 253–255.

J. M. Campbell, *Principal-School Library Media Relations as Perceived by Selected North Carolina Elementary Principals and School Library Media Specialists* (Doctoral dissertation, University of North Carolina, 1991).

Executive Summary: Findings from the Evaluation of the National Library Power Program (Madison, WI: University of Wisconsin at Madison School of Library and Information Studies and School of Education, 1999).

M. A. Grant, "The Principal's Role in the Achievement of Learning Through the Library Media Center," *Catholic Library World*, vol. 60, no. 2 (Sept–Oct, 1988), pp. 71–74.

A. E. Hambleton and J. P. Wilkinson, *The Role of the Library in Resource-Based Learning—SSTA Research Center Report #94-11*. Available at <http://www.ssta.sk.ca/research/instruction/94-11.htm> 2001.

D. Hamilton, "The Principal and the School Library," *Education Canada*, vol. 23, no. 3 (Fall 1983), pp. 31–35, 38.

K. Haycock, "Fostering Collaboration, Leadership, and Information Literacy: Common Behaviors of Uncommon Principals and Faculties," *NASSP Bulletin*, volume 83, no. 605 (March, 1999), pp. 82–87.

D. Oberg, *Principal Support: What Does It Mean to Teacher-Librarians? Paper presented at the annual conference of the International Association of School Librarianship* (Worcester, England, July 17–21, 1995) ERIC Document ED 400 851.

I. Pfeiffer and P. Bennett, "The Principal and the Media Program," *The Clearing House*, vol. 62, no. 4 (December 1988), pp. 183–185.

I. Schon, G. C. Helmstadter, and D. Robinson, "The Role of School Library Media Specialists," *School Library Media Quarterly*, vol. 19, no. 4 (Summer 1991), pp. 228–233.

R. B. Senator, *Collaborations for Literacy* (Westport, CT: Greenwood Press, 1995).

C. C. Walker, *The Role of the Principal in the Provision of Effective Library Services in Selected Indiana Elementary Schools* (Doctoral dissertation, Indiana University, 1982).

P. P. Wilson and J. A. Lyders, *Leadership for Today's School Library: A Handbook for The Library Media Specialist and the School Principal* (Westport, CT: Greenwood Press, 2001).

27 A. K. Mishra, "Organizational Responses to Crisis: The Centrality of Trust," In R. M. Kramer and T. R. Tyler (Eds.), *Trust in Organizations: Frontiers of Theory and Research* (pp. 261–287) (Thousand Oaks, CA: Sage Publications, 1996).

28 R. B. Shaw, *Trust in the Balance: Building Successful Organizations on Results, Integrity, and Concern (*San Francisco: Jossey-Bass, 1997).

29 R. B. Shaw, *Trust in the Balance: Building Successful Organizations on Results, Integrity, and Concern* (San Francisco: Jossey-Bass, 1997).

30 B. Barber, *The Logic and Limits of Trust* (New Brunswick, NJ: Rutgers University Press, 1983).

J. J. Gabarro, "The Development of Trust, Influence, and Expectations," In A. G. Athos and J. J. Gabarro (Eds.), *Interpersonal Behavior: Communication and Understanding in Relationships* (pp. 290–303). Englewood Cliffs, NJ: Prentice-Hall, Inc., 1978.

G. R. Jones and J. M. George, "The Experience and Evolution of Trust: Implications for Cooperation and Teamwork," *Academy of Management Review*, vol. 23, no. 3 (1998), pp. 531–546.

R. J. Lewicki and B. Bunker, "Developing and Maintaining Trust in Work Relationships," In R. M. Kramer and T. R. Tyler (Eds.), *Trust in Organizations: Frontiers of Theory and Research*, pp. 114–139 (Thousand Oaks, CA: Sage Publishers, 1996).

P. L. Schindler and C. C. Thomas, "The Structure of Interpersonal Trust in the Workplace," *Psychological Reports*, vol. 73, no. 2 (1993), pp. 563–573.

31 M. C. Clark and R. L. Payne, "The Nature and Structure of Workers' Trust in Management," *Journal of Organizational Behavior*, vol. 18, no. 3 (1997), pp. 205–224.

32 F. Dansereau, G. Graen, and W. J. Haga, "A Vertical Dyad Linkage Approach to Leadership Within Formal Organizations: A Longitudinal Investigation of the Role Making Process," *Organizational Behavior and Human Performance*, vol. 13, no. 1 (1975), pp. 46–78.

G. G. Graen and T. Scandura, "Toward a Psychology of Dyadic Organizing." In L. L. Cummings and B. Staw (Eds.), *Research in Organizational Behavior*, Volume 9, pp. 175–208 (Greenwich, CT: JAI Press, 1987).

33 R. J. Deluga and J. T. Perry, "The Role of Subordinate Performance and Ingratiation in Leader-Member exchanges," *Group and Organization Management,* vol. 19, no. 1 (1994), pp. 67–86.

R. C. Liden, S. J. Wayne, and D. Stilwell, "A Longitudinal Study of the Early Development of Leader-Member Exchanges," *Journal of Applied Psychology*, vol. 78 (1993), pp. 662–674.

34 D. Good, "Individuals, Interpersonal Relations, and Trust," In D. Gambetta (Ed.), *Trust: Making and Breaking Cooperative Relations*, pp. 31–48 (New York: Basil Blackwell, 1998).

35 D. H. McKnight, L. L. Cummings, and N. L. Chervany, "Initial Trust Formation in New Organizational Relationships," *Academy of Management Review*, vol. 23, no. 3 (1998), pp. 473–490.

36 R. H. Fazio and M. P. Zanna, "Direct Experience and Attitude-Behavior Consistency," In L. Berkowitz (Ed.), *Advances in Experimental Social Psychology, Volume 14*, pp. 162–202 (New York: Academic Press, 1981).

37 J. K. Butler and R. S. Cantrell, "A Behavioral Decision Theory Approach to Modeling

Dyadic Trust in Superiors and Subordinates," *Psychological Reports*, vol. 55, no. 1 (1984), pp. 19–28.

J. J. Gabarro, "The Development of Trust, Influence, and Expectations," In A. G. Athos and J. J. Gabarro (Eds.), *Interpersonal Behavior: Communication and Understanding in Relationships* (pp. 290–303). Englewood Cliffs, NJ: Prentice-Hall, Inc., 1978.

R. C. Mayer, J H. Davis, and F. D. Schoorman, "An Integration Model of Organizational Trust," *Academy of Management Review*, vol. 29, no. 3 (1995), pp. 709–734.

P. L. Schindler and C. C. Thomas, "The Structure of Interpersonal Trust in the Workplace," *Psychological Reports*, vol. 73, no. 2 (1993), pp. 563–573.

38 J. J. Gabarro, "The Development of Working Relationships," In J. Galegher and R. E. Kraut (Eds.), *Intellectual Teamwork: Social and Technological Foundations of Cooperative Work*, pp. 79–110 (Hillsdale, NJ: Lawrence Erlbaum Associates Publishers, 1990).

39 F. Dansereau, G, Graen, and J. W. Haga, "A Vertical Dyad Linkage Approach to Leadership Within Formal Organizations: A Longitudinal Investigation of the Role Making Process," *Organizational Behavior and Human Performance*, 1975, 13(1), 46–78.

G. B. Graen, R. C. Liden, and W. Hoel, "Role of Leadership in the Employee Withdrawal Process," *Journal of Applied Psychology*, 1982, 67 (6), 868–872.

G. B. Graen, M. A. Novak, and P. Sommerkamp, "The Effects of Leader-Member Exchange and Job Design on Productivity and Satisfaction: Testing a Dual Attachment Model," *Organizational Behavior and Human Performance*, 1982, 30(1), 109–131.

G. B. Graen and W. Schiemann, "Leader-Member Agreement: A Vertical Dyad Linkage Approach," *Journal of Applied Psychology*, 1978,63(2), 206–212.

R. C. Liden and G. B. Graen, "Generalizability of the Vertical Dyad Linkage Model of Leadership," *Academy of Management Journal*, 1980, 23(3), 451–465.

D. Tjosvold, "Power and Social Context in Superior-Subordinate Interaction," *Organizational Behavior and Human Decision Processes*, 1985, 35(3), 281–293.

40 E. M. Eisenberg and H. L. Goodall, Jr., *Organizational Communication: Balancing Creativity and Constraint* (New York: St. Martin Press, 1993).

Chapter 8

The Principal III: Building a Better Working Relationship

To this point, the discussion of ways to develop an understanding of your principal has focused on abstractions. The approach has asked you to accept theoretical models and make subjective analyses and interpretations. Those ideas are useful in understanding your relationship with the principal, and in coming to appreciate your principal's responsibilities and motivations, but they don't suggest very much to help you get a handle on how he or she works. This chapter's purpose is to operationalize some of those ideas and offer suggestions of specific things to look for in your principal's working style. Without this information, you can inadvertently precipitate unnecessary conflict and misunderstanding.

The Elements of Your Principal's Working Style

If you can build a profile of your principal and his or her working style, you can make comparisons with your own and then make adjustments. While the superior/subordinate relationship is one of mutual dependence, it's not usually one of equal dependence. With the authority of position, the principal remains more the person to accommodate than you do.

The questions below collectively attempt to sketch a working description of your principal. You will see that some of the questions connect with David McClelland's ideas of leader/manager needs, and others reflect the effects of hierarchical position or the role outlined in Mitchell's and Spady's conception of schools, both of which you read about in Chapter 6.[1] With that in mind, see if you can ascertain the answers to these questions:

• **What are your principal's primary objectives? That is, where does he or she place real emphasis? Is it on order and discipline in the school? On activities and athletics? On public relations? On the college bound student? On instruction in general?**

Chris Argyris at Harvard makes an interesting case that we all have two sets of theories that inform our performance.[2] The first is espoused theories, those theories that we tell others—and often ourselves—guide our behavior. The second is action theories. That is, the things we actually believe, perhaps at a subconscious level, that demonstrably explain our behavior. An assistant principal gave me a good example one day when he described how much his principal believed in empowerment (espoused theory). "Oh, yes," he said, "my principal believes in empowerment. We're truly empowered to do whatever she tells us to do" (action theory). The greater the divergence between our espoused theories and our action theories, the more difficult we can be to work with.

Knowing the difference with your principal can be a critical factor in your ability to harmonize your work style with his or hers. I could take you to a principal I know and, after a half-hour discussion, you would come away convinced that this administrator has no other focus than student achievement—that is until you proposed a study plan that gave students any kind of unsupervised research time. The truth is that this principal's driving value is order in the school. Everything else is second to that, and programs only exist if they fit the principal's concept of appropriate command and control. Providing the administration with independent study proposals in that school is a waste of time and would make you suspect in the principal's eyes.

This is not necessarily to say that the principal is wrong for that particular school at this particular time. The point is that you need to know what the principal really values, whatever that may be. For some principals, it is student achievement. For others, it can be early childhood education or at-risk children or sports supremacy or reading growth. Whatever it is, you need to know what it is.

With this information, you can make judgments about areas to select for information dissemination, for getting involved in projects, and for discussion. Knowing what your principal truly values also provides a measure of his or her philosophy and makes it easier for you to see opportunities.

• Is your principal on the way up? How ambitious is he or she for advancement?

You can anticipate that a principal strongly pursuing advancement will have emphases different from one who plans to retire out of his or her current position. If nothing else, think about the differing effect each of the two perspectives might have on your long-term project proposals.

The aggressively upward mobile principal may also have a different take on how credit should be shared. It's not uncommon to see principals who want to draw notice as a foundation for their own enhanced futures claim a large share of the credit for whatever is good in the school. Knowing your principal's goals can only help you in deciding how much to invest in the relationship and what kinds of research and other information to share with him or her.

• How does your principal get along with the superintendent? Are they philosophically aligned? Do they work well together? What can you tell about how the board members feel about your principal?

Principals are always trapped in the middle between the demands and desires of the faculty on one hand and the district office on the other. If there's tension between the superintendent and the principal, the likelihood is that the principal will be pretty conservative in initiating certain activities.[3]

Knowing something about how the superintendent and board members perceive your principal will let you assess what kinds of pressures your principal is under. It will give you an idea of who is leaning on him or her and how much support he or she can look for in times of conflict. If you can discern the issues, other than personality conflicts for which there are no cures, you might be able to provide research and model program information that will help your principal meet the pressures and tighten relationships with the central office.

• What experiential path did your principal follow to the office? Did he or she come from outside the district? Outside the building? What position(s) did the principal hold before this one? What was his or her reputation there? Out of what teaching discipline did the principal come?

This information is useful in several ways. First, a new principal has motivations and needs different from those of an experienced administrator.[4] A seasoned principal has been socialized to the job and can more quickly come to focus on technical issues. A neophyte has to first work through a variety of socialization and self-definition issues. Each will require different kinds of information and support.

Second, a principal who was a teacher in the same school has a "history" with people that newcomers brought in from outside don't have. This affects their relationships because outsiders coming in are perceived differently than insiders promoted. This perceptual difference can include a presumption of competence which, accurate or not, can put a lot of pressure on the principal.[5]

Third, there is evidence that an assistant principalship may or may not be adequate preparation for the principalship.[6] If your principal served in only one narrow capacity as an assistant, he or she may have an uneven distribution of knowledge and skills and require more assistance in some areas than in others.

Fourth, the teaching discipline from which the principal came may still remain an important interest area and may be something you use to open lines of communication. More than one of the librarians with whom I worked used my enduring interest in western history to entice me into the library.

• How formal or informal is your principal?

This information may help you measure your principal's self-perception. Some administrators like to interact on a first name basis with the people they see every day. Others want to be addressed by title, many particularly do if the title is "doctor." You get a sense of your principal's perceptions, for example, if he or she addresses you by your first name but expects you to use a more formal mode in responding.

Preferred formality levels also may let you glimpse the principal's sense of humor. How formal your principal is will help you to understand if you can use humor to help build a relationship, or if you would hurt yourself by so doing. John Cleese sums up humor's power in persuasion efforts: "If I can get you to laugh with me," he says, "you like me better, which makes you more open to my ideas. And if I can persuade you to laugh at the particular point I make, by laughing at it you acknowledge its truth."[7]

Humor is analogous to electricity in some ways. It's one of the great human connectors and relationship energizers if properly employed, but it's dangerous when the wires get crossed or different currents intersect. The fuse box often is sex. Know your principal well before venturing into that area.

• How much control does the principal maintain in delegating tasks or in working with committees?

Think back to the Needs Survey you took for yourself at the end of Chapter 6. You might now take the inventory again, but this time, answer the questions as you think your principal would answer them. This information may give you a glimpse of the principal's mix of needs for achievement, power, or affiliation. If you pursue a close working relationship with the principal, you will be subject to these needs.

How work is delegated, if at all, is a good example. Suppose you are asked to work on a project for the duration of the spring semester. Will your principal expect you to meet with him or her every few weeks throughout the term or will you just be expected to show up at the end with the completed product?

Suppose your principal wants you to report in March 1, March 15, April 1, April 15, and so on until the completion deadline in May. It might be easy to be offended at this, particularly if you're a strongly independent worker. As you wrestle with your feelings, it's important to keep in mind that it's the principal's personality you're assessing here, not your own. Your principal would have shown trust and confidence in you just by selecting you to take on the project. The need to have you check in periodically may have nothing to do with you and everything to do with your principal's inability to surrender power and control.

• What are the major issues facing the principal today in your school? In your district? Where does he or she stand on these?

The answers to these questions can provide more measures of both the pressures on your principal and his or her philosophy. It can tell you how close or far apart you and the principal are on given subjects. It's useful to know whether you see the same things the same way or see them differently. If your views are similar, there is an opportunity here to tighten the relationship. If you're very different in your philosophies, this information may help you decide which discussions and projects to avoid.

Knowing the major issues in your school and district can also tell you where he or she may have to put priority attention for the foreseeable future.

• How does your principal relate to the teachers' and support staff unions?

Dealing with the union is always one of a principal's more interesting experiences. Having a sense of how he or she perceives the union—and depending upon how the union has actually conducted its affairs—might give you some insight into how your principal perceives both allies and adversaries. It is a very different experience to work with someone who sees opposition as a free and proper expression of a legitimate, though different, professional point of view than to work with someone who sees adversaries as professional or even personal enemies.

• Has your principal been involved in attempts, successful or not, to terminate any teachers' employment in your school? Has he or she been involved in conflicts over student rights, club activities, or contents of the student newspaper or other publications?

Knowing whether this has occurred—and, if so, how often—can give you a sense of how aggressive your principal might be in pursuing his or her philosophy or authority. Trying to fire someone is a time consuming, expensive—both financially and emotionally—endeavor. Student issues, especially in a high school, can get you into the newspaper all too quickly. A principal has to be seriously committed to undertake these challenges.

The more important question, though, is how each incident was handled. The number of incidents may or may not be a trustworthy measure of the most important feature of the situation. In a troubled school with a difficult faculty or a contentious student body, continual confrontation may be inescapable, even desirable. Whether due process was observed, discretion maintained, and goal displacement avoided are much more important considerations.

• How well does your principal handle criticism?

This information can be useful in determining how to approach your principal regarding a problem. Some people can handle criticism of programs, policies, practices, and other global issues very well but, at the same time, are unable to gracefully handle criticism of themselves. Some can take personal criticism, but are very protective of programs they've created or shepherded. Others, of course, handle both very well, and still others handle neither.

There are two ways to discern how and how well your principal handles criticism. One way is to express your criticism to him or her. The other, and perhaps the wiser, at least at the outset of your relationship, is to observe how your principal responds to others' critical statements. Chances to observe will be abundant. Principals never go very long without someone voicing criticism of some sort.

• How does your principal react to stress?

Knowing how your principal reacts to stress can help you in several ways. First, if you can read the signs, you will know those times when you should not to make an approach. Second, you might see opportunities to reduce the intensity of the situation and thereby improve your standing. Third, you may be able to compare behavior during stress periods with how you are treated other times, which will help you avoid taking personally things that aren't meant to be personal.[8]

• Is your principal a morning, an afternoon, or an evening person?

A major purpose in building a profile of your principal's working style is to maximize the odds that any idea you present will receive a favorable hearing. Knowing when your principal is most productive and receptive can help you better gauge when to approach him or her about things of interest and importance to you both.

Discerning this characteristic can be difficult and may take a good deal of time and observation. It's sometimes easy to be fooled. I knew an administrator who used to get to work very early in the morning. Many people assumed that that meant that he was a morning worker and that an early approach was a good approach. The simple fact was that he had a small house, several teenage children, and too few bathrooms. It just was easier to come to the high school to take a shower in the gym and then go on to his office. The best time to approach him with an idea was actually about 4:00 in the afternoon.

• How direct is your principal in language use?

As Andrew DuBrin points out, managers sometimes attempt to soften their really non-negotiable demands through polite language.[9] Problems result if you interpret "If it's not too much trouble ..." as an option when the message really is "Do it ... and soon," or interpret "May I suggest ..." as a real suggestion instead of as an expectation. It's important that you get clarification if there is the slightest doubt on your part of exactly what your principal means when he or she uses a particular phrase.

- **Does your principal prefer dealing with a wide range of things at once, or is there a preference for concentrating on a single issue?**

Knowing this can help you prepare materials and adapt to the principal's style. The goal, again, is to structure the situation so any proposal you make has the greatest chance of getting a favorable hearing. Some people like to work on just one idea at a time, methodically analyzing its components, setting it in the context of the moment, and then making a decision. Others, like one administrator with whom I worked, have minds like the Windows screens on a computer and like to entertain several ideas at once to see if they can interlink them. If you have two or three ideas to float with your principal, give them to him or her in the manner he or she best receives them, whether it's one at a time or all together.

- **How does your principal best receive information?**

Peter Drucker classifies managers as "readers" and "listeners." You need to know if your principal is someone who prefers written or oral presentations and whether the presentations should be terse or elaborate. The implications, according to Drucker, are clear. If your principal is a reader, send a written report first and follow it up with a face-to-face discussion. If your principal is a listener, brief him or her on the subject, or make a presentation, depending on the principal's preference, and then send a written report afterward.[10]

- **Is there something your principal considers absolutely unforgivable in interpersonal relations?**

Finally, we all have idiosyncrasies. Find out what your principal's might be, and then stay away from them. For some people, they're issues of protocol and command and control—"everything has to go through this office!" For other people, they're personal in some way or another. I worked with a principal who was as delightful a person as you'd ever encounter, unless he perceived that you were trying to intimidate him in some way. Then he would turn on you like an enraged grizzly. Think of the old joke about the patient telling the doctor that "It hurts when I do this," and the doctor says, "Then don't do that." It's good advice.

Strategies and Tactics for Building Your Relationship with Your Principal

The rest of the chapter is divided into two parts. The first describes strategies useful in constructing a strong relationship with your principal. These are general approaches to working with him or her. They outline broad behaviors rather than specific activities. The second part lists specific tactics you might employ to capture your principal's attention, increase your usefulness to him or her, increase his or her dependence on you, and give him or her a reason to support your activities and requests.

Strategies

1. Get early and continuing clarification of what the principal expects of you and from you.

You and your principal both need to clearly understand what your responsibilities are. Congruent views of your role, duties, rights, and opportunities are critical to the overall relationship. They must be constructed at the outset, so you don't waste time, energy, or resources on things that neither the principal nor other members of the faculty and staff will value.

These perceptions must be continually monitored and updated for two reasons. First, schools are not static institutions and conditions change. This is particularly true if your school is caught up in change as a result of shifts in community resources or demographics or if it is involved in internal restructuring. New projects and programs may lend themselves to a reordering of responsibilities and roles. Second, many of your own activities will precipitate changes in your expectations and in others' expectations of you as you go about building influence with teachers, students, parents and others in the building and district.

If you can regularly get clarification of what the principal expects, especially if you are attempting to simultaneously shape some of those expectations, you'll be in a better position to sense what he or she wants to have happen. You will also be in a better position to make the right decisions when unforeseen events arise, as they always will.

Change has an ebb and flow to it. There are likely to be periods of loosening and tightening as concerns about resources and people's feelings surface and are dealt with. You want to avoid being boxed in by contractions or overwhelmed by rapid expansion of opportunities or support. The only way to do this is to actively seek shared understandings of what is going on and what your role is in it.[11]

A librarian who is made uncomfortable by change, who doesn't see the superior/subordinate relationship as a mutual dependency, or who feels that the library can remain a protected arena, may be tempted to withdraw and minimize contact with the administration. The most common result of this tactic is misunderstanding, which, in turn leads to mistakes, poor performance, and loss of the principal's confidence.[12]

2. Take the initiative instead of simply waiting for the principal or others to come to you.

If you wait for the principal or the teachers to see your value and the value of your library, you will wait a long time. There is too much going on in schools today to always wait for others to give direction or guidance. As Geoffrey Bellman observes, you have your position because of your expertise. You need to search out opportunities to put to work what you know. Instead of waiting until the administration or teachers, parent groups, or student groups ask you for help, you would do better to be out there offering it. You gain the respect of the organization by anticipating its needs.[13]

Webster's dictionary tells us that initiative is the "energy or aptitude displayed in the initiation of action; self-reliant enterprise; self-initiated activity."[14] That's a good beginning, but initiative takes on four additional characteristics when applied to the workplace.

First, taking the initiative at work means more than just working beyond or even without someone else's direction. As Robert Kelley at Carnegie Mellon University explains, initiative "involves moving out of your own protective job description to bridge the spaces between job spheres."[15]

For librarians, this means bridging spaces between the library and the various classrooms, the counseling center, and the administration offices. This is a real challenge in schools because it is counter-cultural. One of the great contradictions in how schools run is that we know from research that both teachers and students benefit from collaboration among the adults, but the pervasive paradigm of school in America is one adult in one room with one group of students for one period of time.[16]

Of course, you cannot afford to spend every moment in initiatives that take you away from your own environments. Part of being perceived as conscientious involves effort and effectiveness in your specific day-to-day job responsibilities. Initiative is exercised above and beyond the job description. Students and teachers who need help now must have it. Forging links to other teachers, counselors, and administrators is done in addition to your prescribed duties.

The second additional characteristic of workplace initiative is that its result must benefit others as much as it benefits you. Absent a visible benefit to others, people who press into areas outside their own job descriptions are likely to be perceived as self-serving. One of the reasons that initiative is appreciated by others is that it benefits them. This helps to explain why you need to make contributions in meetings and on committees concerned with school-wide issues and why you need to be involved in the activity program. People value that which makes their jobs easier, makes them look more effective, helps them succeed, and makes them look good.

Third, while the dictionary cites initiative as beginning something, workplace initiative requires a commitment to completing it. False starts and withered dreams are not initiative. This doesn't mean that everything you start must be overwhelmingly successful, but it does mean that ideas need to be carefully thought through to raise the odds of success.

Fourth and last, initiative is shown as much in small ways and small-scale efforts as it is in massive institution-changing projects.[17] The Mississippi River is born of droplets. An accumulation of small successful initiatives is perhaps a better measure of initiative than a few great attempts at change. Not only is there less chance of failure in small steps than in large, but small projects do not consume so much of your time and effort that you neglect your primary responsibilities. It's not just trying; it's doing that counts.

"This sounds good," I suspect you're saying, "but what does it really mean when I go to work tomorrow?" Let me offer five specific ways you can begin to demonstrate initiative and conscientiousness at work.

Take Action: This notion summarizes everything I've said above. Don't be passive—that's the librarian's stereotype. Don't stop at the idea stage, and don't hesitate to take the lead. To take the initiative is to take a risk. The two are inseparable. Don't, of course, wander off into an organizational or academic swamp, but—at the same time—don't be too afraid to try things with which you are not completely familiar. After all, the Ark was built by amateurs and the *Titanic* by professionals.

I'm speaking more of an attitude here than of a skill set. Given the unique culture of each school building and the individual nature of each of the people who make it up, you will have to decide on specific activities that fit your time and place. Still, the idea of action can be operationalized in even the smallest of ways, sometimes by nothing more than by changing a few words here or there. For example, instead of telling someone to call you if he or she needs help, you can do a little homework, learn about someone's situation, and then seize the initiative in a conversation by saying something like, "I see you have a new assignment this year. I have all kinds of things in the library that you might like to use. I'd be glad to show them to you."

If you tell someone to call if he or she needs help, he or she will probably thank you very nicely—and then never call. To ask for help is to admit a deficiency. Most people don't easily do that. On the other hand, if you take the initiative and offer the help before it may be needed, you have helped the person save face; the odds go up considerably that he or she will accept what you offer (though perhaps some time later), and you will have opened the door to a collaborative relationship.[18] He or she doesn't have to admit anything. That person can just come back and say, "You know those things you mentioned the other day? Are they still lying around? I might like to come by sometime and take a look at them." Then you have him or her.

How do you find people like that? You take the initiative and review your school's assignment roster each term, looking for people new to the school, people in new jobs (including administrators), and people whose assignments have been changed within their existing jobs. Then you seek them out. This is what Tom Peters and Bob Waterman called "a bias for action" in *The Pursuit of Excellence*.[19] Initiative is akin to leadership, and the one universal characteristic of leaders is that they make things happen.[20]

Persevere: Perseverance is pursuit of the objective. The thing that counts is accomplishing the goal; the method is secondary. It's like what we try to do with mission statements in schools and fail so miserably at.[21] The mantra of initiative and conscientiousness is "the goal, the goal, the goal." It's like Winston Churchill's targeting the destruction of Hitler as England's only goal. "That alone. That all the time. That to the end." Multiple methods in pursuit of a single goal reflect initiative. It's what researchers call a belief in equifinality—the idea that there are many equally effective ways to reach the same end.[22]

Try to build bridges with whomever you can. If one teacher or grade or department or administrator doesn't respond, move on to another. If the department head isn't listening, try a teacher who has his or her ear. If grants don't pay off, talk to local groups like the Rotary or Kiwanis. Just keep trying.

Search for Problems to Fix: I try to teach my administrative students that there is no one best way to do anything. Everything is context-bound. What works with you might not work with the next person; what works today might not work tomorrow. Consequently, everything in school work is a judgment call. If everything is a judgment call, then you must do your homework so you can make the most informed judgments.

You can analyze your own performance and product. You can watch for danger signals in your relationships. You can watch for changes outside your own area that might have implications for you and for your library media center. Beyond client surveys, you can use the technology you have to analyze budget and usage trends in your library, collection status, collaborative efforts with others, volunteer personnel contributions, and other library functions, programs, and operations. Get useful feedback from your principal by pressing the administration to accept or to develop an evaluation instrument geared to library media personnel instead of the teacher evaluation form or some variant of it. Develop close associations with the assistant principal, dean, or other person who handles discipline in the school to raise the odds of quick and effective assistance and support when the inevitable discipline problem emerges. If you're in an elementary school, get down on the floor regularly—seeing the facility the way the children see it—to spot hazards and temptations and to improve your perspective. Go to board meetings regularly and identify emerging issues. Tap your professional organizations for information on trends, challenges, and problems that could affect you.

Look for Opportunities: Problems are not the only places where you can find opportunities to establish a presence. As organizational researcher Robert Kelley has pointed out, people who seize the initiative at work often look into those areas between the boxes on the organizational chart, between the job descriptions that not only define but also limit the activities of many others.[23]

You can examine student assignments for pathways back to teacher interests. Teachers who accompany their students to the media center can be observed and engaged in conversation to assess their information retrieval and technology skills. Over time, you can draw a profile of the faculty that will show you the places where you might make a staff development contribution. Administrators always need the latest information and research on curriculum and instruction, law, policy, finances, and model programs. You can tap your electronic databases and the Internet to find that information for them—before they ask for it. Identifying what people need before they think to ask for it is to strike the mother lode of opportunity.

Do the Unexpected: Initiative is not demonstrated just in finding things that need doing and new things to do. It's also shown in how you deal with those things once you've found them. Initiative is, in many ways, a breaking out. Instead of being bound by tradition, you show initiative in trying to create new traditions. This kind of behavior is what Edgar Schein at M.I.T. had in mind when he wrote about "creative individualism" and "role innovators."[24] These are people who perceive the pivotal behaviors, values, and norms of their positions as the foundation rather than as the limitation of their jobs. Using those as an initial framework, they try to extend the concept of the role in ways that are both satisfying to them and good for the organization. How they do this, of course, depends upon their own personalities and the unique characteristics of their workplaces.

For someone like you as a school librarian, creative individualism in pursuit of role innovation could include such things as attending department or grade level meetings. You could arrange for team or departmental showings of new acquired materials. You could volunteer to work with teachers at different grade levels and departments to develop research activity packages that substitutes can employ. You can involve teachers in library policy development, or invite them to help you weed the collection, or offer the library as the site for an "idea bank" of materials, lesson plans, project descriptions, quizzes, and examinations. Beginning teachers who are creating lesson plans, veteran newcomers who need help to learn the culture and the preferred approaches in their new schools, and people who teach outside their areas of preparation all need and are likely to be grateful for ideas.[25]

It takes work to craft people's perceptions—not just more of what you've already been doing, but work that is qualitatively different from what they expect of you. Bringing all of your research resources to bear as a member of a committee or task force can be a start. Depending on the topic under discussion, you possibly can bring more useful information to a meeting than just about anyone else there. This is initiative because it reaches beyond the borders of your job and will deliver the greatest benefit to others. This will help you take the lead—or at least be a leading contributor—to an important achievement. At the same time, it will show others that your perspective is not limited to library media, an important alteration in the perceptions of many other educators.

Most managers value initiative in their subordinates, particularly if it prevents problems, solves problems, or multiplies the value of existing resources. Initiative also demonstrates a desire and willingness to take on new responsibilities. A reputation for being interested and concerned about the school, doing things your job description doesn't call for, and reaching out to others will keep you in mind when decisions are made about who should receive opportunities. Such a reputation is a necessity if you have aspirations for an administrative position later in your career.

3. Do your homework before going to see the principal; try to deliver possible solutions when you deliver problems.

If you only come to see the principal with problems, after a while you may become associated in his or her mind with problems. Recall the discussion of likability and the delivery of bad news in Chapter 3. Someone who solves problems and thereby makes the principal successful is going to be more influential than someone who only uncovers and defines problems.

It is important, however, that you report problems—not just immediate problems, but those that you see beginning to emerge. Principals can only appreciate early warnings, but you do not want to develop a reputation as an alarmist or a negativist. Whenever possible, delay making your report until you have had a chance to investigate the situation and can generate a range of possible counters or solutions.

Christopher Hegarty points out another advantage to this strategy, especially if the problem involves you or the library: it reduces the odds that the principal will impose a solution that might be unacceptable to you.[26]

4. Be your own publicist and promoter, but be subtle rather than strident.

This idea is a theme that runs through the whole of this book, and only a reminder need be entered here. Influence is based on perceptions. In order to have supportive perceptions of the library and librarian, in fact, to have any perceptions at all, the principal has to be aware of them. Competence must be made visible. The principal has to evaluate your performance. It is in your best interest to help him or her do that in a way that is both accurate and positive.

5. Get out and talk to people before you talk to the principal.

The principal needs current information in order to make the best decisions for the school. You need current information in order to make the best decisions for the library and to be able to influence the principal. Stale information is usually not very persuasive. Further, the principal is not likely to be much impressed with your knowledge if it is out of date.

Henry Mintzberg, the prominent organizational researcher, has perceptively pointed out that formal systems of communication in organizations provide people with past, not current, information.[27] If you wait for the department or faculty meeting to take place, or, worse, wait for the minutes of the meetings you didn't attend, you are condemned to being a step behind. Department, school, and district newsletters are even worse. Quarter, semester, and year-end reports going to or coming from the district have virtually no current value. If you are going to be able to offer assessments of current situations, you need to know what they are. That means you need to get out and talk to people.

6. Don't get caught up in jargon or titles.

In talking with the principal, you need to stress what you can do for him or her and for the school. These are ideas best communicated in straightforward language, not in jargon. Given the typical principal's background and interests, the odds are good that terms like "shelflist," "accessioning," "vertical file" are next to meaningless.[28] These serve to distance the principal from you and can even create an invisible barrier.

If you must employ language other than layman's language, use the principal's own. It wouldn't take much for you to pick it up. Read through the administrative journals in your professional library, and pay close attention to the terms the principal and other administrators use in conversation.

One of the terms the principal, teachers, students, and parents are likely to use is "librarian" rather than "school library media specialist." Don't fight it. From the typical principal's point of view, the title means nothing, and to be constantly reminded of it is an irritation. To press too hard on the title without a significant change in the function is to invite ridicule. You create a caricature of professionalism and reinforce the fussy stereotype. Whether you are called the "school librarian" or the "school library media specialist," "teacher-librarian," or "library media teacher" will make no difference in terms of faculty, student, parent, or administrative respect for you or the extent to which you will be able to garner administrative support.

If the title is important to you, get it on the memo pad, in the job description, in the faculty roster and phone book, in the accreditation report, and anywhere else you can get it written. Introduce yourself with the title, ask to be introduced with the title, but once past that point, let it go. Don't disrupt the flow of the principal's thought or action, or the thoughts or actions of anyone else upon whom you are dependent for support, by calling your title into question whenever it is misspoken. People will say the title for you, but inside they'll be saying something else.

7. Establish a strong relationship with the assistant principal(s).

Assistant principals are often undervalued in schools. They are too often only thought of in association with discipline. The truth is that assistant principals are involved with virtually every aspect of school operation, especially in secondary schools. For teachers and students in all but the smallest secondary schools, as often as not, the assistant principal is the administrator of involvement. The assistant is the person most frequently and readily available, the one turned to when something is needed immediately.[29]

For your purposes, there are several reasons why it is in your best interest to build a strong relationship with the assistant principal. First, the assistant principal has the principal's ear. There are few closer working relationships than that between the principal and the assistant. Words of praise about your performance, attitude, and abilities communicated from the assistant will go a long way with the principal. The assistant principal who perceives you as valuable can facilitate your relationship with the principal by lobbying for you and your needs.

Second, assistant principals can provide you with a lot of information about the principal: priorities, likes and dislikes, wishes, working style, and so on. The assistant can help you shape reports and proposals, inform you of opportunities, and keep you up-to-date on important issues across the school.

Third, assistant principals frequently oversee the activities of one or more academic departments. An assistant convinced of the value of the library and the librarian can be of great assistance in opening doors and minds to your expanded role. Conversely, a resistant assistant can retard, perhaps sabotage, your efforts.

Fourth, sooner or later you will have a discipline problem in the library. You will want the assistant principal's enthusiastic support.

Fifth, the single largest group in the pool of principalship candidates is made up of assistant principals.[30] A good relationship can be an investment in the future.

The strategy for building a relationship with the assistant principal is fundamentally the same as the strategy for building the relationship with the principal. There are some significant differences between the principalship and the assistant principalship, but many of the driving forces are the same.

The differences lie in four distinct areas: (1) the assistant's work is much more specialized than the principal's; (2) the assistant is perceived more as one of the led than as the school leader; (3) the assistant shares jobs with other faculty members rather than having sole responsibility; and (4) the assistant is not involved in as much boundary spanning as the principal.[31] These characteristics make the assistant principal of particular importance to the school librarian looking to build influence in the school.

First, with more specialized tasks, the assistant principal has a set of particular interests which can be specifically connected to library services. Second, as one of the led and yet in the ranks of administration, the assistant principal represents a linkage between the two. Some writers have even defined the job that way.[32] Third, by having shared responsibilities, the assistant is required to do a great deal of lateral communication and is drawn into all parts of the school. This makes the assistant an excellent channel for disseminating and gathering information. Lastly, without major boundary spanning responsibilities, the assistant's attention is focused inward, which places his or her attention squarely in the realm where you will want to do your most intense influence building.

It is worth your time to do an analysis of the assistant principal(s) similar to the one you do on the principal. The assistant can be of great help in reaching into the principal's office and into other corners of the school.

8. Build a strong relationship with the principal's secretary.

For many of the same reasons you would want to build a good relationship with the assistant principal, you will benefit from a positive association with the principal's secretary.

One of the critical elements in working successfully with the principal is having an understanding of his or her idiosyncrasies, habits, and working style. Few people know these better than the secretary. The secretary who sees you as valuable may squeeze you in for a needed appointment that an indifferent secretary would never consider making. The secretary can look over written material you want to submit and offer ideas and corrections. Even if his or her input is small, you have complemented him or her by asking. You gain an advantage when the secretary delivers your message to the principal if he or she presents it with a smile and a positive word. On the other hand, you lose a lot if he or she presents it with a derisive laugh or a comment that indicates you are a bother or your paper is a waste of time.[33]

You need to be very careful in building relationships with secretaries and other classified employees in a school. They very often see themselves as treated less than professionally by the certificated staff, and they are very sensitive to being used. It is very important that your relationship with the secretary be as honest as you can make it.

9. Learn the preferred chain of command.

Find out the protocol for communicating with people at other schools in the district and at the central office.

Some principals require that all upward communications be routed through their offices. There may be different channels for dealing with policy matters and for dealing with curriculum matters. Find out. You do not want to rupture relations by being perceived as having gone over the principal's head or of having made an "end run."

Tactics

1. If you don't have it, ask for department head status in your school.

If you're in a high school, ask for department head status. If you're in an elementary school or a middle school or junior high that is organized without departments, ask to sit in on team or grade level meetings.

Department head status offers several benefits. It will increase your visibility and will offer you opportunities to showcase your resources and services. You will be present when new and important issues are raised, and you can help to frame them. Department head status will put you in contact with a wider range of people who control resources and information useful to you. It will increase your familiarity and offer opportunities to develop alliances and coalitions. Most of all, it will put you in continual contact with the principal.

2. Seek to develop an evaluation instrument that recognizes that the work you do is fundamentally different from what teachers do.

Librarians across the country suffer from inaccurate—even inappropriate—evaluations. I'm sure it's no surprise to you—and surely is no secret to many school librarians—that the processes used to evaluate your performance often have little relationship to the work you actually do.[34] Unfortunately, many administrators remain unaware of this and, as a result, the value of librarian performance appraisals is often severely diminished. The problem this represents is important both to librarians and to principals.

Evaluations are supposed to have utility. They should yield information that identifies needed change or that validates what is being done as appropriate and worthy. Inaccurate evaluations are unfair to you and misleading to your principal. In the long run, the cost can be very high. Principals are key figures in quality library media programs,[35] but their ability to make appropriate personnel, resource, scheduling, and support decisions is impaired if the librarian's evaluation doesn't provide a realistic picture and assessment of the librarian's role and contribution.

Strive to get elements in the evaluation that recognize your contributions to teacher and program success—things that will help to break the "staff" image and enhance the "line" personnel image. The goal with this tactic is to become clearly aligned with the school's central mission. You want to stress that you perform tasks critical to the success of others, but you have unique needs of your own. There are many models available in the literature.

If you can't make this happen because of union rules or unbreakable tradition, develop a clear written job description. Make sure it contains reference to public relations contributions and stresses educational involvement, staff development, collaboration, and planning with teachers.

3. Ask for assignment to accreditation teams.

You will demonstrate energy and focused effort. You may bring back useful new ideas from the other schools you evaluate and may deliver social proof to support them. You will broaden your contacts with educators from other schools, which will enlarge your alliances and friendship network. You will better understand what will happen when your school undergoes accreditation and can assist better with development of your school's self-study, which will again increase your contacts, associate you with the main thrust of the school mission, and enhance your visibility.

4. Volunteer for committees.

First, no matter how good you are, your reputation depends on other people. Committees provide opportunities for you to make contributions that others will remark upon. If the principal chairs the committee, first-hand observation of your talents will be possible. Familiarity can be built and expertise demonstrated. If the committee is successful, especially if there is some fun to be had in the work of the committee, you can increase your association with positive memories.

Second, committees are wonderful sources of information. You can establish contacts, do favors in order to invoke reciprocity, and increase the breadth of your alliances. Information you gather can increase your sensitivity to the needs of others.

Third, committees are often the site of issue generation. Your presence allows you to help frame the issue and shape the agenda. In developing alternative solutions to whatever issues emerge, you may be able to elicit public commitments to support the library's role.

Last, principals care about how departments relate. High-level attention is given to coordinating activities among varying departments, grade levels, and programs. The library can serve as a link-pin between them, reinforcing the image that the library is critical to school success.

5. Build the professional library through subscriptions to educational journals.

Seek input on what to buy; subscribe to certain journals as a clear favor to the people who want them in order to invoke reciprocity.

Don't route the journals. The fall issue may not reach someone until the spring and you won't be able to track where it is if you need it. Make photocopies of the table of contents and send them to each of the administrators with a note.

Depending on your budget, you may be able to send the principal or assistant a copy of the specific article in which he or she is interested. That way, they can have it to keep, mark up, use, and not worry about returning. This tactic showcases your resources, creates a dependency, demonstrates expertise, and invokes reciprocity.

6. Use the professional library, subscriptions, and the newsletters of your particular library/media professional organizations to track events that could have an impact on your library, your school, or the staff in your school.

For example, provide the principal with the knowledge that a textbook used in your school or a book in your library has been the target of a lawsuit somewhere. Administrators abhor surprises. This information could be of considerable value if the topic just "pops up" at a parent meeting or a board meeting sometime.

This tactic demonstrates expertise and a sensitivity to the needs of others, showcases your resources, ties you to the central mission of the school, and encourages reciprocity.

7. Design a logo for use on all communications coming from the library.

The logo should be neat, non-obtrusive, and professional. No cutesy designs, koalas, or happy faces. This creates a professional image within the culture of the school and enhances familiarity.

8. Write a monthly report.

Hold your monthly report to one page. More than anything, include listings of activities, projects, and collaborative instruction. As space allows, include circulation statistics, new materials, and ideas for improvement of service. Keep statistics to a minimum. Maybe report them like the automakers report sales—up or down for the same period last year and an estimation of why. The principal can use this for reports to the superintendent or board. They should always be typed and always be professional.

This tactic illuminates your administrative skills, gains recognition for accomplishment, demonstrates linkages to the central mission of the school, and provides a rationale for requesting additional resources.

9. Offer to write a column in the principal's newsletter to parents.

Writing a column lightens the principal's burden, draws the principal's attention, and gives you access to parents. This tactic increases visibility and can increase familiarity if written in a personal style. It offers opportunities to showcase expertise and library resources and services. At the same time, it provides a vehicle for giving recognition to others. Because it does a favor for the principal, it has the potential to invoke the reciprocity principle.

10. Invite faculty meetings to be held in the library.

Get the principal and the staff to see the facility and feel comfortable in it. See if a two-minute maximum library report can be a part of each informational faculty meeting. Have a handout to give to teachers and staff; customize the handout to grade level or department whenever possible. This will keep your operation in the light of attention, showcase resources and services, increase familiarity and the opportunities for networking, and invoke reciprocity.

11. Invite PTA or equivalent groups to meet in the library.

The principal or assigned assistant principal will be there. You will build your familiarity base and have opportunities to showcase resources and services. Listening to the discussions will increase your information base, disclose opportunities for acquiring outside resources, and promote sensitivity to the needs of others as the parents perceive them.

12. See if you can schedule a quarterly meeting with the principal.

Save questions and ideas in a file; use the file as the basis for a short agenda for the meeting. This increases the principal's familiarity with you and the library, demonstrates administrative skills, and provides a foundation for requesting information and additional resources.

13. See if you can get a permanent position on the new student orientation program and on the program for the parents of new students.

This will increase your visibility and associate you with the school's mission. It will give you a chance to tie the library to teaching and to promote its resources. It can provide you with an opportunity to solicit donations of funds, materials, and services, which will further increase your resources. The principal will be there and hear your presentation, which will increase your familiarity and give you a chance to demonstrate expertise.

14. Develop an orientation program for student teachers and for new hires.

If there is already an orientation program in place, find a way to be part of it. The principal will be there and hear your presentation, plus you will open communication channels with teaching staff and increase the odds of developing mentor relationships. This also will increase your alliances and contacts throughout the school and will put more people in your debt.

15. If you're in a high school, consider becoming a field deputy registrar of voters.

Voter registration offers a service to students and staff that the administration can use for recognition. It also provides you with a resource that can be restricted or eliminated at a later time.

16. Invite the principal or appropriate assistant principal(s) to the presentations of sales representatives when you are considering major purchases.

Even if they don't come to the presentations, you'll get credit for the invitation and the opportunity for involvement. You will build a reputation for openness. If the prices are just a shade beyond your current budget, you may be able to make a case for increased marginal resources, especially if you can demonstrate linkages with other departments that might have use for whatever it is that you want to purchase. If you can either get the administration to contribute the added funds or can get the administration to encourage another department to put in a few dollars, you will be able to purchase a resource you otherwise could not have acquired—and, because your contribution is far and away the largest, you will be in a position to claim possession of it and control of its use.

17. See if you can write a regular column for the school newspaper.

It will, of course, be geared to student interests, but the administration always reads the school newspaper, enhancing your visibility. This can also be a support for the teacher in charge of the paper, invoking reciprocity, and a link to the central office administration and to the parents.

18. If you have the equipment, offer to produce visuals for the principal's use in presentations to faculty, district personnel, parents, and so forth.

One of your responsibilities is always to make the boss look good. Over time, there is the possibility that the principal will come to depend on you for presentation support.

19. If you have the equipment, produce a video on the library and its services that administrators can use at meetings with the public.

You will have made their jobs easier, showcased services and resources, and tied the library operation to the school mission. Updatings will keep pulling the library to their attention and may provide a rationale for requesting additional resources.

20. Credit the administration when you receive compliments on the library and its services.

Praise and compliments are major influence tools. They enhance likability and open communication networks. Over time, they can invoke the reciprocity principle.

21. Seek outside funding and donations for the library/media center.

These may range from large scale grants to donations from the Rotary or Soroptimists to a program for donating books or materials to the library in memory of a student, graduate, staff member, or former staff member who has died (easily done with a prepared book plate).

Administrators deal in opportunities and wrestle for the dollars to create them. A person who creates opportunities and funding for programs is noticed and valued, particularly if these efforts also produce recognition for the school.

A successful grant proposal also puts more resources under your control.

22. See if you can be a lunchtime speaker for the Rotary, Lions, Optimists, Soroptimists, Kiwanis, community coordinating council, chamber of commerce, or other local civic group(s), especially if the principal or another administrator is a member of it.

Talk on some general educational topic, but emphasize how the library/media center has a vital role and how supportive the principal is. This can help the principal by highlighting the school in the community and can help fulfill any responsibility he or she may have for providing a program to the organization. It will increase your visibility and image of expertise. It may also draw in resources that will increase your internal influence potential.

23. Develop a "brag" sheet or book for the principal, assistant principals, and counselors to have in their offices.

Make it look professional; it is for adult consumption, not student consumption. Many parents "shop" for schools when they move into an area, and with the movement toward choice in America and with the growing emphasis on student capabilities and outcome-based education, many parents shop without moving. This can help an administrator or a counselor make a solid presentation of the virtues of your school. You will have performed a task that increases the odds of success for another.

24. If you get major and consistent support from your principal and other administrators, see if you can find a way for them to be honored for it by some organization.

The principal will know you made the nomination, but the award will not look self-serving if it comes from an outside agency.

25. If you are in a district where the principals attend school board meetings, attend such meetings yourself now and again.

The exposure is good. You'll be seen and recognized as involved. You'll be up-to-date on issues, and you'll have fodder for conversation. The influence potential can be multiplied if you have an opportunity to speak in support of something the principal wants to have happen. It will also improve your information resources and possibly offer opportunities to be involved in framing issues.

26. Write something for one of the magazines, journals, or newsletters in the library field.

The topic is not of importance. Drawing recognition to you and your school is.

27. Write something for one of the administrator organization publications on the relationship between administrators or curriculum or teaching and the importance of the library.

Writing for outside publications enhances your visibility by enhancing the principal's. It draws attention to you, the school, and the principal in a forum of particular interest to an administrator. This will especially gain credit with your administrator if you can describe something worthwhile going on in your school to the whole state or nation. National Association of Secondary School Principals' publications, like the *NASSP Bulletin, Schools in the Middle,* and *High School Magazine,* for example, reach into more than 40,000 schools across the country every school-year month.

Breaking into these journals can sometimes be difficult if you're not an administrator. One way around that is to co-author a piece with your principal or assistant principal. It means sharing the credit for what really will be your work, but that's not the point. The point is to draw positive attention to your administrators and school. If they know that you're the one responsible for recognition they'll receive, it doesn't matter if anyone else does. The fact that you garnered recognition for them will invoke the reciprocity rule.

28. Develop an annual report that can serve multiple purposes.

Report activity and inventory, educate constituents, project a specific image, highlight a unique service, demonstrate progress, undergird a proposal you want to make, provide an evaluation tool, and so on. You probably already do the statistical reports; think now of how to expand it to serve other goals. Be sure to include descriptions of collaborative projects with teachers and, as much as possible, identify student learning outcomes. Disseminating this kind of information will increase your visibility, demonstrate the range of your interactions, invite responses that will increase communication, and demonstrate expertise. This is such an important opportunity, in fact, that it is the central concern of Chapter 15.

Building Influence with the Principal by Building Influence with Those Above the Principalship

None of us is an independent actor. All of us are in some way subject to the authority or influence of the people who surround us. This section suggests how you might build influence with the people who occupy hierarchical positions above the principalship.

1. Volunteer for district level committees.

The benefits of committee service at the district level are the same as those at the building level. Such service will enhance visibility, familiarity, and the image of expertise. It will tie your work to the central mission of the enterprise and expand your communication networks.

2. Attend board meetings regularly.

Visibility, familiarity, and opportunities to demonstrate expertise can be found at board meetings.

3. With the other librarians in your district, create a position of "librarian to the board" and rotate it among you.

This might be an even stronger tactic if the other librarians don't want to take part. The board will want access to research and model practices from time to time and from sources separate from the usual. Be careful not to get put in the position of an adversary of the administration in doing this. The tactic can provide visibility, a chance to demonstrate expertise, and opportunities to develop alliances, expand communication networks, and invoke the reciprocity principle.

4. Make regular presentations to the board of education.

The opportunity to develop visibility is important. A caution here, however: Be careful not to usurp the role of the district library media coordinator if your district has one. But if it's the appropriate thing to do in your district, take advantage of making these reports to deepen the image that the library is an integral part of the instructional program and tied to the central mission of the school. This can work especially well if the part of the report is delivered in cooperation with one or more teachers, which can help you build alliances and develop a rationale to request more resources.

5. Be prepared for questions whenever you go to the district or out into the community.

If you were suddenly asked at a board meeting, some district wide committee meeting, or a civic or parent meeting to justify your existence, what would you say? How would you answer the charge that anyone can check out books? Think this through and have a prepared answer that outlines three or four short but critical points.

It's not enough to say that the library media center should have a high priority because it helps students or because it is the key to processing materials and providing informational access. Tell what you do to facilitate the central mission of education. Explain the dependence of teachers and students on your resources and facility. Talk about your contributions to school climate and culture. The best answers depend upon the conditions in your school, but an answer that shows thought—whatever it is—is required. See Chapter 18 for additional information on preparing for surprises at meetings.

6. If it is appropriate within the culture and size of your district, make an appointment to meet with any new superintendent, assistant superintendent, or board member when he or she first comes into office.

Make sure he or she receives a copy of your "brag" sheet, your annual report, and an invitation to visit the library during class hours. Let it be known that you can research things of interest or react to parent or community requests for information. This tactic offers the chance for visibility, the opening of communication channels, the building of alliances, and association with the main mission of the school. The visit will allow display of resources and expertise.

If it is not appropriate to visit with new appointees, find out who handles new administrator or new trustee orientation and see if you can get your library on the tour.

7. Invite school board members and central office staff to any special programs you may have; acknowledge their presence if they come.

Central office personnel and board members receive many more negative communications from the public than positive. This tactic can help to restore the balance and associate you with good news and experiences. It also increases visibility, familiarity, and likability.

8. Make sure the appropriate district officials and the board members receive information about any research reports that support the role of the library and the librarian in student achievement.

The goal is to become thought of as holding a "line" position. To do that, you have to demonstrate a direct contribution to student accomplishment. A search of the ERIC database will help you accumulate such materials, but there are periodic reports in such journals as *Library Media Connection (LMC)*, *School Library Journal*, *School Libraries Worldwide*, and *School Library Media Activities Monthly*. *The Teacher-Librarian* (what used to be the *Emergency Librarian*) runs a monthly column. A quick perusal of a nearby university library catalogue will turn up any number of books containing research summaries. Provide central office officials and board members with every reason to approve your resource requests, and try to cut away every reason not to.

Conclusion

Building influence with the principal is a laborious, time consuming, and ceaseless undertaking, but it is absolutely essential if you are to be as effective and influential as you can be. Some people resent having to do so many things outside their job descriptions, actually in addition to their job descriptions, to manage their relationships with principals. These people fail to realize that these activities are investments. As John Kotter and John Gabarro of the Harvard Business School point out, these activities can simplify jobs by eliminating potentially severe problems and miscommunications. If you view yourself in the final analysis as responsible for what you achieve, then you know that you need to establish good working relationships with everyone on whom you depend, including the principal.[36]

References

1 D.C. McClelland, "Toward a Theory of Motive Acquisition," *American Psychologist*, vol. 20, no. 5 (May 1965), pp. 321–333.

D.C. McClelland, "The Two Faces of Power," *Journal of International Affairs*, vol. 24, no. 1 (1970), pp. 29–47.

D.C. McClelland, *Power: The Inner Experience* (New York: Irvington Publishers, 1975).

D. E. Mitchell and W. G. Spady, *Authority, Power, and Expectations as Determinants of Action and Tension In School Organizations.* Paper presented at the annual meeting of the American Educational Research Association, New York City, April, 1977.

2 C. Argyris, Reasoning, *Learning and Action* (San Francisco: Jossey-Bass, 1982).

C. Argyris, R. Putnam, and D. McLain-Smith, *Action Science* (San Francisco: Jossey-Bass, 1985).

C. Argyris and D. Schon, *Theory in Practice: Increasing Professional Effectiveness* (San Francisco: Jossey-Bass, 1974).

3 There is some interesting research on this relationship emerging. An example to begin with is C. H. Glascock and D. Taylor's, "The Elementary Principal/Superintendent Relationship as Perceived by Teachers and Its Effects on the School: A Case Study Comparison," in *Education Policy Analysis Archives,* 9(45). Retrieved June 1, 2003, from <http://epaa.asu.edu/epaa/v9n45.html>.

4 H. B. Alvy, *The Problems of New Principals* (Doctoral dissertation, University of Montana, 1984).

F. W. Parkay and G. E. Hall, *Becoming a Principal: The Challenges of Beginning Leadership* (Boston: Allyn and Bacon, 1992).

5 D.C. Feldman and J. M. Brett, "Coping With New Jobs: A Comparative Study of New Hires and Job Changers," *Academy of Management Journal*, vol. 26, no. 2 (1983), pp. 258–272.

N. Nicholson and M. West, *Managerial Job Change: Men and Women in Transition* (Cambridge, England: Cambridge University Press, 1988).

6 W. D. Greenfield, C. Marshall, and D. B. Reed, "Experience in the Vice Principalship: Preparation for Leading Schools?" *Journal of Educational Administration*, vol. 24, no. 1 (1986), pp. 107–121.J. M. Koru, "The Assistant Principal: Crisis Manager, Custodian, or Visionary?" *National Association of Secondary School Principals BULLETIN*, vol. 77, no. 556 (November 1993), pp. 67–71.

7 In R. H. Carpenter, *Choosing Powerful Words* (Boston: Allyn & Bacon, 1999, p. 47).

8 C. Hegarty, *How To Manage Your Boss* (New York: Rawson, Wade Publishers, 1980).

A very useful and readable little book that can give you a quick handle on stress concepts and ways of assessing stress at work is Walter Gmelch's *Beyond Stress to Effective Management* (New York: John Wiley and Sons, 1982).

9 A. DuBrin, *Winning Office Politics: DuBrin's Guide for the '90s* (Englewood Cliffs, NJ: Prentice-Hall, 1990).

10 P. Drucker, *The Effective Executive* (New York: Harper and Row, 1967).

11 A very useful book for understanding the effects of the reform movement and the processes of change in educational institutions is Michael Fullan's *The New Meaning of Educational Change, Second Edition* (New York: Teachers College Press, 1991). Written with the assistance of Suzanne Stiegelbauer, Fullan examines the processes of change with individual chapters giving attention to the effects on the principal, teachers, students, district administrators, and parents and community members. There isn't a chapter on school library media specialists, but there isn't any surprise in that. The book will provide you with useful insights as you plan your influence strategy.

12 E. H. Neilsen and J. Gypen, "The Subordinate's Predicaments," In E. C. G. Collins (Ed.), *The Executive Dilemma: Handling People Problems at Work* (pp. 112–124) (New York: Wiley, 1985).

13 G. M. Bellman, *Getting Things Done When You Are Not In Charge: How To Succeed From a Support Position* (San Francisco: Berrett-Koehler Publishers, 1992).

14 *Webster's New Collegiate Dictionary* (Springfield, MA: G. & C. Merriam Co., Publishers, 1960).

15 R. E. Kelley, *How to Be a Star at Work* (New York: Times Books, 1998), p. 60.

16 S. Feiman-Nemser and R. E. Floden, "The Cultures of Teaching," in M. C. Wittrock (Ed.), *Handbook of Research on Teaching, Third Edition* (pp. 505–526) (New York: Macmillan, 1986).

J. W. Little, *Conditions of Professional Development in Secondary Schools* (Stanford, CA: Center for Research on the Context of Secondary Teaching, 1988).

17 R. E. Kelley, *How to Be a Star at Work* (New York: Times Books, 1998), p. 60.

18 An interesting and useful discussion of "face" can be found in *Working Through Conflict: Strategies for Relationships, Groups, and Organizations, Third Edition*, by J. P. Folger, M. S. Poole, and R. K. Stutman (New York: Longman Publishers, 1997).

19 T. Peters and B. Waterman, *In Search of Excellence: Lessons From America's Best-Run Companies* (New York: Harper & Row, 1985).

20 A good introduction to this notion can be found in *Leaders: The Strategies for Taking Charge by Warren Bennis and Burt Nanus* (New York: Harper & Row, 1985). A readable summary of theory and research can be found in *Contemporary Issues in Leadership, Third Edition*, edited by William E. Rosenbach and Robert L. Taylor (San Francisco: Westview Press, 1993).

21 Robert Evans has an insightful section on school mission statements in *The Human Side of School Change* (San Francisco: Jossey-Bass, 2001).

22 W. K. Hoy and C. G. Miskel, *Educational Administration: Theory, Research, and Practice, Sixth Edition* (New York: McGraw-Hill, 2000).

23 R. E. Kelley, *How to Be a Star at Work* (New York: Times Books, 1998).

24 E. H. Schein, "Organizational Socialization and the Profession of Management," *Industrial Management Review*, vol. 92, no. 2 (1968), pp. 1–16.

25 Teachers assigned to teach grades and subjects outside their areas of preparation is a major problem in the United States and likely to grow worse in the face of the impending teacher shortage. A good place to find introductory information about the problem—and to gather arguments to use with teachers and administrators—is "The Problem of Out-of-Field Teaching" by Richard M. Ingersoll in the June 1998 issue of the *Phi Delta Kappan* (volume 79, no. 10, pp. 773–776).

26 C. Hegarty, *How To Manage Your Boss* (New York: Rawson, Wade Publishers, 1980).

27 H. Mintzberg, T*he Nature of Managerial Work* (New York: Harper and Row, 1973), p. 20.

28 R. Pennock, "Trading Places: A Librarian's Route to the Principal's Office," *School Library Journal*, vol. 35, no. 1 (September 1988), pp. 117– 119.

29 D. B. Austin and H. Brown, Jr., *Report of the Assistant Principalship, Vol. 3: The Study of the Secondary School Principalship* (Washington, D.C.: National Association of Secondary School Principals, 1970).

J. T. Hentges, *A Normative Study of the Assistant Principalship in Selected Minnesota Secondary Schools.* (Specialist in Educational Administration thesis, Mankato State University, 1976), ERIC Document ED 168 148.

L. O. Pellicer, L. W. Anderson, J. W. Keefe, E. A. Kelly, and L. E. McLeary, *High School Leaders and Their Schools, Volume I: A National Profile* (Reston, VA: National Association of Secondary School Principals, 1988).

D. B. Reed, *The Work of the Secondary Vice Principalship: A Field Study. Paper presented at the annual meeting of the American Educational Research Association*, New Orleans, April 23–27, 1984. ERIC Document ED 246 527.

D. B. Reed and A. Himmler, "The Work of the Secondary Vice Principal," *Education and Urban Society*, vol. 18, no. 1 (1985), pp. 59–84.

J. A. Smith, *A Comparative Study of the Role of the Secondary Assistant Principal: New Demands, New Realities, and New Perspectives* (Doctoral dissertation, Seattle University, 1984).

30 D. B. Austin and H. Brown, Jr., *Report of the Assistant Principalship, Vol. 3: The Study of the Secondary School Principalship* (Washington, D.C.: National Association of Secondary School Principals, 1970).

L. O. Pellicer, L. W. Anderson, J. W. Keefe, E. A. Kelly, and L. E. McLeary, *High School Leaders and Their Schools, Volume I: A National Profile* (Reston, VA: National Association of Secondary School Principals, 1988).

31 D. B. Austin and H. Brown, Jr., *Report of the Assistant Principalship, Vol. 3: The Study of the Secondary School Principalship* (Washington, D.C.: National Association of Secondary School Principals, 1970).

G. N. Hartzell, "The Assistant Principal: Neglected Actor in Practitioner Leadership Literature," *Journal of School Leadership*, vol. 31, no. 6 (November 1993), pp. 707–723.

J. T. Hentges. *A Normative Study of the Assistant Principalship in Selected Minnesota Secondary Schools.* Unpublished thesis for the degree of Specialist in Educational Administration, Mankato State University, 1976, ERIC Document ED 168 148.

L. O. Pellicer, L. W. Anderson, J. W. Keefe, E. A. Kelly, and L. E. McLeary, *High School Leaders and Their Schools, Volume I: A National Profile* (Reston, VA: National Association of Secondary School Principals, 1988).

D. B. Reed and A. Himmler, "The Work of the Secondary Vice Principal," *Education and Urban Society*, vol. 18, no. 1 (1985), pp. 59–84.

J. A. Smith, *A Comparative Study of the Role of the Secondary Assistant Principal: New Demands, New Realities, and New Perspectives* (Doctoral dissertation, Seattle University, 1984).

32 Z. J. Clements, "Enriching the Role of the Assistant Principal," *National Association of Secondary School Principals BULLETIN*, vol. 64, no. 436 (1980) pp. 14–22.

33 Several of the ideas in this section came from C. Hegarty, *How To Manage Your Boss* (New York: Rawson, Wade Publishers, 1980).

34 J. Taylor and M. Bryant, "Performance Based Evaluation and the School Library Media Specialist," *NASSP Bulletin*, vol.80, no. 581 (1996), pp. 71–78.

P. Tucker, J. Stronge, "How Do You Evaluate Everyone Who Isn't a Teacher?" *The School Administrator*, vol.5, no. 11 (1994), pp. 18–23.

E. Young, "Evaluating School Library Media Specialists: From Performance Expectations to Appraisal Conference. *Journal of Personnel Evaluation in Education*, vol. 9, no. 2 (1995), pp. 171–189.

35 "The Role of the Principal is the Key Factor in the Development of an Effective School Library Program," *Emergency Librarian* (January–February, 1989), p. 31.

K. Bishop and N. Larimer, "Literacy Through Collaboration," *Teacher Librarian,* volume 27, no. 1 (October, 1999), pp. 15–20.

R. Blazek, *Influencing Students Toward Media Center Use: An Experimental Investigation In Mathematics* (Chicago: American Library Association, 1975).

B. S. Campbell and P. A. Cordiero, *High School Principal Roles and Implementation Themes for Mainstreaming Information Literacy Instruction.* Paper presented at the annual meeting of the American Educational Research Association (New York, April 8–12, 1996). ERIC Document Number ED 399 667.

J. B. Charter, *Case Study Profiles of Six Exemplary Public High School Library Media Programs* (Doctoral dissertation, Florida State University, 1982).

Executive Summary: Findings from the Evaluation of the National Library Power Program (Madison, WI: University of Wisconsin at Madison School of Library and Information Studies and School of Education, 1999).

P. P. Wilson and J. A. Lyders, *Leadership for Today's School Library: A Handbook for The Library Media Specialist and the School Principal* (Westport, CT: Greenwood Press, 2001).

36 J. J. Gabarro and J. P. Kotter, "Managing Your Boss," *Harvard Business Review*, vol. 71, no. 3 (May–June 1993), pp. 150–157.

Chapter 9

The Principal IV: Communicating with Your Principal

Sooner or later, the quality of just about every relationship comes down to communication. This certainly is true in your relationship with your principal. No matter how good your ideas, no matter how strong your evidence, they count for nothing if you can't get them across to your target. The message is important, of course, but there is no message apart from the mechanism that carries it. How then do you maximize the odds that you'll be able to capture your principal's favorable attention? Organizational and communication research offer some useful suggestions. Considering this half-dozen might pay substantial dividends the next time you craft a proposal.

1. Lay Some Advance Groundwork.

Before you think about how best to present your idea, develop support for it among at least some of the people who might be affected by it. Before you go to the principal, spend some time with key players at lower levels: teachers, lead teachers, department chairs, counselors, assistant principals. Especially target anyone whom you know is in the principal's favor. Circulating an idea to get people's input before you present it to the boss generally strengthens your position. Ask them, "What do you think? Would this be helpful? Is there something I'm missing?" It's important to get informal reactions, especially any that might be negative. Find out if others are bothered by some part of your proposal and look for ways to accommodate any reasonable concern. Once you've sorted those things out, you can take your idea to the principal knowing that some number of people, particularly people in whom he or she has confidence, buy into it. Informally eliciting concerns in advance, and addressing them, raises the odds that your idea will not be shot down the moment you present it.

2. Decide on the Initial Format.

You need to decide whether to make your proposal orally or in writing—or both. Research suggests that written presentations foster greater understanding, but face-to-face presentations are more effective in persuasion efforts.[1] Pretty clearly, you'll want to do both. Redundancy increases both the richness and the accuracy of the information you want to communicate.[2] The question becomes which method should you use to first approach your principal.

Remember Peter Drucker's designation of leaders as either "readers" or "listeners" discussed in Chapter 8? If your principal is a reader, send a written report first and follow it up with a face-to-face discussion. If your principal is a listener, brief him or her on the subject, or make a presentation, depending on his or her preference, and then send a written report afterward.

In making the presentation or submitting the report, you also need to know if your principal prefers terse or elaborate communications.[3] Some principals want you to talk them through an entire idea, others want just a synopsis. Some want a full written report, others just an executive summary. Your goal is to get your idea the most positive hearing you can. Delivering it in the format the principal prefers is the first step.

3. Speak Your Principal's Language.

Remember that, in many ways, the principal speaks a language different from your own—and, once you learn it, you can more meaningfully translate your ideas to him or her. Every part of an organization develops its own particular lexicon.[4] Teachers, counselors, librarians, and administrators all use different terminology. Sometimes people within the same division even have specialized vocabularies. Look, for example, at the varying vocabularies of special education, industrial technology, music, foreign language, English, and art teachers. This disciplinary lexicon variation is a challenge to principals who have to deal with people from all across the educational spectrum, and it's one reason we so often hear in education about "developing shared meaning" in both goals and processes.

How do you learn your principal's language? There are at least three things you can do: First, read through the administrative journals in your professional library and pay close attention to the terminology used. Second, take every chance you get to listen carefully to the principal, assistant principal, or any other decision-maker you want to influence. Ask yourself what their burning issues and concerns are. Pay attention to the buzzwords they're using. What metaphors do they frequently use? Do they describe schooling as sport, combat, construction, travel, or something else? Take in it as you would take in a second language if you were abroad, with the intention of using it yourself.

Last, another good way to learn how to frame your ideas in administrative terms is by getting some administrative education of your own. That doesn't necessarily mean getting certified as an administrator, although that might be a good idea. In the long run, nothing would advance library visibility and support as quickly or solidly as former librarians becoming administrators. Assuming, though, that you're not going to make that career change, most universities do offer access to individual classes. Think about taking a class in the principalship as a way of acquiring both perspective and vocabulary.

You also may want to assess your principal's personality in writing your proposal and marshalling your supporting arguments. Communication research argues that individuals' personal characteristics affect their ability to be persuaded.[5] Intelligent people are best influenced by communications that rely on strong, logical arguments. But it doesn't stop there. Authoritarian personalities, those who believe that status and power differences do and should exist among organizational employees, also are more swayed by authority. Logical arguments and clear evidence can carry the day with non-authoritarian types, but your odds of convincing an authoritative personality go up if you appeal to authority in your arguments. Remember the social proof and authority heuristics discussed in Chapter 4? Appealing to authority helps you overcome what researchers call a "status incongruence" reaction.[6] Such reactions occur when someone of higher organizational status and an authoritarian personality (as some principals have) perceives himself or herself being pushed by someone of lower organizational status (such as a librarian). Citing higher authority—recognized names in the field, professional organizations, leaders in a number of other schools or districts, or researchers—reduces the focus on you as the compelling force behind the idea.

4. Frame Your Proposal From Your Principal's Perspective.

One of my mentors long ago used to talk about the invariable importance of the WIIFM principle: *W*hat's *I*n *I*t *F*or *M*e? People have a natural tendency to see the world in those terms. One key to persuading people to support any proposal is to demonstrate "what's in it for them." This isn't easy to do. Because we naturally see things from our own perspectives, we also tend to speak and write from our own perspectives—rather than from the perspective of the person to whom we are trying to sell our ideas. The challenge is to put yourself in the other person's place, think about what he or she might be looking for, and then speak to that.

As you craft your proposal, ask yourself, "What motivates the principal (or the teachers or students involved)? What is in this for the *people* it will affect? Which of their problems will it address? What problems might it create for *them*? What benefits will they realize?" Rather than focus on how your proposal might affect the library media program, analyze the potential savings, gains, or enriched opportunities that your idea offers to other school constituents—students, teachers, counselors, administrators—and then link your proposal to those benefits. The greater the connection people can see between your idea and what *they* do, the greater the odds of support.

Don't talk about how your proposal might help the library media program. Principals tend to be "big picture" people. They're looking for ideas and operations that will enhance student achievement and school performance. Make one or both of those the leading edge of any proposal you advance. Never ask for anything for the library or the library program itself. Always couch it in terms of what the students need, the teachers need, or a particular program needs.

5. Put the Bottom Line at the Top.

A fundamental part of any good proposal is an executive summary paragraph right at the beginning. Provide an overview of your proposal, put it in context, and outline its costs and benefits. We often try to proceed in a logical fashion, putting our conclusions at the end because we want a chance to build our case before asking for support. This can be counterproductive in dealing with someone as busy as your principal. He or she is likely to turn immediately to the last paragraph anyway or see that the conclusion is not stated at the beginning, set it aside to read later, and never get back to it. The first paragraph may be all that your principal has time to read—so make it one he or she remembers.

6. Be Brief.

Principals don't have time to read everything they receive. The pieces that are quick and easy to read make their way to the top of the pile. The first thing many busy people look at is a document's thickness or, if they open it up, its length. The shorter it is, the more likely it is to be read. Length has to vary with complexity, of course, but it's a good idea to try to keep proposals somewhere between two and three pages. Supporting documentation and implementation plans should be available on request, but don't add to your principal's paper load by submitting them with the proposal.

Brevity also is a function of medium. Time is the question here—your principal's time. You might be tempted to send your proposal via e-mail. In some instances and with some people, technological transmission may indeed be the way to go. However, it's a good idea to assess your principal and the situation before you do that. Some principals are very adept at using the available technology; others are not. It's neither your intent nor in your best interest to cause your principal work or frustration. Whatever the person's skill-level, the odds are that your principal will eventually print the information anyway if he or she senses that it may be useful. You will have saved some of your principal's precious time if you've already taken care of that.

Communication is a game of odds. Education is in such flux today, and there are so many competitors for resources, there can be no guarantee that your principal will react favorably to even the best thought-out and presented proposal. This means that your ideas must be competitive. The first step in competing for resources is getting the power-holder's attention; a well-crafted proposal raises the odds of your being able to do that.

References

1 L. W. Porter and K. H. Roberts, "Communication in Organizations," in M. D. Dunnette (Ed.), *Handbook of Industrial and Organizational Psychology* (pp. 1533-1589) (Chicago: Rand-McNally, 1976).

  W. C. Redding, *Communication Within the Organization* (West Lafayette, IN: Purdue Research Council, 1972).

2 W. C. Redding, *Communication Within the Organization* (West Lafayette, IN: Purdue Research Council, 1972).

3 P. Drucker, *The Effective Executive* (New York: Harper and Row, 1967).

4 E. M. Hanson, *Educational Administration and Organizational Behavior, Fourth Edition* (Boston: Allyn & Bacon, 1996).

  W. K. Hoy and C. G. Miskel, *Educational Administration: Theory, Research, and Practice, 6th Edition* (New York: McGraw-Hill, 2001).

5 M. Karlins and H. I. Abelson, *Persuasion: How Opinions and Attitudes are Changed, Second Edition* (New York: Springer Publishing, 1970).

6 R. K. Shelly and M. Webster, Jr., "How Formal Status, Liking, and Ability Status Structure Interaction: Three Theoretical Principles and a Test," *Sociological Perspectives*, vol. 40, no. 1 (1997), pp. 81–107.

  W. Shrum, "Status Incongruence Among Boundary Spanners: Structure, Exchange, and Conflict," *American Sociological Review*, vol. 55, no. 4 (1990), pp. 496–511.

  W. F. Whyte, "The Social Structure of the Restaurant," *American Journal of Sociology*, vol. 54, no. 4, Industrial Psychology (January, 1949), pp. 302–310.

Chapter 10

The Principal V: Capitalizing on a Rare Opportunity

If there is one thing the research incontrovertibly shows, it is that the principal's support is vital to library media program success.[1] So, if and when you get the rare opportunity to be part of a principal selection team and get to interview principal candidates, you want to make the most of the opportunity. The question is: What do you ask them? What you ask is an important consideration. You need to elicit the most accurate information you can regarding candidates' views about libraries, library media services, and librarians. Success in any school improvement effort rests in hiring talented, knowledgeable, and committed people. Administrators who don't know or appreciate the role and potential of library media services not only can stymie your best efforts, they can undo what progress you have made. At the same time, insightful and supportive administrators can provide you with even greater opportunity to make a contribution and a difference where you work.

Moreover, an interview is your first opportunity to interact with the person who will eventually be hired as your boss. You want to leave him or her with the most positive impression you can. New administrators usually like to initiate new programs and build new teams, and they need information in great quantities. An incoming principal who remembers you as thoughtful, perceptive, and articulate may offer you an early opportunity to show what you can do in a larger arena. Finally, if someone ultimately is hired who has only a minimal understanding of what you and your library can offer, the answers he or she gives to your questions will help you target the starting point of the education you'll have to give that position. Of course, if you are not part of the principal selection team—which will often be the case—you still can profitably use these questions when you schedule your first meeting with your new boss.

The challenge is to craft questions that will force the candidates to think through their answers. You want to catch a glimpse of how they structure their priorities while narrowing or eliminating their opportunity to dodge your questions or to tell you what they think you want to hear. Few questions are more predictable, easier to answer generally, less impressive, or more forgettable than "What is your philosophy regarding ...?" You will rarely get a clear picture of a candidate's views from such questions. General shapes may emerge, but the important features will be indistinct—the kind of image you get when you look at the back of a tapestry. You want to ask questions that will provide you with specifics. Then you can take those specifics as you would take a handful of stones to create a mosaic, placing each idea in appropriate relation to another, letting a philosophical image emerge. It won't be perfect, and it won't be complete—the length and nature of job interviews simply doesn't allow you to gather enough information for that—but it will be a lot sharper than you could create out of more general questions.

Here are nine questions you might use as a starting point when you interview administrative candidates. Other than the first one, they are not in any particular order. You can think of more and better questions, and certainly can devise queries directly focused on the unique conditions in your school or district, but these will give you a sense of the approach argued for here.

1. "What do you think are the most challenging issues facing this district/school?"

This question can tell you whether candidates have done their homework on your school or system and on your community. It will ask them to identify such challenges as reading, information literacy, and technology to you rather than having you bring these issues up to them, as they are likely to expect you to do if they know that you are a librarian. If a candidate doesn't mention one or more of these issues, then you will know that you are dealing with someone to whom you and your program are largely invisible. If a candidate does bring up one or more of them, then you can follow up with questions specific to library media as a field and to conditions in your school or district in particular.

2. "Most of the recently promoted instruction and curriculum reform measures are calling for increased independent study where students take greater personal responsibility for their own learning and are called upon to locate, access, organize, interpret, and persuasively present concepts. Do you think this is a step in the right direction? If not, why not? If so, what implications do you see in this for how our schools should operate over the next five years? What implications do you see in this for staff development in this school/district?"

This series of questions should again tap into candidates' philosophies without ever using the word. It should also tell you whether they see a role for the library and librarian in reform and restructuring, curriculum, instruction, and staff development.

You can follow this question with another aimed at getting at the candidates' sense of library media services: "If this concept of instruction and learning becomes the dominant model, what do you think the role of the library and librarian should be?" The answer should give you some insight into their perceptions of your role, potential, and limitations.

3. "Where in your list of priorities do you rank reading achievement?"

Whether we're talking elementary, middle, or high schools, local building or district-wide, reading is fundamental to student success in school as in life. This is a critical question in any setting. Whatever the answer, you can follow up by asking what candidates see as the role of the library media program in raising and sustaining reading achievement.

4. "Should technology be a part of the library media program or should it stand as a separate program or should it be in the hands of individual teachers?"

Candidates' answers to this question can give you a glimpse of their ideas on organizational structure and will tell you something about where they do or do not see the library. Depending upon the answers you receive, you can follow up with questions that will indicate what candidates know about technology in your school or district as well as what they know about the attitudes and personalities of the people involved in technology in your workplace.

5. "How do you feel about Internet filters? What is your view on Internet and e-mail access and use policies for students in elementary school? Middle school? High school?"

The answers to these questions should tell you something about candidates' philosophies without you ever having to ask that dull and deadly question, "What is your philosophy regarding ...?" On the hopeful chance, if you're in a small district, that you ever get to interview superintendent candidates, the answers may give you information about their abilities to recognize the significant differences that exist between elementary, middle, and high school students.

6. "The average copyright date on materials in our libraries is 19xx. What does that imply to you?"

This question requires you to do a little homework, but it should pay dividends. If the copyright date is old, you should hear something about the need for students to have access to up-to-date material. Or the candidate might suggest that a dated collection implies neglect or misplaced priorities. It certainly has financial implications, which might logically segue into a funding question. This gives you a more anchored approach to asking funding questions than to ask a general question about how much support libraries should have.

If the copyright date is recent, you may get not only a glimpse of how the candidates feel about library materials but also something about their willingness to recognize the successful efforts of others. See whether the candidates commend you and the current administration and express a need to keep materials current.

7. "On what criteria do you think libraries and library media programs should be evaluated?"

This may tell you a little something about whether candidates have any sense of the contributions your program makes or could make in the school(s). Evaluation is critical to professional and financial support. You can hit the bull's-eye every time, but it won't matter if you and your boss aren't looking at the same targets.

The logical follow-up question has to do with the criteria on which library media specialists should be evaluated. The answer candidates give to this question will alert you to whether they recognize that the work you do is in many ways qualitatively different from what classroom teachers do.

8. "Where in your list of priorities do you rank professional collaboration as a value?"

This question is closely aligned to the evaluation question, and its answer may let you see how candidates feel about your role in working with teachers, counselors, and others. If candidates answer that they rank collaboration highly, then you might follow up by asking for specifics on how they would encourage such collaboration. Many, perhaps most, teachers are not naturally collaborative. The cellular structure of the school and the continuing paradigm of one teacher in one room with one group of students for one period of time work against it. Administrative encouragement of collaboration is essential if it is to take hold in the culture of the organization. A follow-up question might address what the candidate sees as the ideal relationship between teacher and librarian.

9. "Are there any ways in which the library and librarian can be of specific assistance to you and your administration?"

It's always interesting to see whether candidates come up with anything in response to this question. Their answers will give you more information about how they perceive libraries and librarians. If a candidate does have some specific ideas, and if that candidate ultimately is the person hired, acting on these ideas can be a starting point for strengthening your relationship with him or her. Of course, it's a good idea for you to have an answer to your own question in the event that the candidate throws it right back at you, either during the interview or later. The candidate may want to understand your views because she or he is your new administrator or because she or he wants to do a better job in her or his next interview.

Principal support for library media services doesn't develop by accident. Educating an administrator about the library's and librarian's value is a long and difficult undertaking. It's a worthwhile endeavor, but you can go so much further so much faster if you are able to hire principals and superintendents who bring a good measure of library media understanding and appreciation into the job with them.

References

1 A quick review of this research is available in a theme issue of *School Libraries Worldwide* (vol. 8, no. 1, January 2002), the International Association of School Librarians' refereed journal.

Other sources can be found in *Capitalizing on the School Library's Potential to Positively Affect Student Achievement: A Sampling of Resources for Administrators*, prepared for the White House Conference on School Libraries, June 4, 2002. Available at <http://www.imls.gov/pubs/whitehouse0602/whitehouse.htm> and at <http://www.unocoe.unomaha.edu/ghartzell/library/>. Accessed June 1, 2003.

Chapter 11

Building Influence with Your Colleagues

Opportunities for building influence with teachers are plentiful now, and it appears likely that the situation will remain that way for at least the next few years—for as long as schools remain in crisis.

Why This is a Good Time to Build Influence with Teachers

Change is everywhere and change is tremendously unsettling. How then does that offer an opportunity for you? Change, the researchers tell us, always precipitates three effects. It causes confusion, it challenges competence, and it creates conflict.[1] Each of these represents an opportunity for school librarians to step up and make a difference.

Confusion is inevitable because changes in goals and structures push us all back to ground zero in the sense that none of us has had experience in the new environment. And the environment is unstable. The next board election, the next state or national election, or the next state or federal Supreme Court decision can revise and redirect all that we do. Comparatively few teachers in our schools—the average teacher in the United States today is in his or her late forties[2]—were either trained to deal with or grew up in a world of high stakes testing, standards, extreme ethnic diversity, school choice and vouchers, charter schools, site-based management, higher level technology, block scheduling, or any of the myriad other changes sweeping through their world today. It's no wonder than many are confused. In uncertain times, the ability to develop influence increases among people who possess clarifying information that can help others make sense of the situation in which they find themselves.

Changing goals, standards, and methods challenge our competency. They create a dual anxiety in us—first, how to recognize appropriate ways to respond to the new environment, and, second, from among those possibilities, how to select the one that best fits the present situation.[3] Unable to use traditional norms and values to screen the choices and predict how others may respond to our selections, we face a situation in which whatever we choose seems to carry a roughly equal probability of drawing support, criticism, or some mix of the two.[4] Researchers term this "behavior-outcome uncertainty," resulting from not knowing how to achieve a desired outcome in the new environment. This, in turn, is followed by "effort-behavior uncertainty," which is basically analogous to self-doubt, where we're concerned about our ability to perform the new behavior once we've figured out what it should be.[5]

It takes time to learn and become proficient at new methods, let alone rebuild the confidence we once had in the previous methods and in our ability to effectively implement them. In the process, we always encounter what Michael Fullan terms the "implementation dip," that period of time when we truly are not as effective as we once were in implementing plans.[6] Given enough time, he argues, we eventually will become effective in selecting and implementing new methods in the new environment, and—assuming that the mandated changes are, indeed, improvements over past approaches—we will eventually come to perform at an even higher quality level. The difficulty, as you well know, is that schools rarely give faculty members the time they need to make such adjustments. The pressure is tremendous on teachers and administrators to immediately change what they've been doing and to be immediately proficient in meeting new demands. Moreover, schools are not going to shut down in order to give them time to find and learn what they need to know. As the old line goes, they're going to have to build the boat and row it at the same time. They are going to need help.

Many districts and schools are turning to their staff development people or hiring consultants. There are two difficulties with this, however. The first is the state of the economy, which is strapping the staff development budgets in many, if not most, districts across the country.[7] The second is the yet fundamentally unchanged teaching culture in which teachers passively, but effectively, resist the imposition of top-down mandates and are suspicious of outside experts.[8] The effect of short funds and resistance to internal and external authority is to throw faculty members back on their own devices. Philip Turner, Dean of the School of Library and Information Studies at the University of North Texas, makes the astute observation that if teachers are going to have do all this, but are going to resist or reject imposed techniques and outside authorities, the only source of in-house assistance is likely to be the school library media center and the librarian.[9]

The individual teacher in transition time needs as much help as the collective faculty. Your greater opportunity probably rests in assisting the continuing faculty member caught in the whirlpool of change, the teacher new to your school—either the beginner or the veteran newcomer—the teacher whose schedule has been radically changed, or, perhaps most desperate, the teacher teaching outside the area for which he or she was prepared.[10]

You will have a great opportunity here to capture lasting support from several if not many faculty members if you are ready to seize the moment. If you can have warning a year or more in advance that your school is going to move into a particular activity or mode of operation, you can have the lead time you need to research model programs, discover best practices and pitfalls, and prepare materials and resources that will make a pivotal difference in your colleagues' abilities to adjust to the new order. Armed with material and information that will help to make them successful, you will gather debts and commitments to cash in on later.

Last, change causes conflict. This is because every change involves a redistribution of resources, status, prestige, power, and opportunities. As quickly as we might reach agreement that schools do, indeed, need changing, our cohesive feeling will dissipate just as quickly when we ask, "OK, then how should we change?" The real struggle will erupt when we finally reach the point of determining whom should decide how we will change.

Despite the fact that conflicts often are driven by perception rather than by reality, that too many are fueled by personal enmity as much as by professional perspective, and that there simply are not objectively right or wrong answers in many human situations, people in every kind of organization generally make a concerted attempt to appear rational in their decision-making.[11] Rational decision-making models all demand that participants have as much relevant information as possible to consider.[12] In fact, there is a growing trend in education today toward formalizing data-driven decision-making as a process.[13] No one in the school has access to more information, recent research, model programs, case studies, or professional association position papers than you do. The long and short of it is that this is a rich time to try to capture teacher loyalty and support.

The Librarians' Choices

This upheaval represents a wonderful opportunity for librarians to build closer working relationships and increase their influence with teachers. Some will immediately embrace the opportunity upheaval presents, others will capitalize on parts of it, while still others will just allow its effects to wash over them. In effect, librarians have three choices in responding to the opportunity to increase their levels of influence with teachers in this environment.

The First Choice: Do Nothing Different

The first choice, of course, is to do nothing different. The result probably still will be an increase in influence simply because the changing context of schooling will increase the value of the library to the typical classroom teacher.

The Second Choice: Active Generalized Involvement

The second choice is to become actively involved with teachers, but at a generalized level—to solidify the role of information specialist called for in *Information Power*. Teachers are going to need more information about their subjects and about ways of teaching their subjects in the shifting environment, and they are going to want their students to spend more time in the library working on individual research projects. Establishing visible expertise in those activities and controlling the information resources of the school will put librarians in a much improved position, but only so long as teachers don't develop alternative teaching modes that can be delivered in the classroom setting alone.

The Third Choice: Aggressive Engagement

The third choice is full engagement with teachers and aggressive library promotion. The librarian's goal is to carve out a critical role in curriculum development and instructional design processes. To do that means the implementation of the values and model described in *Information Power*.

This will not be an easy job. If successful, it will materially affect the school's organizational culture, and cultural changes are always resisted. Some teachers will oppose librarian role expansion, but others will welcome it if they see it as being of direct benefit to them. Those who will welcome your expanded role are the important targets. Capturing their support will lay a foundation for the later expansion of influence with others.

On the positive side, the growth of library prominence should have administrative support. It is in the principal's best interest to support it, as current research by Keith Lance and his associates and others has demonstrated.[14] Officially, the principal, the school's instructional leader, will be looking for ways and means of helping teachers succeed in the new environment. This is a clear example of the dependency principle: The principal's reputation as a leader and successful educator is going to ride on how teachers and students perform. Helping the teachers will be helping the principal.

Hesitancy to Engage: The idea of school media specialists engaged with teachers as curriculum and instructional partners and consultants didn't originate with *Information Power*. In a dissertation study more than 30 years ago, M. A. Jetter was predicting the assumption that the instructional consultant role would be the greatest single change in the school librarianship in the 1970s.[15] But it didn't happen, and it hasn't happened on a terribly widespread basis yet.

Part of the reason is that librarians themselves are slow to act, claiming that they are largely unprepared for the role. In fact, a series of research studies done between 1975 and 1990 repeatedly found that many school librarians are at odds with parts of the *Information Power* model. They have predominantly negative attitudes and assign expanded roles very low priority.[16]

Still, the opportunity is here now, and there is a lesson to be drawn from an old fur trade story about a young man out with trappers on his first expedition into the wilderness. Thinking there was some secret to being a mountain man, he kept asking an old hunter for advice and counsel. One morning the subject of bearskins came up. In all ignorance and innocence, and certain there were myriad signs he would have to recognize in the forest, the young man earnestly asked how he could know when was the best time to shoot bears. The old man looked at him like the youth wasn't quite bright, squinted down at him over his pipe, and said, "Son, the time to shoot bears is when bears are around."

The academic woods are full of bears right now. Librarians who seek the maximum in influence building can create and take advantage of every opening they see to define and expand their roles in schools. If you decide to try it, every success in that endeavor will put several of the strongest principles of effective influence into operation. Your visibility will be enhanced. You will become more closely identified with the central mission of the school. The value of the resources you control will be increased. Your image of expertise will brighten. You will become more familiar to more people. Perhaps most importantly, you will invoke the reciprocity rule with every teacher you help.

Tactics for Building Influence with Teachers

The tactics that follow are aimed at creating initial collaborative contacts with teachers, capturing their interest and attention, developing opening wedges into their thinking, and getting them to at least semi-automatically think of you when they think about instructional planning. The goal is to get teachers to see you as one of their own and integral to their individual success.

Your ability to be accepted by the faculty as a fully involved curriculum and instructional consultant is not something that can be properly addressed here. Your odds of success in achieving that status will be affected by a number of variables, including such things as the nature of your current status, the culture of your building, the extent of the resources you control, and your current relationship with the principal. And at least two other things will have a major impact on your efforts to gain acceptance: (1) your level of expertise in curriculum and instruction, and your ability to promote its image with teachers and administrators, and (2) your commitment to building influence through integration into the teachers' world as it exists in your school.

A fundamental decision to make before embarking on an influence campaign is whether you want full engagement with teachers. Full engagement will significantly change and increase your workload. You might feel that you don't need the depth of influence full engagement could provide. You might feel, like some of the librarians surveyed in the research cited previously, that this realm of activity is not congruent with your definition of school librarianship, and you really don't want to do it. You might believe that you can build enough influence with teachers to protect the integrity of your library and sufficiently inject your voice into policy decisions short of becoming a teacher yourself, or a teacher of teachers. There isn't any right answer to this. It's a judgment call.

If you decide to expand your curriculum and instruction role, it may take a heavy toll in time and energy. The amounts of time and energy required to become an acknowledged expert in those fields depend on the kinds of formal training you have had and the level of good fortune you've had in finding opportunities to learn and practice new skills.

Secondary school curriculum and instruction are more difficult to master than their elementary school counterparts. Secondary teachers have to contend with greater specialization and sophistication in subject matter and with greater variances in student abilities, motivations, and responsiveness. The literature offers a wealth of books and articles regarding the role of the librarian in curriculum and instruction, but those works must be approached carefully. Study and application in this area, as in almost every area of educational research and recommendation, has been far more extensive in the elementary setting than in the secondary.

Building expertise in secondary curriculum and instructional design might require intensive study of general principles and methods and some rather targeted study of specific disciplines. A lot of useful information and succinct overviews can be found in publications coming from the Association for Supervision and Curriculum Development (ASCD) and the National Association of Secondary School Principals (NASSP), but building expertise still will require a major commitment on your part. As the Romans told us, no great thing is created suddenly.[17]

Whatever your decision, building influence with teachers, as with all others, is based in building a positive relationship and shaping their perceptions of you and your program in a positive fashion. The tactics that follow can help to begin that work.

1. Regardless of the size of your school, know the names and responsibilities of every teacher in the building, even the ones you only see at faculty meetings. This will enhance likability and speed your work when the opportunity comes to connect people, compliment people, or send them notification of appropriate material acquisitions.

2. Take time to socialize. Librarians are often isolated from teachers because the students' lunches and breaks are the same times as the teachers', so the librarian is needed in the library. If this is your situation, look at your school's master schedule and find out who has a preparation hour at particular times. Rotate your breaks and go to the lounge, cafeteria, or other location where teachers congregate. Do not stay in the library every day and only have coffee and lunch with your own staff.

This tactic is built on the internal autonomy the librarianship offers. It produces familiarity, enhances likability, and opens informal communication channels. Informal settings provide opportunities to discuss the extent of your resources, find out areas of individual interest which can be acted upon later, and identify likely targets for joint projects, such as participation in grant proposal development.

3. Pass on compliments that you hear about teachers from students, other teachers, and staff as you go about your duties. Don't pass on any negatives to anyone. This enhances likability. You might look back at Chapter 3 for some specifics on using compliments to enhance likability and build your influence.

4. Develop an orientation program for student teachers and for new hires. There are few times in a teacher's professional life when he or she is more vulnerable than during the first year of service—whether it's the first year in a new school or the first year of a new career, or both. This is the time when teachers are most hungry for information, insight, and discretely delivered assistance.[18]

If there is already an orientation program in place, find a way to become a part of it. These are great opportunities to offer services and partnerships to teachers who are hungry for all the support they can get in their new and unknown environments. This will enhance visibility, encourage mentorships, build alliances, tie you to the newcomers' notions of success, and provide an opportunity to demonstrate expertise.

5. Get early retirement teachers assigned to the library. Many districts have early retirement incentive programs where a teacher agrees to work a specified number of days each year in exchange for a stipend or retirement supplement of some sort. If you can arrange it, get the principal to assign one or more of these early retirees to the library. These people will still have very close contacts with continuing teachers in the building and district; they can be of considerable assistance in making contacts with individuals you want to target for an influence attempt, and they can serve in a number of capacities that will vastly increase your information gathering capacity and enhance your connectedness with the major goals of the school.

6. Survey the teachers and ask (1) for an evaluation of current library services and (2) how the library can be of more service to them in their classes. Where you can identify individuals, grade levels, programs, or departments, follow up the results with visits to these people to ask for details and ideas. This will contribute to your visibility, demonstrate that your ego is under control, open informal communication channels, sharpen your sensitivity to the needs of others, and identify areas for expanded services. These visits also, in a very subtle fashion, will showcase your resources simply by asking teachers if they use a particular thing.

7. Involve teachers in the development of library policies that affect them, everything from putting materials on reserve to student behavior policies. This will enhance visibility and familiarity, allow you to compliment them for their contributions, and invoke the commitment and consistency principle.

8. Work to convince the principal, department heads, and individual teachers that you should be a part of any curriculum committees, especially those considering interdisciplinary curriculum development. When new programs are being discussed, it is appropriate that the librarian be able to describe to what extent the library/media center can support the program in terms of materials, space, teaching assistance, and so on.

A role in curriculum planning will again increase visibility and familiarity and open communication channels. It will also tighten your association with the central mission of the school and give you an opportunity to demonstrate expertise. Once a curriculum is developed, the next logical question has to be how it will be delivered. You will be in at the origin of those discussions. You can help to frame the issues and may be able to elicit commitments for library support. Full integration of the library into new curriculum projects puts you in the position of performing tasks critical to the success of others.

9. Volunteer to sit in with textbook selection committees so they can know what complementary, supplementary, and more in-depth materials are available in the school for lessons and projects they may want to develop around particular contents in the texts they are considering. This will enhance visibility, familiarity, and a sense of expertise. It will allow you to describe the resources you have and provide a rationale for requesting additional resources to support specific classes and programs.

10. Involve teachers in the process of weeding the collection in their areas of interest. You may end up keeping a few volumes you would like to be rid of, but the influence value will compensate you for the shelf space.

More importantly, involving teachers in weeding will provide direct evidence to teachers across the faculty that your library needs more and better material. Too few teachers—as well as administrators, legislators, and community members—recognize that there is more to a quality library collection than just the number of books it contains. They need to be taught that the age of those books, particularly in the natural and social sciences, is of equal if not surpassing importance. In some ways, it can be worse to have outdated books than to have no books at all. As the American Association of School Librarians' Harriet Selverstone observes, "Outdated books give students misinformation. Our mission is to give them correct and credible information."[19] Outdated books distort what we know in the sciences and social sciences, perpetuate errors, and keep stereotypes alive. Old books also are less likely to attract the young student reader. Ironically, in elementary schools, where reading habits are established, the average age of fiction titles—which can retain their literary value through the years—tends to be more recent than the average age of nonfiction titles which lose their value with changing times.[20]

A recent national survey asked school librarians across the country to examine and estimate the currency of their collections.[21] Sixty-six percent of the respondents reported that somewhere between 11% and 70% of their collections were out of date. While the very largest of schools with sizeable collections can probably give reasonable service with some small percentage of their books out of date, any substantial percentage of out of date books is crippling. Outdated books pose even more of a problem in smaller schools—the typical American school library—where even very low percentages of out of date works severely damage their utility.

These figures represent a national survey. Some specific examples describe darker situations in many places. The average age of books in New Mexico school libraries, for example, ranges between 16 and 20 years, depending upon the grade level and school location.[22] A recent survey of Philadelphia's elementary schools indicated that library collections are, on average, 25 to 30 years old.[23] An Indiana study showed an average copyright date of 1975 on books in science, geography, and other key areas.[24] As of the spring of 2000, only 12.4% of high school collections and 22.3% of middle school collections in Baltimore, Maryland, had books averaging copyright dates in the 1990s.[25]

Even though there has been a nation-wide proportional average increase in school library funding over the last four years, the increase mainly has been spent on technology rather than on books.[26] The flatlining of book expenditures, and in some places their reduction, coupled with book price increases, implies that the number of books per student reported in surveys taken three or four or five years ago may actually be the same books reported currently.[27] The collection may remain adequate in size but may be less than adequate in the currency of the material it contains.

There is progress in some places, but it is slow, inconstant, and clearly insufficient. For example, in 1995, the average copyright date of books in California school libraries was 1972. By 2000, the average had risen to 1982, but that still is two decades behind.[28] Several states have made commitments to increase funding, but state budget problems either have reduced, delayed, or eliminated their implementation. The difficulty you and most school librarians face is that so few others are aware of the situation. Having your teachers help weed the collection puts the problem directly in front of them in a way that they cannot ignore.

Depending on district regulations, you might offer the discarded books to the teachers. Be very careful in choosing what to give away, however. There is no gain if outdated books end up in classrooms. Not only will the students still have access to misinformation, but, in point of fact, they will have both easier access and encouragement to exercise it.

If discarded books can be sold, commit at least some portion of the revenues to strengthening the section from which they were taken.

Involving teachers in library operations provides exposure for your resources—in this case, also the lack and deficiency of them—and can invoke both the commitment and reciprocity principles. The fact that you ask teachers to exercise their judgment is complimentary.

11. Volunteer to work with teachers at different grade levels or in different subjects to develop library research activity packages that substitutes can employ. These must be customized for each unit taught and need to be regarded by the teacher as an important part of the students' experience and grade, so students will not just fool around while in the library.

This will enhance visibility and familiarity, invoke reciprocity with both teachers and substitutes, and more closely identify you with the central mission of the school. Out of this may come an expansion of alliances and your friendship information network.

12. Utilize every Internet source and subscription database you can access to retrieve the latest research, theory, model program, and case study information available. Do research for curriculum committees or for teachers contemplating development of a new idea for a class. To the extent that you can provide information about model programs or evaluations of existing programs in the literature, your contributions become increasingly important to the group or person.

Over time, tapping these resources will increase others' dependence on you, open communication channels, and demonstrate an expertise.

13. Surf the Internet when you have the time, just to stay current with the standards, frameworks, trends, and particularly the vocabulary— formal and buzzwords—relating to the grades and subjects taught in

your school. The goal is to impress teachers who come to you with your knowledge of *their* areas.

14. Track events that could have an impact on teachers in your school through discipline-based professional publications, the newsletters of your particular library/media professional organizations, and posting questions on LM_NET or other listservs where you can get quick answers, advanced warning, and differing perspectives. Provide teachers with information about theories, approaches, books, software, and other materials in their fields and, especially, with the knowledge that a textbook used or being considered for use in their program or a book or media piece in your library relating to their subject has been the target of a lawsuit somewhere.

This will enhance visibility and a sense of expertise, back your recommendations with social proof, create the image you are interested in their fields and that you are watching out for them; reciprocity will be in order.

15. Invite teachers to attend sales presentations made by book, media, software, and equipment representatives in their area(s) of interest. This will show respect, compliment those invited, and provide you with better information about what is going on in each of the programs in your school. Along the same line, if local distributors will cooperate, arrange to have exhibits of software and other resources for teachers to preview. This may also offer opportunities to increase your resources by entering into cooperative purchasing agreements with departments and programs.

16. Don't throw out advertisements for new materials; recycle them to teachers. You undoubtedly get an endless stream of advertisements across your desk for new books, media, software, and other products. If you just toss it after looking it over, you may be missing an opportunity to build some influence with teachers.

As you go through your mail, just sort the advertisements you don't want to follow up on into a series of piles—one for each department, grade level, or teaching team that might be interested in the subject of the ad. Have a student aide bundle them and send them along to teachers who might be interested with a form note to the effect that "I thought you might be interested in this. If you are, please let me know."

The tactic lets teachers know that you are the focus of a lot of attention from venders, that you are familiar with what is emerging in their fields, and that you are supporting their activities and watching out for their interests. You will enhance visibility and communication and invoke the reciprocity principle.

17. Make the professional library both accessible and attractive to teachers. It's typical for teachers, especially in secondary schools, to generally have divided but connected interests. That is, they are particularly interested in their individual discipline, but they are also interested in how to teach that specific discipline, how to understand, motivate, and control students, and how to generally be more effective in the school.

In many school media centers, the discipline-based materials are accessible and attractively arranged. Someone interested in the history of art can find all the works you have on the arts and artists. But the books and media in the "professional library" that deal with art instruction, art students, and teaching as a profession are frequently out of sight in a back room away from student access. Moving materials away from student access also often means moving them away from adult access.

Undisplayed resources too often are unseen resources and cannot serve to build your influence. If the goal is to be perceived as integrally involved in curriculum and instruction, then materials relating to such subjects should be prominent. Make them easy to find and use. If there is any way your facility can support it, create a faculty reading room, or at least a cubbyhole. See if you can get a comfortable chair or two in there. Provide access to coffee. The objective is to get teachers to come into the library for their own purposes as well as for student purposes. Familiarity, enhanced visibility, association with the school's mission, similarity, resource display, and increased communication flow can all be addressed to some extent by this tactic.

18. Use some of your computer disk space to create teacher obligation. Many teachers came into the profession before the advent of the desktop computer and are afraid of it. Still, they would like to have the advantages it provides. Others appreciate the computer but don't have access to one at work or at home. If you can use your computer to help with things that all teachers need, but can't do for themselves because of fear or inaccessibility, you will have created a new resource.

One idea, for example, is to invest a few dollars in a test construction software program. These are programs where once a pool of test questions has been typed in, the computer will select, format, and print the test according to the teacher's instructions, including multiple forms to reduce the opportunity for students to cheat by looking on a neighboring student's paper. This tactic will draw people into the library and so increase familiarity. It will create a dependency, new alliances, and expanded information networks.

19. Provide instructional support services, such as test make-ups. A major problem in teacher scheduling is arranging for a student to make up a missed exam. If you establish a file, teachers can place tests in it for students who are absent on the day of an examination. When the student returns to class and has been given a deadline for test completion, he or she can later come to the library (either out of that class, at lunch, from a study hall, or at any other mutually convenient time) and take the test. The finished paper can be time-stamped to verify that it was completed before the established deadline.

Don't send the test back to the teacher or allow a student aide to pick it up; make sure the teacher comes to get it in person. That way, not only is the test itself secure, but, perhaps more importantly, the teacher is in the library and vulnerable to other influence tactics such as visibility, familiarity, and direct communication.

This tactic provides a valuable service for the teacher and can invoke the reciprocity principle. It involves the library in a central mission activity. But this tactic also has a danger to it. Test security is always a concern. The files need to be kept in a secured location, accessible only to adults. A problem in this regard can only be charged to you and can undo all the gain. In fact, it can leave you worse off than if you had never undertaken the project.

20. If your school has a teacher of the month program, see if you can get a copy of the display, if not the original and only one, to set up in the library. People will go where they are recognized. Setting up the teacher of the month poster, or some other award, in the library associates the library with the award.

21. Be sure the section in each year's edition of the faculty handbook on the media center is comprehensive and updated to enhance visibility and to showcase resources.

22. Make display space available for teacher-led projects such as fund raisers. Teachers, especially in secondary schools, often are involved in fund-raising activities and in student recruitment projects for athletic teams, organizations, and clubs. The success of the projects impacts the teacher's image in the school. To whatever extent you can help the teachers in these endeavors, you invoke the reciprocity principle.

23. Attend department or grade-level meetings. See if a two-minute maximum library report can be a part of each or alternating department meetings. Arrange for individual, departmental, or grade-level showings of newly acquired materials. Inform teachers that you have catalogs and reviews of new materials in their fields of interest. Have a handout to give to teachers and staff; customize the handout to grade level or department. Invite departments and grade levels to periodically hold their meetings in the library. These actions will enhance visibility and familiarity, promote the perception of expertise, allow promotion of your resources, improve communication, increase sensitivity to the needs of others, and invoke reciprocity.

24. Get the principal to allow you to make a two-minute presentation at each faculty meeting. Provide the faculty with an update of new acquisitions, new services, pending proposals, answers to questions asked since the last meeting, and so forth. Hand out a blank suggestion form to be returned to you at the end of the meeting; it will draw more ideas than a suggestion box in the hallway or media center. Keep it to two minutes or less unless you have prior permission to go beyond that. To violate that time line is to put the opportunity in jeopardy.

This tactic will increase familiarity, give you an opportunity to showcase resources and expertise, and enhance informal communication lines. It will demonstrate energy and focused effort and promote sensitivity to the needs of others.

25. Keep accurate records of teachers who bring their classes to the library, who check out large numbers of books themselves, or who consistently assign research assignments to their students. These are the prime candidates to approach about team teaching opportunities, from whom to seek public statements about the value of the library, and to watch for opportunities to compliment.

26. Seek out teachers to join you in funding proposals to outside agencies. Success will acquire new resources, help to cement your interpersonal relationship, tie their programs to the library, build your reputation for success, and gain you joint recognition. Even failure can give you a common experience on which to build a continuing relationship, but *only* if the time you spent in preparing the application or project was a positive experience in itself.

27. Seek funding for extended library hours or the opening of a "night library" program to be staffed by paid teachers. It is best if they can be paid at their professional rate. If that's not possible, see if they can be paid at the substitute rate, curriculum writing rate, or adult school rate, driver training rate, or whatever other rate is highest. This offers teachers an opportunity to earn some extra money, shows they are trusted with the facility, shows respect for their abilities, and encourages them to assign research work and to encourage their colleagues to do the same. It also gives them a glimpse into your world that they otherwise could not get. Try to build in an expansion or contraction of the open library hours over time depending upon how many students use it. If it is funded, it will enhance your reputation as effective.

Even if the idea is not funded, teachers will hear of it and it will improve their perceptions. Do not do it if it is not funded. Influence is *not* gained through the creation of burdens for either yourself or others.

The odds of its success might be increased by the simultaneous meeting of volunteers from the parents and community to help students who need assistance with their homework. Honor society or scholarship federation students or cross-age tutors might also be used. Students could submit requests for the types of assistance they need some time in advance so particular talents could be assembled at the library at that time.

This tactic creates a new resource and creates a dependency in the teachers and students who would benefit. It makes the library more visible and it ties it more to the school mission. Once in place, threats of discontinuation could invoke the scarcity principle.

28. Develop a proposal that the school adopt one bibliographic style for all research projects, term papers, and the like. Propose a team that includes you, a group of appropriate teachers, and the assistant principal (if you have one) who oversees either curriculum and instruction or the programs most likely to require research projects and reports (certainly English and social studies). Be sure to survey all the teachers, however, and check for their input along the way.

Workshops done by a teacher and librarian team on how to do particular types of papers or projects could be scheduled for students. You can handle the technical questions; the teacher can present techniques specific to the discipline being studied.

This tactic can offer several influence opportunities. It can project the image of the library as an integral part of the instructional program. It will invoke the commitment and consistency principle. It will allow you to demonstrate expertise and provide a service that teachers will want to protect. New alliances can be formed and communication networks expanded.

29. Develop an assignment form that teachers can forward to the library before they assign the work to the class. Have it describe the assignment (including a copy of any and all handouts the students receive), estimate the kinds of materials the students will be after, indicate the approximate number of students involved, and list any class library trips planned and any particular service the library might render or should not render (like giving certain answers to students). All of this allows you to know what to expect and to be able to inform the teacher of any potential problem, such as student and teacher frustration because the library cannot support this project with the materials it has.

This form could be done electronically or on NCR paper so a copy or an e-mail version could be sent to the local public library and improve your relationship with them as well. These documents also provide materials for a multipurpose year-end report and can give life to circulation and reference statistics.

It might be a good idea at some point, possibly through the PTA or its equivalent, to have a workshop that brings teachers, parents, the school librarian, and a representative from the public library(ies) to look at the problems and possible solutions in making good assignments.

This tactic increases visibility and ties the library to the teaching mission. It will increase the odds that the teachers will think of the library when they plan assignments, and, over time, they may begin to seek your expertise in planning their projects.

30. See if you can devise a "for-credit" workshop of some kind for teachers that will help them fulfill their in-service requirements or advance them in some other way. This tactic will enhance your resource base, provide a service teachers will not want discontinued (especially if the workshop is really tailored to meet some need they have), open communication lines, and let you demonstrate expertise. You will have done a favor for teachers and can invoke the reciprocity rule.

31. Begin an "Adventures into Intellect" program. Arrange for a series of interesting presentations by asking teachers if they will come to the library at an appointed time and give a talk on their favorite subject, or do a reading, or debate an issue, or otherwise make a presentation to their colleagues and other adults. Then make sure they have an audience by enlisting administrative support, inviting classified staff, or inviting parents. The topics should not have anything to do with teaching or education. This is not a staff development program; it's an intellectual "adventure." These are programs for adults, not students. These presentations are a service for members of the school community because they deserve it.

The tactic taps into several influence principles. It increases visibility. It compliments teachers, gives them recognition by their peers, and enhances your likability. It gives teachers an opportunity to display expertise and talents in areas heretofore unknown, and it may invoke the reciprocity principle. Your knowledge of their talents may be turned into a resource for you if you are ever asked to get someone to speak at a Rotary meeting, PTA meeting, or other event. It impacts the climate of the school.

32. Reverse the "Adventures into Intellect" idea and go out to classes to make presentations yourself. Whether you do it in their classrooms or in the library, teachers expect you to make presentations to their classes on library and research subjects. There's an influence gain to be made in being able to teach other subjects. Develop a current interest, find a new one, or create one. Get to the point where you can make a high quality classroom presentation on it. Then find teachers who will let you make the presentations in their classrooms.

This tactic strikes directly at the similarity principle. If teachers see you teach their subject to their students on their turf, the impact of similarity is geometrically multiplied. Some librarians may resist this idea. There is a small risk in it: You have to be very good. But consider this: It is very much like the presentations you make to classes on the use of the library. We are talking about a single presentation, on a topic you like and enjoy, focused in the way you want, practiced and perfected, presented to an audience of your choice, at a time of your preference. If you can't be good in that situation, you have other things to worry about.

If you select topics that will never go out of date, once you have the lesson down pat, it will serve you indefinitely. The students move along, but the teachers stay and teach the same subjects again to the next class the next year. When you have accomplished mastery, select another topic and start over. The broader your exposure, the greater the influence benefit.

Beyond similarity, the tactic promotes familiarity and visibility. By enriching a class for students and simultaneously relieving the teacher of responsibility for the period, you have done a favor and the reciprocity principle is invoked. The tactic also enhances perceptions of your expertise. It fact, it brings a whole new dimension to its image. Students will also identify you with the teachers. Successfully executed, this tactic lays a solid groundwork for laying a claim to involvement in curriculum development and instructional design. Besides, wouldn't it be fun to compete with the teachers at their own game?

33. Offer the library media center as the site for an "idea bank." Many teachers moving into new class and time configurations are going to be scrambling for teaching ideas. For example, one of the reasons for going to secondary school block scheduling with its 90-minute to three-hour classes is to reduce teacher tendencies to lecture for the full period. Whatever style of teaching an instructor currently employs, it will be severely taxed if it becomes the only act he or she has to fill an expanded time.

New teachers are also always looking for ideas. The research on first-year teachers indicates that one of their real challenges is the development of a repertoire of teaching approaches and techniques.[29] An idea bank can also serve to assist teachers whose assignments are changed as a result of restructuring, whether the change involves simply changing subjects within a discipline field (teaching literature is different from teaching grammar) or assuming responsibility to teach something never before taught as a result of curriculum innovation.

Getting teachers to contribute written descriptions and documents associated with the units and lessons they teach can provide a real service to newcomers and to people with new responsibilities. They will owe a debt of gratitude to the library if they can come there, peruse the files, and walk away with workable plans for their classes.

The idea bank will constitute a new responsibility for you but also a new resource over which you will have control. You can enhance its value over time by continually adding to it, and by adding bibliographies and lists of audiovisual materials (materials over which you also have control) to individual entries. A teacher making a contribution will invoke the commitment and consistency principle. Substantial numbers of teachers doing so will activate social proof that this is a good idea.

34. Develop a library media center newsletter to enhance visibility and to showcase resources.

References

1 R. Evans, *The Human Side of School Change* (San Francisco: Jossey-Bass, 2001).

L. G. Bolman and T. E. Deal, *Reframing Organizations* (San Francisco: Jossey-Bass, 1991).

2 R. Evans, *The Human Side of School Change* (San Francisco: Jossey-Bass, 2001).

3 D. E. Berlyne, *Conflict, Arousal and Curiosity* (New York: McGraw-Hill, 1960).

4 E. E. Jones, H. B. Gerard, *Foundations of Social Psychology* (New York: Wiley, 1967).

5 J. M. Brett and J. D. Werbel, *The Effect of Job Transfer on Employees and Their Families, Baselined Report* (Washington, D.C.: Employee Relocation Council, 1978).

J. M. Brett, and J. D. Werbel, *The Effect of Job Transfer on Employees and Their Families, Final Report* (Washington, D.C.: Employee Relocation Council, 1980).

6 M. Fullan, with S. Stiegelbauer, *The New Meaning of Educational Change* (New York: Teachers College Press, 1991).

7 L. Dianis, "Spending Report: Getting By With Le$$," *District Administrator*, vol. 39, no. 3 (March, 2003), pp. 24–30.

8 R. Evans, *The Human Side of School Change* (San Francisco: Jossey-Bass, 2001).

S. Feiman-Nemser and R. E. Floden, "The Cultures of Teaching," In M. C. Wittrock (Ed.), *Handbook of Research On Teaching, Third Edition* (pp. 505–526) (New York: Macmillan Publishing Company, 1986).

G. Nadler and S. Hibino, *Breakthrough Thinking* (Roseville, CA: Prima Publishers, 1998).

S. Purkey and M. S. Smith, "Effective Schools: A Review," *Elementary School Journal*, vol. 83, no. 4 (March, 1983), pp. 427–453.

9 P. M. Turner, *Helping Teachers Teach: A School Library Media Specialist's Role, Second Edition* (Englewood, CO: Libraries Unlimited, Inc., 1993).

10 There is a real crisis in this last area. Many people currently teaching mathematics, science, and social studies, especially in secondary schools have no formal training in the subject or in related subjects. See R. Ingersoll, "The Problem of Underqualified Teachers in American Secondary Schools," *Educational Researcher*, vol. 28, no. 2 (March, 1999), pp. 26–37 or for a general overview see R. Ingersoll, "Out-of-Field Teaching: An ERIC Digest," ERIC Document ED 449 119, October 2000.

11 W. K. Hoy and C. G. Miskel, *Educational Administration: Theory, Research, and Practice, 6th Edition* (New York: McGraw-Hill, 2001).

J. Pfeffer, *Managing With Power* (Boston: Harvard Business School Press, 1992).

12 There's a good overview of these models in W. K. Hoy and C. G. Miskel, *Educational Administration: Theory, Research, and Practice, 6th Edition* (New York: McGraw-Hill, 2001).

13 Even something as simple as a quick Google search of <"schools" AND "data-driven decision-making"> turns up multiple pages of models, research, opinion papers, position statements, and case studies.

14 For a quick summary of this research and argument, see such works as

G. Hartzell, *Why Should Principals Support School Libraries?* ERIC Digest, November 2002

K. Lance and D. Loertscher, *Powering Achievement: School Library Media Programs Make a Difference—The Evidence* (San Jose, CA: Hi Willow Research and Publishing, 2001).

E. G. Smith, T*exas School Libraries: Standards, Resources, Services, and Students' Performance*. ERIC Document 455 850. Available online at <http://www.tsl.state.tx.us/ld/pubs/schlibsurvey/index.html>.

15 M. A. Jetter, *The Roles of the School Library Media Specialist in the Future: A Delphi Study*. (Doctoral Dissertation, Michigan State University, 1972).

16 J. G. Coleman, Jr., P*erceptions of the "Guiding Principles" in Media Programs: District and Library Trends* (Doctoral dissertation, University of Virginia, 1982).

S. T. Kerr, "Are There Instructional Developers in the Schools? A Sociological Look at the Development of a Profession." *A V Communications Review*, vol. 25 (1977) pp. 243–268.

L. Kvalness and P. La Croix, *Levels of Involvement in the Consultant Role of the School*

Library Media Specialist. A presentation at the American Association of School Librarians Research Forum, Chicago, 1990.

S. E. Staples, "Sixty Competency Ratings for School Media Specialists," *Instructional Innovator*, vol. 26 (November 1981), pp. 19–23.

17 Epictetus (c. 50–120 AD). In J. Bartlett, edited by E. M. Beck, *Familiar Quotations, Fifteenth Edition* (Boston: Little, Brown and Company, 1980), p. 121. The full quote is: "No thing great is created suddenly, any more than a bunch of grapes or a fig. If you tell me that you desire a fig, I answer you that there must be time. Let it first blossom, then bear fruit, then ripen." From the *Discourses*, book I, chapter 15.

18 D. C. Feldman, "The Multiple Socialization of Organization Members," *Academy of Management Review*, vol. 6, no. 2 (1981), pp. 309–318.

C. D. Fisher, "Organizational Socialization: An Integrative Review," In K. M. Rowland and G. R. Ferris (Eds.), *Research in Personnel and Human Resource Management: A Research Annual, Volume 4* (pp. 101–145). Greenwich, CT: JAI Press, 1986.

19 *Outdated School Libraries: What Can You Do to Update Yours?* <http://www.education-world.com/a_admin/admin181.shtml>.

20 C. A. Doll, "Quality and Elementary School Library Media Collections," *School Library Media Quarterly*, vol. 25, no. 2 (Winter 1997), pp. 95–102.

21 M. L. Miller, "New Money Old Books," *School Library Journal*, vol. 47, no. 10 (October 2001), pp. 50–60.

22 *The New Mexico Task Force for School Libraries Report.* <http://www.iema-ia.org/IEMA405.html>.

23 *Association of Philadelphia School Libraries.* <http://www.iema-ia.org/IEMA405.html>.

24 D. J. Callison, *Indiana School of Library and Information Science, personal communication,* July 19, 2002.

25 *Outdated School Libraries: What Can You Do to Update Yours?* <http://www.education-world.com/a_admin/admin181.shtml>.

26 M. L. Miller, "New Money Old Books," *School Library Journal*, vol. 47, no. 10 (October 2001), pp. 50–60.

27 *Fast Facts: Recent Statistics from the Library Research Service*, no. 133, October 21, 1997. <http://www.lrs.org>.

28 <http://www.cde.ca.gov/library/libstats.html>

29 M. Huberman, "Teacher Careers and School Improvement," *Journal of Curriculum Studies*, vol. 20, no. 2 (1988), pp. 119–132.

P. J. Sikes, L. Measor, and P. Woods, T*eacher Careers: Crises and Continuities* (London: The Falmer Press, 1985).

Chapter 12

Building Influence Through Your Clientele

Anyone who doubts the power of student influence ability need only read "Social Action Saves the Day" by Barbara Lewis and Jeanette Woolley in the January 1994 issue of the *School Library Journal*.[1] Their article describes how students in a Salt Lake City elementary school successfully lobbied the school board for funds to keep the media center open year round and wrote grant proposals for funds to buy books and support technology. Secondary schools students are every bit as capable of doing those things and more.

The process of student involvement in influence building is circular and presumes that the driving force behind the librarian's actions is based in good intentions and moral commitment to student welfare. It works like this: School librarians wielding influence with students undertake activities with two motives: (1) to benefit students, and (2) to cause students, in turn, to take actions that will encourage adults to support the library. The adult support translates to opportunities, resources, and protection. As the library's resources, status, and range of possible activities grow, so does its ability to better serve students and its capacity to further influence both students and adults. At one level, you could say that we help students in order to help ourselves develop greater ability to help students. It is with this in mind that the activity suggestions listed below for building influence with students are offered.

Tactics for Building Influence with Students

There is a rich literature of books and articles suggesting ways to improve library services to students. Most of them have a single purpose, usually to improve student motivation or to make student library use more effective. The tactics outlined in the text that follows may have one or both of those effects, but that is not why they appear here. These tactics aim to capture student support for the library and its operation. Their objective is to build influence with students, and they have to be seen in the light of that purpose.

1. Make arrangements with the librarian(s) or teachers at the feeder school(s) for students to be able to use your school's library.

The chances are that your library will have much greater resources than the feeder school library and will be very impressive to the younger students while helping them to succeed with where they are right now. The students will come to value the library, and their parents will value their students' success. The connection will not be lost on them. This tactic does a lot to increase your visibility and tie your operation to the central mission of education even before students are in your school.

2. Be part of the team that makes presentations about your school to incoming students, and their parents, while they are still in the feeder school.

This helps to set the image that the library is an integral part of the school's program. The objectives are to increase visibility and to plant the seed of the idea that effective school library use is a necessity for student success. Presentations to the parents of incoming students also offer the opportunity to make a pitch for donations and volunteers, which will expand your resource base.

3. Get on the new student orientation programs at the opening of school in the fall semester and try to get to any class (grade level, freshman, sophomore, junior, or senior) meetings.

Plan short presentations and have handouts that invite student use of the library. These can be strengthened if they are prepared in conjunction with and endorsed by teachers popular with the students at each level.

This tactic also helps to solidify the library's image as an integral part of the school's program. The objectives are to increase visibility and to nurture the idea that effective use of the school library is a necessity for success as a student.

4. Develop a "tape tour" of your library for use in a portable tape or DVD player with earphones and use it to orient students who enter the school after the start of the year.

This provides personalized service in a medium of student choice. It is very difficult to invoke the similarity principle with adolescents, but an appreciation of their communication channels pays dividends. The tactic enhances likability, offers an opportunity to showcase resources, and is perhaps a chance to recruit student aides.

5. Learn as many names as you can.

Students respond to individual recognition. If the library is one of the few places where they are well known, as it may be for some students in some schools, they will be more likely to speak well of it to parents and others. The tactic works on the components of likability.

6. Survey the students about how they see the library and what they would like to see in the library.[2]

See if you can give the survey through English or social studies classes or through classes in some other discipline where you anticipate teacher support. Find out what the students think. Where you can identify individuals, grade levels, programs, or departments, follow up the results with visits to randomly chosen classes to ask for details and ideas.

Some of the results will be foolishness, some will probably be obscene, and some will surely be funny. If nothing else, the survey will tell you the level of student awareness and give you a clear picture of the work you need to do in education, publicity, and public relations. But there may also be gems in the results. Student calls for more materials, more help, longer hours, and the like can be powerful additions to your proposals to the administration and to community support groups.

The motives for this are the same as for surveying the faculty. This tactic will contribute to your visibility and familiarity, show students respect, and open informal communication channels. Public statements made by students will also invoke the commitment and consistency principle. Of course, your reputation will soar if you actually enact any of their suggestions.

7. Develop a program of cross-age student tutoring in library skills.

Younger students look up to older students. The tutored students will take in the value of the library because it is presented to them as valuable by the older students. The students doing the teaching are every bit as much targets of influence, however. The tactic employs the principle of public commitment and cognitive dissonance. The older student, who will be working to convince the younger student of the library's value, will convince himself or herself in the process. The tactic also increases visibility. If the program is clearly identified as a library program, you will raise the odds of the library being perceived as critical to student success.

8. Develop a course that provides class credit for working as a library assistant.

Go the full route: Develop a curriculum, identify significant duties, and establish performance standards.

Make the first part of the course academic in nature; have the youngster become the resident student expert on the library. If you have a number of student aides at any one time, give each specific areas of expertise to develop. Then give each significant duties that assign responsibility and show trust; have them help other students who come to the library or have them tutor students. Treat them in a first class fashion, sharing the soft drinks and cookies in the back room; perhaps make them laminated nametags with titles on them.

Get the strongest, most involved students you can to take the course. The aim is to get them to speak in support of the library with their influential friends and parents. Few things could help you more than to have students at graduation give you credit for part of the quality of their education.

The tactic draws on the familiarity, commitment, communication, and likability principles. To the extent that you can do any favors for these students, you may invoke the reciprocity principle.

9. Request that a small number of at-risk students be assigned to the library as aides.

Your approach with these students would be different than with the strong students in your assistant's class. Here your focus is on establishing a personal relationship. Interviews of students who drop out of school have revealed time and again that one of the reasons they left school was because no one showed an interest in them personally; there was no bonding to the institution.[3] Not only will you do a real service to a vulnerable student, but word of you and your operation will reach into a segment of the student population that is usually very hard to reach. And, again, what could be better than to have a student who was not predicted to graduate attribute his or her graduation to an association with you. This can only help your reputation.

10. If your district requires that you have some sort of penalty for overdue materials, develop a system whereby students can work off fines or the cost of lost or damaged books or materials instead of paying cash.

This can accommodate students of every socio-economic level in your school, will allow them to get to know you and your staff a little better, and will educate them more to what goes on in a library and what it can offer. This tactic works on the components of the likability principle. The work they do may invoke the commitment and consistency principle at some level.

11. Consider adapting the "adopt-a-highway" idea to an "adopt-a-shelf" or "adopt-a-section" format involving clubs or teams in the school that could see to the care of the section and to the raising of funds for adding to its collection.

This can create an investment/ownership in the library and invoke the commitment and consistency principle while it builds familiarity and visibility and showcases resources.

12. If you're in a secondary school, offer sessions on how to take tests as semester finals time approaches.

Certain teachers, counselors, or others can probably be recruited to run these. The library can recommend books or articles or even create a one-page "guideline" sheet for students. This increases visibility with both students and staff, ties the library to the central mission of the school, associates the library with student success, and does students a favor to stimulate reciprocity.

13. Get the student council to create a library liaison office.

Give modified versions of the reports given to teachers and administrators to the student leaders. This places one or more students already influential with other students in a position of publicly speaking for the library. It appeals to the commitment and consistency principle and to the familiarity principle. Depending on how closely you work with the office holder(s), you may be able to invoke the likability principle. This tactic also increases visibility, not only with students but with the adult who supervises the student council.

14. Develop a materials selection committee composed of students.

The idea is to give the students two tasks. The first is to provide reviews of selected books, media, and software that the library intends to purchase for the general collection or for particular subjects. The second is to set aside a certain amount of money for them to spend on books they and their peers want to read; software programs might also be considered. For the second task, students might be required to survey the student body for suggestions and requests and then to justify which items were chosen for purchase.

Make sure the students have full copies of all selection policies, regulations, and guidelines. This teaches them more about how the library operates, what its constraints are, and what it can offer.

The tactic improves visibility and familiarity. It gives students recognition and real respect through investing them with the resources of limited decision-making power and a budget. It also invokes the commitment and consistency principle since they become a part of the library operation itself.

15. Think about establishing a student behavior advisory committee for the library.
A student committee that reviews and develops library rules can also invoke the commitment principle.

16. Develop a program that emphasizes skills for the non-college bound.

Clearly be able to demonstrate how libraries have social, personal, technical, political, and economic information that students will want and need to have after high school. Work with teachers in elective subjects to develop and deliver this notion. Model it by distributing public service pamphlets and other materials free for the taking.

This tactic offers recognition of the needs of less academic students and shows respect for their aspirations. Students will speak well of places that will provide what they need and can't always get elsewhere.

17. In secondary schools, work with the coaches to develop a study support plan for athletes.

Don't limit the program to athletes in danger of losing eligibility; make it a "study table" program for everyone. The coaches will support you because this is will serve as another element in developing close relationships between players and improving team cohesion.

This tactic will increase your visibility and familiarity and allow you to demonstrate expertise. This will carry word of your program into another segment of the student population. It will improve the odds that students will identify you with the teaching staff.

18. If you are a member of the Rotary, Lions, Kiwanis, Soroptimists, Optimists, Chamber of Commerce or some other civic group, take one or more students with you to meetings on a regular basis.

This tactic is much stronger if you can get opportunities for students to be recognized or, better yet, to speak. This tactic will increase visibility and promote familiarity and likability.

19. Devise a student version of "Adventures into Intellect" (see Chapter 9), but call it something more in line with student jargon.

These kinds of programs can again draw in students from previously untapped segments of the student population, increasing your visibility and familiarity. It will also provide recognition for students and associate the library with the central mission of the school.

20. Go out and teach a class lesson on a subject you love other than library science or research skills.

See the description of this idea in Chapter 9 as part of teacher influence tactic number 25. The objective is to have students identify you with the teaching staff and regard you as a "line" person. This increases visibility and gives you a chance to showcase expertise.

References

1 B. A. Lewis and J. M. Woolley, "Social Action Saves the Day," *School Library Journal*, vol. 40, no. 1 (January, 1994), pp. 33–35.

2 Mike Eisenberg has offered a good initial model in "A View From the Other Side," in the *School Library Journal*, vol. 26, no. 11 (December, 1980), p. 39.

3 R. B. Ekstrom, M. E. Goertz, J. M. Pollack, and D. A. Rock, "Who Drops Out of School and Why: Findings From a National Study," *Teachers College Record*, vol. 87, no. 3 (Spring 1986), pp. 356–373.

M. D. LeCompte and A. G. Dworkin, *Giving Up On School: Student Dropouts and Teacher Burnouts* (Newbury Park, CA: Corwin Press, 1992).

Chapter 13

Parents & Community: Building Influence Through Your Constituents

Parents and community members can support you or cripple you by speaking out, voting one way or another, acting in court, or deciding how they will spend their money and time. School boards and administrators listen to parents and community members both because they should and because they have to. If parents and community members perceive the library media center as vital to school success, they will pressure the board and administration to see it the same way.

Tactics for Building Influence with Parents and Community Members

There is a wealth of books and articles available on fashioning the public relations of the library media center. They offer a host of wonderful ideas for establishing linkages between the library and the people outside the school building. It will be well worth your time to explore publications like Julieta Dias Fisher's & Ann Hill's *Tooting Your Own Horn: Web-Based Public Relations for the 21st Century Librarian* (Linworth Publishing, 2002), Sandy Schuckett's *You Have the Power: Becoming a Successful Political Advocate for School Libraries* (forthcoming from Linworth Publishing in 2004), Richard Halsey's *Lobbying for Public and School Libraries: A History and Political Playbook* (Scarecrow Press, 2003), and Leslie Farmer's *Teaming with Opportunity: Media Programs, Community Constituencies*, and *Technology* (Libraries Unlimited, 2001). As you read the ideas these works contain, however, mentally try to see which principles of influence any given idea may invoke. Virtually all of them will enhance your library's visibility, but particular ideas may well do a lot more. The selection of ideas presented here demonstrates the influence building potential of carefully selected and structured activities. You will be able, no doubt, to find, adapt, and create many many more.

Parents

1. Review your records of students who check out books. Say nothing to anyone in advance, but at the end of the semester or the year write a short note of commendation to the student or to the parents (whichever seems appropriate at your grade level). Parents thrive on recognition of their children. These are the kinds of things that end up on refrigerator doors all over your attendance area. Keep the commendation general enough that it will not offend any notions of student privacy or violate any law. Be very careful in doing this.

The tactic associates the library with the central mission of the school and increases visibility. It may invoke the reciprocity principle; parents are often generous with people who are generous with their children. It promotes likability.

2. Always contribute something, no matter how small, to the multitude of bulk mailings that go out to parents from the school. The objectives are visibility, an image of activity, linkages to other school functions and activities, and an invitation to open informal communication channels, make donations, and render service.

3. Invite the PTA or your school's equivalent group to hold its meetings in the library media center. Make a two-minute library report somewhere during each meeting. Prepare handouts for parents to take home with them that have the most up-to-date information about the library, its usage, its services, its linkages with other parts of the school, and its needs. Depending upon the relationship that evolves with the parents or parent group, you might prepare special reports on selected topics of interest.

This tactic increases visibility and familiarity while it tightens your association with the central mission of the school.

4. Offer to write a column for the PTA newsletter. This will help out the newsletter's editor and may invoke reciprocity. It will increase visibility and enhance communication. If the column also salutes student achievement, it can become even more powerful. Try to highlight collaborative projects with teachers in order to tie the library to the school's mission and to gain teachers' support.

5. Invite one or more PTA members to the presentations of sales representatives when you are considering major purchases. Becoming part of the library process invokes the commitment principle. Even if they don't come, you will get credit for inviting them. If they do come, you will be able to show them all the wonderful things you could put to work for their children if you just had more resources.

6. Offer to serve as the PTA librarian and researcher. Parent organizations, especially in today's activist and restructuring atmosphere, are doing a lot more than holding bake sales. They are becoming increasingly involved in the development of policy and operational procedures. It can be very helpful to have someone who can provide them with information from research and descriptions of model practices elsewhere.

This tactic invokes both the reciprocity and commitment principles, while increasing visibility and familiarity. It improves communication and allows you to showcase both your resources and your expertise.

7. Get a featured position on the Back-to-School-Night Program. Make a presentation to parents' before they set off to visit their students' classrooms. Invite them to the library for a "parents reception" after the classroom visits for coffee, punch, and cookies where they can mingle with teachers and administrators.

This tactic enhances visibility, familiarity, and likability. The presentation tightens the impression of the library as an integral part of the school's operation. The reception integrates schooling with pleasant surroundings, congenial company, and food.

8. If you can legally arrange it, make materials of interest to parents available for check out. Books, tapes, and other materials on subjects such as adolescent psychology, human growth and development, parenting, career opportunities, and helping your child succeed in school can all be valuable to parents. Another tactic is to make some materials available to parents who are returning to school themselves, especially if they are going into education. Your professional library could be of real help to some one in a teacher preparation program.

The tactic draws parents into the library, tightens its links with the school mission, and increases visibility and familiarity. More importantly, it showcases resources to which parents will want access—a fundamental principle of influence; you are doing something for them as well as for their students.

9. If you have the skills, or can prevail on someone who does, schedule a family computer orientation night. Let students and parents together come learn how to use computers. The lessons will be elementary, but you will have drawn the parents into the library and delivered a service. This will enhance visibility and communication, while it allows a demonstration of resources and expertise.

10. Get parent volunteers to work in the library. This tactic clearly promotes visibility and familiarity. It enhances communication and it gives you a chance to showcase both resources and needs. It is most important that this be a pleasant and rewarding experience for the parent volunteer, not just clerical work. Get parents involved as tutors or as research assistants for you as you work for the PTA, principal, teachers, or school board. Incorporate the volunteers into the library operation as much as possible and give every possible recognition.

It may be that a parent would like to volunteer but cannot maintain a continuing schedule. Build a pool of volunteers who might come for concentrated periods, such as for three or four days in a row, to complete a particular project and then be gone. Whenever you can, arrange for someone other than library staff, such as an administrator or teacher, to "drop in" while parents are there working. Ask them to compliment the volunteers on the work done, thank them, and remark how important the library is in the life of the school.

11. Develop a book donation system for parents who want to donate materials in memory of someone. People look for ways of memorializing the departed. Encouraging parents to donate books allows them to put a physical mark on the school. Develop a book plate to go in any donated volume. Don't just have the donor's name typed in; get someone to write the name in calligraphy. The tactic invokes the commitment principle. If enough people will do it, it can become a social proof driven institutionalized practice.

12. Develop a "how to help your child succeed in ..." program for parents while their youngsters are still in the feeder schools. The transition from elementary school to middle school or junior high, and the transition from either of those into high school, is an anxious event for parents as well as for students. The student's next school is always bigger than the one being left behind. There are always perceptions that the new school will be more difficult and less personal than the current. Parents want to understand the new environment and increase the odds of their children's success.

This tactic allows you to become visible to parents, to open communication lines, to showcase resources and expertise, and to do a service that might invoke the reciprocity principle before the students even enter your school.

Community

1. Join a public service civic organization like the Rotary, Lions, Optimists, Soroptimists, or Chamber of Commerce. These people are always looking for speakers and for worthwhile projects to undertake. By working on their projects, you commit them to working on yours. You can increase the library's visibility and associate its image with the central mission of the school. Any donations or services they may render to you will increase your resources base.

2. If you join a public service civic organization, volunteer to serve as the organization's librarian. Accountants who are members of civic groups all over the country volunteer to keep their club's books. Perform a similar service as the group's librarian. It then makes it in their best interests to support your activities and resource base. This invokes the reciprocity principle and allows you to showcase resources and expertise.

3. Develop a specific version of the "adopt-a-school" idea, narrowing it to "adopt-a-library." Community business donors sometimes wonder how their donations are being used. There is no doubt when they are used in the library. The results should be visible. The tactic makes the library more visible. Depending on the donations you ask for, you might be able to tie the library more closely to the central mission of the school. Once begun, the donations will put the commitment principle into operation. Give every kind of recognition you can every time you can.

4. Instead of a business, get an organization like the Rotary, Lions, Soroptimists, or Kiwanis to "adopt" your library. This will, of course, be easier if you or your principal are a member of the targeted group. But whether you are members or not, support of a school library comes under the umbrella definition of community service espoused by these kinds of groups. Association with one of these kinds of organizations can increase your resource base substantially, and not just in materials. Work crews from organizations such as these are well known for painting, construction, refurbishing, and fund raising.

As an aside, youth organizations also seek community service projects. Eagle scouts and their equivalents in other organizations are usually of secondary school age and capable of making all kinds of significant contributions.

5. Invite businesses that support you to put displays in the library. This will advertise their support of the school and increase the intensity of the commitment principle. This might be strengthened further if the materials are presented in conjunction with some project from an economics or business class, which would allow you to tie a teacher into public support statements.

You must be very careful in doing this, however, and you absolutely should check out every idea with your principal before you issue any invitations. Unless your school or district has a policy that says only certain types of businesses can exhibit displays in school buildings, you may find yourself being forced to display very controversial items. In the long run, controversy erodes much more influence than it builds.

6. If possible, make the library available for community group meetings. The rewards are the same as they are for making it available to faculty and PTA groups.

7. Keep every contact you can with alumni and make whatever services you can available to them. Alumni become professionals, service people, politicians, activists, board members, and parents in your community. Continuing alumni contacts can increase your resources through alumni association donations and support. Individual alumni relationships are investments for unforeseeable support in the future. Every opportunity you can find to invoke the reciprocity principle opens a possibility of support later on.

Active alumni associations often look for worthwhile projects to undertake that will benefit the school. Encourage an alumnae library fund drive. Mark any books, materials, or equipment they provide with a book plate or plaque that recognizes the alumnae association as the donor.

8. See if you can develop reciprocal agreements of any kind with other agencies in your community. Museums, health organizations, galleries, youth centers, police departments, parks and recreation—they all have resources that might be useful to you, and you can think of ways to promote your resources with them. These people compete with you for tax dollars; any resource of theirs you can use is an addition to your own. Every increase in your own resources or in your access to someone else's resources increases your influence potential.

9. Build a relationship with the local media. There isn't room here to go into an extended discussion of the benefits of having a good relationship with your district's public relations officer, the education reporter on the local newspaper, and the people who control the programming for local access public radio and television. Each of those, however, represents a way to increase visibility. Every message they can put in front of the public that draws positive attention and credit to you, your library, and your school scores in two places: (1) visibility with community members, and (2) attention with the board and administration. Board members and administrators favor those who bring them positive press. It conveys the message that the public was correct in electing whom they did to the board and that the board members were correct in appointing whom they did as administrators. Keeping them popular keeps you supported.

10. Write for whomever will print whatever you write. Visibility, visibility, visibility.

11. Join the "Friends of the Library" at the local public library; maybe even volunteer there once in a while. This tactic gives you visibility, allows you to demonstrate expertise, and invokes the reciprocity principle. You can never tell when you may want to borrow something or someone from there. Make their resources augment your resource base.

You might also want to consider having a representative from the public library sit in on selection committees and instructional design groups. It will increase the efficiency of operation and the coordination of materials while it increases visibility, familiarity, and public commitment. It will always be helpful to have a colleague from the public system willing to say important and nice things about you at city council and school board meetings.

12. Let the public library know about major research assignments assigned by teachers. You might even send along a copy of the form you designed for teachers to use to alert you to special materials and services needs for their students (see Chapter 9). By alerting librarians at the public library to student needs, you make their jobs easier, and you make it more likely for them to build a strong reputation for service with their patrons. People support those who increase their chances for success. You also increase the student odds of success, which makes both students and teachers look good.

13. Develop and promote an academic competition built along the lines of the old "College Bowl" television show. Have students compete in teams of four. Set up a tournament that mirrors the college basketball playoffs, appropriately modified to accommodate the size of your school. Start with up to 64 teams the first round; have 32 the second, and 16 the third, then down to eight, four, and the final two. Get local civic groups and businesses to donate prizes at each level of competition. Start with simple certificates at the 64 team level, and progress through T-shirts (which will have the library's name or logo on them somewhere) and other small prizes to savings bonds and other substantial things at the final level.

Hold the early rounds in teachers' rooms at lunch; the last couple of rounds in the auditorium, cafeteria, or other appropriate room. Invite the public and parents to attend any matches they want, but emphasize the last two rounds by holding them in a single evening or at an assembly. Have questions that relate to every single subject taught in the school so every single student will have the ability to make a contribution to a team.

Get parents, senior citizens and other community members, and teachers to develop questions to serve in three capacities:

1. To develop and contribute questions to a quiz bank. Teachers can contribute questions from every class they teach. Get parents and community members to use the library to generate additional questions for use, but be sure they are tied to subjects taught.

2. To serve as question askers, timers, and score keepers. Get them involved in the process of the competition so they will see student enthusiasm and the range of student accomplishment.

3. To serve as award presenters. Let them have the attention of students as they present awards at each level of competition.

A project like this can apply several of the influence principles. It will:

- Greatly increase visibility and tie the image of the library to the central mission of learning and demonstrate what students can do.

- Require people to commit time, energy, money, and thought to the project, which will invoke the commitment principle. The researching portions of preparation will showcase your resources and expertise.

- Open all kinds of new channels for informal communication.

- Bring credit to the teachers and administrators as community members work with them.

These last two points are particularly important. Most community contacts with teachers and administrators are a result of a student's misbehavior. There is always a tension in those conversations and exchanges, no matter how they turn out. This project provides opportunities for interaction in non-threatening, non-problematic settings. It associates the school and its personnel with happy memories.

Section III
Tactics

This final section is an eclectic collection of five influence building tactics. The connection between them is that each offers suggestions for somehow shaping the perceptions others have of you or your library in the public forum—when you are presenting information about you and your library in either a report or a meeting. Here, as everywhere else, your influence derives from the ways in which others perceive you. Impression management is the name of the game, it pays to put thought into how you're perceived when you write and talk about the library.

Chapter 14 begins with a basic: your vision and mission statements. In some instances, these statements deliver the first impression others will have of you because they'll show up in places like school brochures, faculty handbooks, annual reports, and accreditation documents. They'll sometimes be posted in your library or appear on your stationery. Some people will see them before they ever see you.

In other instances, vision and mission statements are used as the foundation for program and personnel evaluation. This can be dangerous. You want to make sure that your vision and mission statements reflect what you really do and shape perceptions that you can fulfill. If they don't, they can become time bombs.

Chapter 15 addresses questions of crafting the reports that you're called on to turn in periodically—especially your annual report. What you report shapes the way others view you. If circulation numbers are the leading edge, then numbers become your library's defining quality, communicating an incomplete picture of library media services at best and a misleading and damaging one at worst. The sharp end of your report should always be the most important activity in which you engage.

Chapter 16 argues for the value of emotion and human experience when you make presentations, whether you're delivering a report or making a library enhancement proposal to the school board, parent association, faculty group, business partner, or anyone else who can make a difference in what you're able to do. Mark Twain observed once that there are lies, damn lies, and statistics. Statistics are necessary because we like to think ourselves rational in all that we do. The truth is larger than that, however, and the simple fact is that the heart can rule the head. Fill your presentations with stories that capture the heart.

Chapter 17 encourages you to get others to make your proposals for you. Getting others up front in library advocacy removes any hint that what you propose is self-serving. Having faculty members, parents, and others speak on your behalf sends multiple positive messages about you, your proposal, and the esteem in which both are held by people who count.

Chapter 18 closes out the section and the book and strikes a different chord from almost everything that came before it. It encourages you to show another side of yourself as a professional librarian—to show your teeth when you're attacked. A retiring image in the face of an assault on your expertise doesn't inspire confidence. Since every incident in a career is linked to prior and subsequent incidents, how you react now influences how you will be treated later. Demanding professional respect is essential for continuing influence.

Chapter 14

Frame Others' Perceptions Through Mission and Vision Statements

Setting a firm and respected foundation for what you do is essential in building workplace influence. Properly constructed vision and mission statements can help in that but crafting them can be difficult. The process requires mixing careful thought with heavy doses of realism. This chapter offers a short analysis of vision and mission statements and some thoughts to consider as you craft or revise your own statements.

As you begin, it's good to keep in mind that there isn't any body of empirical research demonstrating that such statements make any difference in performance.[1] Study results are mixed at best. So why the insistence, sometimes even the state law, that schools and other public agencies adopt and publish them?[2] It's probably because, as so often happens, education has again embraced a popular idea that seems like it has or should have value without first reviewing the research or testing it ourselves. Remember the social proof heuristic? It can be that they're widespread just because they're widespread.[3] Whatever the reason, mission statements seem very attractive to school people. Our problem is that they're also generally boring—and potentially dangerous. This is why you need to be very careful in crafting yours.

Mission statements are attractive because they satisfy some need in us to define our purpose and proclaim our reason for being. For some reason, they help us feel like we've made our goals and priorities explicit, communicating to others both the context within which we work and the contribution we make to the enterprise as a whole. We like to think that they motivate us because they continually remind us of what we're about.[4]

Ironically, though, instead of inspiring us, these statements often end up boring us, probably because there is little in them to really capture our imagination. When did you ever see a really unique school vision or mission statement? Robert Evans nicely sums up what's wrong with most of them in *The Human Side of School Change*.[5] Most are too long, he argues, too fragmented, too impractical, and too clichéd to really grab us. No one can grasp, let alone be motivated by, a statement that goes on for pages. Long lists of impractical and unrealistically lofty goals destroy focus and generate cynicism instead of commitment, especially when they're presented in a cascade of slogans and buzzwords. It's no wonder that so few people take them seriously.

But they're also dangerous because some people do take them seriously and use them as frameworks for evaluation. Any statement promising things that cannot be delivered is an invitation to failure, and you don't want to put a club in the hands of an anti-library administrator or board member.

Paradoxically, it's our good intentions that put us in jeopardy. We want so much for students to be successful that we impulsively turn our desires into promises we can't keep. This is an educator's weakness that doesn't as often afflict other professionals. Compare what educators promise clients with what other professionals promise theirs. Physicians never promise that everyone will be cured. Attorneys never guarantee that every case will be won. They only promise dedicated delivery of the most up-to-date knowledge, skill, and technology. Other factors affecting success or failure—the situation, the client's personal characteristics, and the nature of the problem—are recognized as beyond the professional's control.

So, what does this say to school librarians? It says that you need to recognize the danger of taking responsibility for things you can't control, particularly what others do and become. Despite what *Information Power* suggests, you *cannot* ensure that *all* students will become effective users of ideas and information.[6] All you really can ensure is that all students and the adults who serve them have that opportunity—and that should be your vision and mission.

Educators deal in opportunities, not in certainties. Opportunities are your stock-in-trade. Your job is to provide opportunities in variety and abundance. You're ethically bound to accept responsibility for your own behavior in doing that job, but it's unreasonable to suggest that you can make everyone else accept what you offer or that you can shape everyone else in the school into what you want them to be. The simple truth is that you don't have the power to create effective researchers or produce lifelong learners or instill a love of reading or a love of learning into anyone. The only thing you can really control is you. In light of that reality, your mission or vision statement should describe only what your library is about and what you do as its animator.

You provide your clientele with the advice, instruction, materials, and, for some, the motivation to develop their knowledge and skill. But if some clients—just like the doctor's or the attorney's—won't take instruction or advice, won't perform the prescribed exercise or activity, or won't accept help, there isn't much you can do. This doesn't mean that you fail in your professional obligation if what you offer is rejected, assuming that you offered it in a manner appropriate to your client's age and nature. It only means that the people in question weren't ready or able to accept it. Your evaluation should rest on what you offered and how you offered it, and not on whether everyone accepted it.

Given this situation, how then can you develop a vision and mission statement that will broadcast a realistic message regarding what you and your library are and do? The first thing to do is to stop thinking of "vision" and "mission" as interchangeable terms. The words are not synonymous, and we do ourselves a disservice when we treat them as if they were. James Collins and Jerry Porras, organizational researchers at Stanford, summarize clear and important distinctions.[7] A "vision," they contend, is a guiding philosophy of fundamental motivating assumptions, defining the core values and beliefs that drive the organization. It is broad, fundamental, inspirational, and enduring. It "grabs the soul" and will be relevant and applicable 100 years from now. Rather than describe what an organization currently does, it defines its perpetual purpose. A classic example is Steve Jobs' vision for the Apple Computer Company: "To make a contribution to the world by making tools for the mind." No matter how technology changes in the next century, the "vision" of what Apple is about remains the same.

A "mission," on the other hand, is a tangible image that focuses attention on something currently worthwhile. It defines a clear and compelling goal that serves to unify employee efforts. As Collins and Porras put it, "It is crisp, clear, engaging—it reaches out and grabs people in the gut. People 'get it' right away; it requires little or no explanation. A mission has a finish line and a specific time frame for its achievement. A good mission is risky, falling in the grey area where reasons says, 'This is unreasonable,' and intuition says, 'but we believe that we can do it nonetheless.' "[8] President Kennedy provided a good example in 1961: "Achieving the goal, before this decade is out, of landing a man on the moon and returning him safely to earth." Pepsi's "Beat Coke!" goal for the 1970s is another.

What does this have to do with libraries? At least three things: First, both types of statement are short, crisp, and clear. Why is that important? Try this test: Without peeking, recite your library's statement from memory right now. Can you do it? Can you also quote your school's? How about your district's?

Don't feel bad if you can't quote any or all of them. Most of your colleagues probably can't recite them either—and that's why it's important. In theory, every activity in the district is supposed to flow from and support the vision or mission statement, just as every activity in the school is supposed to flow from and support its own vision nested in the context of the overriding district vision. In turn, because your library doesn't exist in an academic vacuum, your statement is supposed to provide the rationale for what you do within the context of both the larger school and district environments in which your facility is imbedded. How can any of that happen if you don't know what those statements are?

Second, visions always are qualitative and continual, but missions can be either qualitative or quantitative and fit in a limited time frame. Kennedy's moon mission was qualitative; there were no numbers involved in it and no partial measures. We couldn't get "close" to it and we couldn't exceed it. We either did it or we didn't. The Pepsi statement was also a do-or-don't proposition, but it was quantitative because success was measured in sales volume. Did we beat Coke? By how much? More than we expected? Less? Or, how much short did we fall? Can we still feel good about our effort?

Why is this important? A vision statement isn't really designed to serve an evaluative function except in the most holistic sense. But a mission statement by its nature is a framework for evaluation. There's a bottom line to it. And why is that important? Because in any worthwhile evaluation, how much you exceeded or fell short of your target is the measure of your performance. This ties very closely to a third point.

Note that vision and mission statements apply only to the organization and to the activities of its members. They define no one else's purpose or behavior. They assign commitment and responsibility to organizational members, not to clients or patrons. In so doing, they allow members to avoid the trap of having their evaluation anchored in how someone else performs. This is important because measuring your success by how other people behave is an invitation to failure. You can't control or measure what they do, so you absolutely should not take responsibility for it. Can you ever tell if you've created lifelong learners? You know the students in your school. Do you really believe that you can ensure that every single one of them will become an effective user of ideas and information? Are you prepared to define yourself and your program as failures if they don't?

The way around this is to craft separate mission and vision statements. If you accept that idea, then your vision statement might describe "A library that offers everyone in the school the opportunity to become a more effective user of ideas and information." This describes the library's ongoing vital function. It embraces both students and adults and is continual because both they and their needs continually change. It's flexible because it doesn't lock you into any one media or method. And it doesn't hold you responsible for things you cannot control.

Then, annually, or at some other recurring point, you can define a specific mission addressing some part of the vision, something that is measurable within a time frame and that describes only the ways in which you will apply your knowledge and skill. For example, the mission might be to initiate an out-reach program to a certain type of student or to develop a particular number or specific types of collaborative projects. Conditions in your school will dictate the priority choices and provide an important and fair basis for your evaluation.

The idea behind a vision or mission statement is to help you do a better job. The idea behind evaluation is to help you do a better job. That only works if vision, mission, and evaluation are aligned. If they're out of alignment, and you cannot live up to any of them, your influence potential is more like to shrink than to grow.

References

1 C. K. Bart and M. C. Baetz, "The Relationship Between Mission Statements and Firm Performance: An Exploratory Study," *Journal of Management Studies*, vol. 35, no. 6 (November 1998), pp. 823–853.

J. A. Weiss and S. K. Piderit, "The Value of Mission Statements in Public Agencies," *Journal of Public Administration Research & Theory*, vol. 9, no. 2 (April 1999), pp. 193–223.

2 J. A. Weiss and S. K. Piderit, "The Value of Mission Statements in Public Agencies," *Journal of Public Administration Research & Theory*, vol. 9, no. 2 (April 1999), pp. 193–223.

3 J. Krohe, Jr., "Do You Really Need a Mission Statement?" *Across The Board*, vol. 32, no. 7 (July/August 1995), pp. 16–20.

4 C. K. Bart, "Sex, Lies, and Mission Statements," *Business Horizons*, vol. 40, no. 6 (November/December 1997), pp. 9–18.

B. Bartkus, M. Glassman, and R. B. McAfee, "Mission Statements: Are They Smoke and Mirrors?" *Business Horizons*, vol. 43, no. 6 (November/December 2000), pp. 23–28.

5 R. Evans, *The Human Side of School Change* (San Francisco: Jossey-Bass, 2001).

6 *American Association of School Librarians and the Association for Educational Communications and Technology, Information Power: Building Partnerships for Learning* (Chicago: American Library Association, 1998).

7 J. Collins and J. Porras, "Organizational Vision and Visionary Organizations," *California Management Review*, vol. 34, no. 1 (Fall 1991), pp. 30-52.

8 J. Collins and J. Porras, "Organizational Vision and Visionary Organizations," *California Management Review*, vol. 34, no. 1 (Fall 1991), p. 42.

Chapter 15
Craft Influential Reports

Once again, when it comes to building influence, perception is everything. How we shape others' perceptions of us directly affects what value they attach to us and to what we do, what they think we can give, and what they think we'll want and deserve in return. Just like every other description of your operation, formal and informal, your annual report and the reports you submit to accrediting agencies contribute to how your principal and district office administrators perceive you and your library. Since you don't have a choice in whether or not to submit a report, the question becomes what kind of report to produce. Carefully thought out and deliberately structured reports shape one kind of perception; unimaginative and sterile statistical reports shape another. This is particularly important if these reports are going to people, perhaps your board members, who rarely or never see your library in operation.

The critical issue in any report lies in the message the report carries. The content of the report is, of course, important in its own right, but content and significance are not synonymous. It's useful here to remember Doug Johnson's admonition: People don't buy a quarter-inch drill bit because they want a quarter-inch drill bit. They buy a quarter-inch drill bit because they want a quarter-inch hole somewhere. By the same token, school officials and the community members that oversee them don't want an active library in order to have an active library. They want student achievement. The active library is the means, not the end.[1]

With that in mind, then, you need to assess what your report actually conveys. You want to be sure that it describes learning outcomes and not just activities and efforts; that it describes the library's human product and not the process; and that it celebrates student growth and development and not just a quantitative profile of your operation.

Ross Todd at Rutgers University has some interesting insights on this.[2] Drawing from medical practice terminology developed in the early 1990s, Todd advises engaging in what he calls "evidence based practice" to show readers how and why your services are important to student learning. Your report, he says, should be an accomplishment statement and a celebration of achievement, not an activity log. What, he asks, have students really learned when they find a particular Web site, CD, article, or book? Nothing, he contends. If simply finding material were sufficient, students could just turn in lists of references to their teachers. It's in coming to understand the information discovered, making connections between one piece of it and another, synthesizing it, and applying it in pursuit of learning that educational goals are achieved. If the library's mission, as the AASL says, is to make library patrons effective *users* of information, a report that centers on how much information they found and how they found it—rather than on how they *used* that information—is incomplete. Finding information is the process; understanding it well enough to apply it is the product.

This notion aligns with Mortimer Adler's model of intellectual attainment.[3] There are, Adler says, four levels or "goods of the mind." The first and the simplest and the most abundant is information. But information by itself has no meaning. It is only through connection and context that information becomes the second good—knowledge. Knowledge by itself, however, has little value. The value of knowledge is in its application. Only when knowledge is filtered through human experience and linkages are established between one piece of knowledge and one or more other pieces of knowledge that understanding, the third good, is created. Wisdom, the fourth good, derives from being able to judge what knowledge is relevant and appropriate in a given set of circumstances. Wisdom is the prudent application of knowledge.[4] To some extent, when we talk about higher order learning in schools, we're connecting with Adler's typology. This is what libraries are about, not just finding information. That's one reason why using an "information center" metaphor (see the discussion of this in Chapter 3) for the library communicates such a limited and misleading view of what libraries really are.

From an influence perspective, the problem is greater than just an incomplete picture of library operation. By focusing on only the initial part of the library experience, quantitative annual and accreditation reports obscure its greater value. Worse, they perpetuate perceptions of the library media center as an information storehouse instead of casting it as a learning center. If the library is perceived, in Todd's words, as an information space instead of as a knowledge place, emphasizing collection over connection, then the value of the librarian is drawn into question.[5] As information retrieval technology becomes ever more sophisticated, perceptions of a librarian's value can only diminish unless people understand that librarians offer more than just guidance in finding information. They must understand the rich multidimensional nature of librarianship.

How can you use these ideas to shape your own image and advance your own influence potential at work? There are at least three things you can do.

First, unless your district or accrediting agency locks you into a standard reporting form, craft a report that targets the most important things you offer and do. Describe the students with whom you worked with in the past year, both individually and in classes. Explain what they learned and how it relates to a given state standard or district curriculum mandate. Don't just list the number of collaborative projects in which you and one or more teachers engaged. Instead, describe the objectives of those projects and lessons, how the students demonstrated what they learned, how that learning related to standards or mandates, and what you and your library contributed to their success. Describe circulation figures and computer use in the context of a given project, unit, or lesson.

The difficulty in preparing such a report, of course, is controlling its length. You may not be able to report on every good thing you did, but those on which you do report will much more effectively portray the power and potential of the library than any set of numbers could. If, of course, you feel compelled to report the standard numbers you've always reported, attach them as an appendix, but keep student achievement as the leading edge of your report.

The importance of defining student achievement in the context of library work is difficult to overstate. Unless you can keep the connection between student learning and your library in the forefront of your report, you'll suffer again from the librarian's curse of "absorbability." You empower others in the work you do. Unless you keep surfacing the contributions you make, they get absorbed by others, and you fade from the picture. You may help a student tremendously, but ultimately whatever that student was working on becomes his or her project, paper, or presentation—and what you did to contribute is lost to sight. The same thing happens when you work with a teacher. Whatever you contribute to that teacher's instruction can easily be lost. The lesson becomes a part of the teacher's course configuration and delivery. You need a way to draw these contributions back out of the shadows. As Roseabeth Moss Kanter of Harvard has observed, power flows to the person whose work is visible.[6] Your annual report or accreditation report can help to do that if it is carefully structured to capture and record those contributions.

Second, if you are locked into a standard reporting form, then reverse what I've just suggested. Put the learning narrative as an appendix. There probably is room on your standard form for an asterisk or footnote number here or there. Insert them and lead readers to the human translation of your numbers. Illustration and example always enhance quantitative arguments.

Third, don't limit the distribution of your report to your principal, your district office, or the accrediting agency. Once you've gone to the work of crafting the narrative and compiling your illustrated numbers, use them everywhere you can to multiply the return on your investment. Give your report to library-friendly faculty members. Get on the parent group's agenda, give the president a copy, or see if you can get some of it into the group's newsletter if it has one. Offer to write a piece for the principal's newsletter. Even if you have a principal who doesn't want you to submit a new kind of report, he or she is still likely to welcome your help in dealing with the burden of writing a newsletter every week or month. See if the school newspaper might be able to use some of it as fodder for an article. You'll no doubt post the report on your library's Web site, but see if you can get it on the larger school or district Web site as well.

Doing these last things might seem like a weak substitute for giving your principal the kind of report you want to give. But don't feel that you've failed at your attempt to shape administrative perceptions. The objective is to convince those in power that you and your library make significant contributions to student achievement and the accomplishment of the school's overall goals. It's of minimal importance whether administrators are exposed to the idea in a document you give them, see it in an alternate form such as a newsletter, or hear it from people to whom they must pay attention—like parents and faculty. The important thing is to get the idea in front of them. As Ross Todd argues, whole new perspectives open up when you celebrate the understood instead of the found.[7] Once you've captured their attention, the odds go up that they'll begin to ask you directly for information. Once that begins, your influence increases.

References

1 Doug Johnson is the Director of Media and Technology for the Makato, Minnesota, schools. <http://www.doug-johnson.com/>.

2 R. J. Todd, "Irrefutable Evidence," *School Library Journal*, vol. 49, no. 4 (April 2003), pp. 52–54.

3 M. Adler. *A Guidebook to Learning* (New York: MacMillan, 1986), pp. 110–134.

4 There's an interesting discussion of this notion in *Walt Crawford's and Michael Gordon's Future Libraries: Dreams, Madness & Reality* (Chicago: American Library Association, 1995).

5 Todd had previously elaborated on this notion in a keynote address given to the International Association of School Librarians in 2001. It's something that every school librarian should consider. It is available at <http://www.iasl-slo.org/virtualpaper2001.html>. Accessed June 1, 2003.

6 R. Kanter, *Men and Women of the Corporation* (New York: Basic Books, 1977).

7 R. J. Todd, "Irrefutable Evidence," *School Library Journal*, vol. 49, no. 4 (April 2003), pp. 52–54.

   R. J. Todd, "School Libraries and Evidence: Seize the Day, Design the Future," *LMC-Library Media Connection*, vol. 22, no. 1 (August–September 2003), pp. 12–18.

Chapter 16

Exert Emotional Influence Through Storied Presentations

Just as in crafting your annual report and accreditation reports, go beyond the mere presentation of facts and figures in your efforts to convince your school board, parent group, business partner, principal, or faculty that supporting you and your library is a good idea. Plan on illustrating your statistics with stories. We all use—and pretty much believe—the idiom that a picture is worth a thousand words, and a picture painted with words can be just as moving as one done with oils.

Why Add Stories to Your Presentation?

A lot of people see persuasion as a straightforward process.[1] First, you enthusiastically make your proposal or proposition. Then you outline your supporting arguments, grounding each in strong statistical evidence, overwhelming potential opposition with irresistible logic. Finally, you enter the deal-making stage and describe what it is possible to do within the context of the existing situation. In other words, you use logic, data, persistence, and personal enthusiasm to get others to buy into your good ideas. Unfortunately, this doesn't work nearly as often as we would like it to. The question is, why not?

What's missing is the human element. Statistical data allow you to connect with your audience on an intellectual level, but not on an emotional one. Psychological and organizational research studies have demonstrated that people can be—and often are—more affected by emotion packed colorful examples than by statistical data.[2] This is not to say that statistical data is not important, because it is. Statistics have persuasive value in their own right, and some people clearly need objective fact to ground their decisions. But many of us, perhaps most, despite our overwhelming desire to appear rational in our decision-making, make decisions as much with our hearts as with our heads. Perhaps more. If you can capture someone's heart, even in a work setting, his or her head most likely will follow.[3]

Research suggests that this happens as a result of one or more of four interacting reasons. They're kind of interesting to think about because they seem so reflective of our own experience. And our own experience is the core element both in understanding our thought processes and in understanding the power of stories in persuasion attempts.

First, there is what is known as the "vividness hypothesis."[4] We know from psychological and communications research that stories and examples may be more effective than statistics in influencing people because they are more vivid. Vivid things command attention and stir interest. They also create more concrete images in people's minds and, thereby, cause people to weigh the information they provide more heavily when they make decisions.

Second, researchers point to what they call the "availability heuristic." Heuristics, you'll remember, are psychological tools we use for judging individuals and situations. Availability refers to how accessible a piece of information is in our memory.

Examples and vivid stories make material about an issue easier to mentally encode and retrieve.[5] The more available or accessible a piece of information is—that is, the easier it is to recall—the more likely we are to include it and give it weight in our deliberations. Because stories and emotionally laden examples are easier to remember than statistics, we are more likely to draw on them in making our decisions.

Third is the "underutilization hypothesis."[6] The underutilization hypothesis argues that many people have difficulty drawing causal inferences from statistical information. Whatever the individual reasons for this, we often underutilize the information available to us in a statistical report.

Last is "cognitive response theory."[7] Cognitive response theory argues that our cognitive responses to information tend to mediate the relationship between the message and our attitudes about that message. If, for example, we feel overwhelmed by reams of statistics, it's not uncommon for us to respond with skepticism. This reaction is common enough to be imbedded in idiom: "Figures can lie and liars can figure." But we all understand stories, and stories tend to make tighter connections with our feelings than do numbers. The result is that we often are less critical of the evidence and arguments presented through stories and human examples than we are of those that come to us through statistics. If we are less critical and create fewer counterarguments when arguments connect with stories that reflect our own experience, it's more likely that our attitudes regarding the subject will be subject to change.

Taken together, this research strongly suggests the value of using stories to supplement statistical information. Statistics can be powerful, but the research indicates that the combination of statistic and story certainly has more impact than the statistics by themselves.[8] The power of story is strong enough that there is research evidence that even statistical evidence is more persuasive when it is accompanied by the story of how and why the research was done.[9]

So, what does this say to school librarians? It says that while it may be necessary to build your case on things like budget figures, escalating book and software costs, the percentage of out-of-date titles in your collection, circulation and library use statistics, and tallies of how many collaborative projects you've engaged in with teachers this year, it's also likely that that's not going to be sufficient by itself. Even building your case for enhanced library funding, staffing, and support on statistics drawn from the recent studies that Keith Lance and others have done of how much a good library media program can impact student achievement isn't likely to carry the day unless you can tie them to something that matters in the minds of your audience members.[10] The key is to identify local relevance. The impact of bullet number three on slide six in your Powerpoint presentation will be greater if you can illustrate it with a personal example or with a story showing how it relates to a pivotal experience in a student's or teacher's life.

What Stories and How?

What Stories?
Unfortunately, there's no formula for selecting stories. Story selection is a judgment call from beginning to end. The only consistent guideline is that the stories need to relate directly to your school, your district, and your audience members' experiences.

Story selection probably should be driven by audience considerations. Remember that the topic and you are only two of the three ingredients in any story situation; the third is the audience. The effectiveness of the story is grounded in the interactive relationship between all three elements.[11]

In some instances, a generic story will best illustrate a point—"This is like the tale of the man who fell off the 10-story building ..." Other times, a personal anecdote will be the better choice—"I couldn't have been a librarian more than 20 minutes before I first saw ..." In other cases, you will need to anchor your arguments in teacher and student experiences—"We all can remember how much ..." "One teacher working this way ..." "A student in this very school last week ..." In still others, you will want to see if you can connect a story to the specific interests and frames of reference represented by members of your audience. For example, if your audience is a leading board member who runs a business or is made up of representatives from your business partner, you might want to tell a short story about what this kind of project has meant to employers in other places because of its effect on student literacy. All of this means that you might vary the stories in presenting the same proposal—and the same statistics—to the school board, the parent group, the faculty, or a business partner.

How to Tell the Stories?

Again, there is no magic formula. But you may have an advantage here because many librarians are in the story business, telling and sharing stories with students as a part of their jobs. The essential differences, however, are (a) the stories used in a presentation are very short, a series of vignettes at most, and (b) these stories are being told to adults—powerful adults who have the ability to give or withhold organizational support. You need to be careful and you need to be good. Fortunately, there are some guidelines from research. You can do a search of the literature yourself to find more, but a good place to start is with the advice Annette Simmons gives in a little book called *The Story Factor*.[12] The ideas that follow are drawn from her work and then augmented with comment and with research from other sources.

1. Don't act superior. Even if you are an outstanding storyteller, the impact you want will be enhanced by treating your listeners as intellectual equals whose commitment to schools and students is every bit as strong as yours. There's a delicate balance involved in trying to get people to change how they think about things and remaining respectful of the decisions they've made up to now. Never allow self-righteousness, guru-itis, or arrogance to open a breech between you and your audience.

2. Don't bore your listeners. This is the greatest sin, and it is unforgivably counterproductive. A major reason to tell a story is to breathe life into boring numbers. A story that is too long or goes nowhere is deadly. Never tell a story just because you can, never tell one to vent your own frustrations, and never tell one to give yourself a soapbox. Watch your audience's faces; continually assess if audience members are still with you. If you find yourself saying things like, "Anyway ...," you know that you've gone on too long.

Simmons offers some strategies for reducing potential boredom. First, be specific. Specifics are always more interesting than hypotheticals. Hypotheticals don't provide enough sensory or emotional data for your listeners. It's far better for you to say, "I know a teacher ..." than to say, "What if a teacher ...?" Second, stop talking.

If you sense that you're boring your audience, stop. Get out of the story as quickly as possible and on to something to recapture their interest. It doesn't hurt, I suppose, to remember Tom Lehrer's great observation from the 1960s: If a person can't communicate, the least he can do is shut up.[13]

As much as possible, be succinct. Succinctness positively affects how easily others understand the issue you're presenting. People dealing with constrained resources truly value clarity in problem definition and succinctness in problem statement.[14] Make sure that your story answers questions through illustrative application instead of raising them.

3. Don't scare people or make them feel guilty. Stories that stir up fear, guilt, or shame might have an immediate emotional impact, but they usually are counterproductive in the long run.

This is a delicate issue. We know from research that people pay more attention when they feel urgency in something, or even feel threatened by it,[15] but you don't want to be perceived as placing blame for the current situation on anyone. Board members, group leaders, or faculty members are not likely to appreciate being put in a position where they feel like they are being made to respond to that kind of implication. In fact, an adverse reaction to the suggestion that they have somehow caused the problem may discourage them from acknowledging it.[16]

4. Do intrigue and captivate. The best insurance for capturing your audience is to illustrate your points with stories about things that interest them—or those which passionately interest you. Authenticity, passion, comedy, and tragedy are interesting; superficiality and general abstractions are not. Invite people into your story with descriptions of the sights, sounds, smells, and emotions we all have experienced.

Dealing with emotion requires some delicacy, however. You want to show your own emotional commitment to whatever it is that you are advocating, but people will doubt your clearheadedness if you are too emotional.

5. Do connect at the level of humanity. The fundamental connection between you and your audience is that you both are human. The secondary connection is that you share the exclusive experience of somehow being associated with your school or district—and schools are human enterprises. Schools only exist because of our concern for our children. The relationships between the adults only exist because of the connection to the school.[17] This is the nature of workplace relationships. The forces that bring us into relationships at work spring from the organization's goals, not from our own desires, but we don't leave our humanity at the door. We all have a human need for achievement and affiliation. Tap into that.

As Lincoln told a friend once, "They say I tell a great many stories. I reckon I do; but I have learned from long experience that plain people, take them as they run, are more easily influenced through the medium of a broad and humorous illustration than in any other way."[18]

6. Do leave them feeling hopeful. The purpose in using a story to illustrate numbers and arguments is to show audience members that what you're proposing is both reachable and worth their effort.

On one level, storytelling is easy. We all do it, nearly all the time—but unconsciously. When we consciously set out to select a specific example or story, and even more when we need to create or craft one, storytelling takes on the semblance of work. But it's good work and it pays high dividends—and here's the irony: There are statistics on that.

References

1   J. Conger, "The Necessary Art of Persuasion," *Harvard Business Review*, vol. 76, no.3 (May–June 1998), pp. 84–97.

2   D.C. Kazoleas, "A Comparison of the Persuasive Effectiveness of Qualitative versus Quantitative Evidence: A Test of Explanatory Hypotheses," *Communication Quarterly*, vol. 41, no. 1 (Winter 1993), pp. 40–50.

3   J. Pfeffer, *Managing With Power* (Boston: Harvard Business School Press, 1992).

4   R. Nisbett and L. Ross, *Human Inference: Strategies and Shortcomings of Social Judgment* (Englewood Cliffs, NJ: Prentice-Hall, 1980).

5   J. E. Dutton and S. J. Ashford, "Selling Issues to Top Management," *Academy of Management Review*, vol. 18, no. 3 (1993), pp. 397–428.

6   D. Kahneman and A. Tversky, "On Prediction and Judgement," *ORI Research Monograph*, vol. 12 (1972), p. 4.

    S. Taylor and S. Thompson, "Stalking the Elusive Vividness Effect," *Psychological Review*, vol. 89, no. 2 (March 1982), pp. 155–181.

7   D.C. Kazoleas, "A Comparison of the Persuasive Effectiveness of Qualitative versus Quantitative Evidence: A Test of Explanatory Hypotheses," *Communication Quarterly*, vol. 41, no. 1 (Winter 1993), pp. 40–50.

8   J. Martin and M. E. Powers, "Organizational Stories: More Vivid and Persuasive Than Quantitative Data," In B. M. Staw (Ed.), *Psychological Foundations of Organizational Behavior, Second Edition*, pp. 161–168 (Glenview, IL: Scott, Foresman, & Company, 1983).

9   J. T. Cacioppo, R. E. Petty, and K. J. Morris, "Effects of Need for Cognition on Message Evaluation, Recall, and Persuasion," *Journal of Personality and Social Psychology*, vol. 45, no. 4 (October 1983), pp. 805–811.

    R. E. Petty and J. T. Cacioppo, "The Effects of Involvement on Responses to Argument Quantity and Quality: Central and Peripheral Routes to Persuasion," *Journal of Personality and Social Psychology*, vol. 46, no.1 (January 1984), pp. 69–81.

10 K. C. Lance, C. Hamilton-Pennell, and M. J. Rodney, *Information Empowered: The School Librarian as an Agent of Academic Achievement in Alaska Schools. Revised Edition* (Juneau, AL: Alaska State Library, 2000).

    K. C. Lance, M. J. Rodney, and C. Hamilton-Pennell, *How School Librarians Help Kids Achieve Standards: The Second Colorado Study* (San Jose, CA: Hi Willow Research and Publishing, 2000).

    K. C. Lance, M. J. Rodney, and C. Hamilton-Pennell, *Measuring Up to Standards: The Impact of School Library Programs & Information Literacy in Pennsylvania Schools* (Greensburg, PA: Pennsylvania Citizens for Better Libraries, 2000).

    K. C. Lance, L. Welborn, and C. Hamilton-Pennell, *The Impact of School Library Media Centers on Academic Achievement* (Castle Rock, CO: Hi Willow Research and Publishing, 1993).

    E. G. Smith, *Texas School Libraries: Standards, Resources, Services, and Students' Performance* (Austin, TX: EGS Research & Consulting, 2001).

11 B. Kaye and B. Jacobson, "True Tales and Tall Tales: The Power of Organizational Storytelling," *Training & Development*, vol. 53, no. 3 (March 1999), pp. 44–50.

12 A. Simmons, The Story Factor: *Secrets of Influence from the Art of Storytelling* (Cambridge, MA: Perseus Publishing, 2001).

13 T. Lehrer, *That Was the Week That Was*, Reprise Records, 1965. A live recording by the Harvard mathematician turned satirist. Also worthwhile are such albums as An Evening (Wasted) With Tom Lehrer, 1959—if you're in to that sort of thing.

14 J. E. Dutton and S. J. Ashford, "Selling Issues to Top Management," *Academy of Management Review*, vol. 18, no. 3 (1993), pp. 397–428.

15 K. K. Reardon, *Persuasion in Practice* (Newbury Park, CA: Sage, 1991).

16 J. E. Dutton and S. J. Ashford, "Selling Issues to Top Management," *Academy of Management Review*, vol. 18, no. 3 (1993), pp. 397–428

17 J. J. Gabarro, "The Development of Working Relationships," In J. Galegher and R. E. Kraut (Eds.), *Intellectual Teamwork: Social and Technological Foundations of Cooperative Work*, pp. 79–110 (Hillsdale, NJ: Lawrence Erlbaum Associates Publishers, 1990).

18 D. T. Phillips, *Lincoln on Leadership* (New York: Warner Books, 1992).

Chapter 17

Get Others Up Front to Speak for You

One of the interesting things about influence is that it often is best practiced out of the target's sight. Some of the best examples of this probably are found in your local advocacy efforts. Here's where you can profit by developing avenues of indirect advocacy. This involves recruiting other educators to plead the library media cause with the principal, superintendent, union, board members, parents, and community groups. After all, as the dictionary tells us, an advocate is "one who pleads the cause of another, as before a tribunal or judicial court; one who defends or espouses any cause by argument; a pleader."

Your library needs a voice, but that voice doesn't necessarily have to be your own. The goal is to get the message across. Within pretty broad limits, the identity of the messenger is a secondary consideration. In fact, you may be way ahead if you can get others to step up front in supporting you and your library. Advocacy messages are more often more attractive, even convincing, if the advocate is someone speaking on behalf of another. To have someone else plead the library's case strips away any taint of librarian self-interest. How can a non-librarian's call for library support be perceived as self-serving?

Who Might Step Up?

You're probably thinking, "That sounds good, but how do I make it happen? I have teachers now who won't collaborate with me. How will I ever get them to advocate for me?" The answer is: You won't. Those are the wrong teachers.

Beginning an advocacy campaign by attempting to recruit teachers secure in the traditional teaching role and practiced in very individualistic approaches is unlikely to enlist many vocal supporters. Ironically, dealing with insecure teachers is more likely to initially produce positive results. When those teachers are committed to the support of library media services, they will open doors to working with more secure teachers. The goal is to get all teachers to speak in support of the library media program, but you need to begin somewhere.

The initial targets for advocacy recruitment are teachers whose professional confidence and security either have not yet been established or whose confidence and security have been shaken and need to be re-established. Those are the people you look for. But please do not mistake what I'm saying here. I am not talking about poor or even mediocre teachers. You must have good teachers speaking on your behalf. But even the best of teachers—or those who will become the best of teachers— go through periods of vulnerability. A period of vulnerability is your window of opportunity.

How Can Vulnerability Become an Opportunity?

A teacher moving through some professional transition is more likely to accept help from you than one who is not. In usual circumstances, teachers rarely admit that someone else might know more than they do about how to present a particular lesson or deal with a specific group of youngsters. It takes a special circumstance to overcome an aversion to admitting a need for help. But, given the nature of today's schools, there are situations in which teachers are likely to experience a decline in confidence and a rise in anxiety severe enough that they will accept assistance. These situations center around periods of personal or institutional transition; periods when individuals are uncertain of both themselves and their environments. Even at those times, they may not be willing to ask for help in making sense of and mastering their situations, but they are likely to be willing to accept it if it's offered—and if they see it as something that promises to help them get back on a steady course without causing them to lose face. This is exactly what you have to offer.

Opening the Relationship

The key to opening a relationship with a teacher you want to recruit as a library advocate rests on a dual ability foundation. One part of it is your ability to recognize his or her vulnerability—another example of the sensitivity discussed in Chapters 3 and 4—and the other is your ability to offer help in a way that doesn't force the teacher to admit any deficiency.

Recognizing Vulnerability

Recognizing vulnerability isn't difficult if you consistently strive to do two things. The first is to know the members of your faculty and to keep up-to-date on changes in their assignments and situations. This can be done through social as well as professional interactions. The second is to scan the schedule and environment each semester for any of five specific situations in which a teacher is most likely to accept help. These are when he or she is (a) a brand new teacher, (b) a veteran teacher just new to your school, (c) a teacher whose assignment has been radically changed, (d) a teacher assigned outside the area of his or her university preparation, or (e) part of a faculty involved in a significant school-wide change.

Initiating the Relationship

Offering assistance to a vulnerable teacher is a skill that takes planning and practice because it runs counter to our natural inclination. In our most generous and sincere desires to be helpful, most of us will turn to someone and say, "Call me if you need help." Unfortunately, to take us up on our kind offer requires an admission from that person that he or she does indeed need help. The most likely response is a hearty "thank you" and then a disappearance into the classroom for the rest of the year.

But it doesn't have to be that way. We can raise the odds of successfully opening a relationship by changing just a few words. Instead of saying, "Call me if you need help," we can open the dialogue by acknowledging the teacher's position and saying something along the lines of, "You're new here, and I know there's a whole lot to learn very quickly. I can help you with part of it"—or even the more gentle, "I see you have a new assignment this year. I have something you might be interested in."

This approach saves face for teachers because it doesn't box them in. In both cases, you only offer to provide something small—"part of it" or one thing "you might be interested in." There's no arrogance or threat, no take-over, and no question of reduced professionalism. The impression is of two professionals interacting. The approach doesn't force them to take the first step and ask for help. It allows them to decline your offer if they wish. It allows them to accept it without having to say that they are accepting help; they can just accept with an inquiry: "Oh, how?" or "Like what?" The question opens the door for you.

Once the door is opened, you have your shot. If you can then deliver on something that helps them master the new situation in which they find themselves, two things happen: (1) they will be in your debt, and (2) they will tell others of what you've done. They probably won't directly tell another teacher that "You should go see the librarian about that" because another teacher will not confess a problem to them either, and the culture of teaching discourages direction from one teacher to another. They're also not likely to go and say that "The librarian really saved me." But they will praise your work to other teachers when a safe opportunity arrives. Many will likely react favorably to serving on some committee or task force with you. Some are likely to be willing to make a presentation to a parent group some evening, and there will probably be at least one who will speak out to the administration if the source of the assistance that was so helpful is threatened. That is the definition of indirect advocacy: People speaking out on your behalf when you are not there and willing to stand up for you so you don't have to do it yourself.

We shouldn't make a mistake here. Building an indirect advocacy support system is a lot like photography: You have to take a lot of pictures to get a few good ones. You may have to approach and assist many teachers to get the few who will openly advocate for you. Many teachers feel just as you feel about being a vocal activist for something. But it doesn't take many teachers talking to the principal or standing before the board on your behalf to have a positive effect.

Five Great Opportunities for Indirect Advocacy Recruiting

A Brand New Teacher

All the research on beginning teachers demonstrates that the first year on the job is dominated by attempts to make sense of the experience and to find ways to survive in the classroom.[1] There is invariably a gap between what someone right out of the university expects teaching to be like and what it really is like. One dimension of teaching for which new instructors frequently are unprepared is what Robert Evans calls the motivational burden—addressing the reality that not all students are as eager to learn as your professors said they were and that your job responsibility includes motivation as well as instruction.[2] Another and related area for which new teachers are often unprepared is how to deal with the wide span of learning styles to be found in any group of children. It is a major challenge to develop a repertoire of teaching techniques that will motivate reluctant learners and address varieties of learning styles.

The first year is the time that a new teacher wants to show that he or she is up to the challenge and is casting about for ideas of every kind. You can be of immense assistance to a new teacher and capture lasting support if you can develop an opportunity to show that you can fill this need. It's here that the reciprocity heuristic kicks in. You might even realize longer-range benefits than you expect. Down the road, the benefits of making a new teacher successful can be multiplied. As an experienced teacher in later years, that same teacher may be called upon to be a mentor to another new teacher. One of the mentoring messages will be to capitalize on what the library media specialist has to offer.

A Veteran Teacher New to Your School

A veteran newcomer experiences some of the same uncertainties a beginning teacher experiences. Becoming a member of any organization involves learning the norms, values, and required behavior patterns of the new group.[3] Because every school has a distinct culture, when a teacher transfers from one school to another, even within the same district, a re-socialization experience is part of the entry into the new situation. It even happens to an employee returning from a leave of absence to the same site and role if there has been a significant change in the environment, such as new administrators or the development of a strong union movement.[4]

Prior experiences affect our ability to make rapid sense of a new situation and to figure out what are the most appropriate responses,[5] and the more similar the old and new environments appear—and schools are very similar, one to another—the more difficult it may be for the veteran newcomer to develop new responses.[6] He or she will have developed attitudes and responses in the last school, especially to uncertainty or perceived threat that may prejudice how the new school is viewed.[7] For example, look at the adjustment you'd have to make if you came from another school where there had been a very different approach to discipline, instruction, community relations, teacher-administrator interactions, or evaluation. It sometimes is very difficult for a newcomer to suppress the inclination to respond to familiar stimuli with familiar patterns of behavior. What was acceptable to previous colleagues, administration, students, and parents may not work with the new ones where norms and values are different.[8]

Moreover, continuing faculty members and administrators are likely to see experienced teachers coming in as needing far less orientation and training than beginners do.[9] They are expected to already be aware of those things the training would provide or be able to find them out on their own and assimilate them. They also are expected to be instantly competent and talented, where beginners are assumed to need a time to get up to speed. Job changers often have more opportunities than beginners, but the price is a higher expectation of performance.

These expectations can place heavy demands on veteran newcomers, especially those who make significant geographical moves, assume new or additional responsibilities, or take on different functions in their new positions, such as teaching a different grade or subject. The way newcomers are perceived is also influenced by the reasons behind the move. In transfers made because the receiving school needs a special talent, or because of some unavoidable situation like enrollment shifts, newcomers are likely to be presumed as competent. The hiring of an experienced person from outside the system is usually interpreted as an affirmation of competence, rather than a test of it. Consequently, co-workers and friends are frequently less likely to see the need for increased levels of support.[10] This is unfortunate because there is wide research evidence to indicate that interpersonal support is an important feature in a person's ability to make a major transition.[11]

The bottom line is that experienced teachers new to your school are also in a very vulnerable state. They are trying to make sense of the new situation. They may not be as much in need of new teaching ideas as a beginning teacher, but they sorely need help in understanding the resources available, what gets rewarded, what gets punished, and how to make a positive impression. You can help them with all those things—and, in doing so, you develop an ally.

A Teacher Assigned Outside the Area of University Preparation

This situation is more likely to occur at the secondary level, but it certainly is not exclusive to the higher grades, especially in K–8 settings. The problem is not in any lack of education on the part of the teachers so assigned; it's in the lack of fit between what they were trained for and what they are called upon to do.[12] The problem is compounded by the fact that beginning teachers and recent hires are given more out-of-training assignments than are experienced continuing teachers. Teachers in these situations are at more of a loss and a disadvantage than beginning teachers and veteran newcomers assigned to grades and students for which they were trained.

These teachers may be the most desperate for help among all who find themselves in a vulnerable state, and you have the resources and skills to help them. In this situation, you might truly be a professional lifesaver. Appropriately assigned beginning teachers and veteran newcomers at least know what questions to ask, are familiar with the challenges they are to face, and have a sense of the materials and resources available to them. The mis-assigned teacher may hardly know where to begin. This is a fertile field for your labors.

A Teacher Whose Assignment Has Been Radically Changed

Radical alteration of a schedule isn't quite as challenging as a first teaching job, the effect is not quite as devastating as movement from one school to another, and it certainly is not in the same league with being assigned outside your field of expertise, but it still shakes confidence and raises anxiety. The experience of moving from teaching second grade to teaching sixth, or the reverse, for example, takes a teacher out of one unique environment and into another. Not only are there subject matter differences, but the nature of the client is substantially changed. Research and common sense indicate that the knowledge and skill base required to deal with seven year olds varies considerably from that required to deal 11 and 12 year olds. Such schedule changes also change adult relationships, as the bonds of common experience in teaching shift from interactions with one group to another.

You can be of real assistance to a teacher making such a change. A given teacher, with, say, a decade's experience at one grade level, may see no gain in working with you on a broad scale. The same teacher, however, moved to a level at which he or she has no experience on which to draw, may develop a whole new perspective on the breadth, depth, and value of library media services. Once more, helping someone make rapid sense of a new situation and become effective in a new environment creates a debt that may be translated into a commitment as it grows.

A Teacher Taking Part in a School-Wide Change

Lastly, there is one situation in which everyone on the faculty becomes vulnerable—and their "recruitability" increases. That is when the school is undergoing a major operational change. In such conditions, everyone is taken back to the beginner's level. Large magnitude change challenges competencies, causes confusion, and creates conflict.[13] In such instances, the usual sources of information and support are absent. This is a void into which you can step, especially if you have any warning that such a change is coming. For example, if your school is moving toward inclusion, making a decision about whole language or phonics instruction after spending years practicing only one approach, is going to go to block scheduling, is revamping curriculum in the face of new standards, or is about to engage in site-based management, the odds are that few if any of your faculty colleagues have had any experience in working in such a setting. In one sense, it makes all of them veteran teachers coming into a new school setting. They all will be concerned with how well they will be able to meet its challenges. They all will be trying to make sense of the new environment and technology. They all will suffer a drop in effectiveness as they go into the "implementation dip" that accompanies all change from old operational methods to new ones.[14] In short, they all will be vulnerable.

You will have a great opportunity here to capture lasting support from several if not many faculty members if you are ready to seize the moment. If you can have warning, a year or more in advance, that your school is going to move into a particular activity or mode of operation, you can have the lead time you need to research model programs, discover best practices and pitfalls, and prepare materials and resources that will make a pivotal difference in your colleagues' ability to adjust to the new order. Armed with material and information that will help to make them successful, you will gather debts and commitments to cash in on later.

What Does It Take to be Ready for Such Opportunities?

Building an indirect advocacy system spares you the unpleasantness of engaging in organizational politics, lobbying, pleading, and making impassioned public statements before large and sometimes hostile groups. But the trade off is a required vigilance. You must engage in activities that will allow you to gather the information you must have in order to be able to assess the vulnerability and needs of others. That means you must serve on committees where you will get access to long-range plans and scheduling decisions. You would do well to carve yourself a role in new employee orientation and mentoring programs, if not in the hiring process itself. You need to attend board meetings and interact with the members of the teachers' organization. These activities will help you build the knowledge base and relationships through which you will be able to analyze new developments and recognize the opportunities they will bring.

References

1 R. Fessler and J. C. Christensen, *The Teacher Career Cycle: Understanding and Guiding the Professional Development of Teachers* (Needham Heights, MA: Allyn & Bacon, 1992).

  M. Huberman, "Teacher Careers and School Improvement," *Journal of Curriculum Studies*, vol. 20, no. 2 (1988), pp. 119–132.

2 R. Evans, *The Human Side of School Change* (San Francisco: Jossey-Bass, 2001).

3 E. H. Schein, "Organizational Socialization and the Profession of Management," In E. H. Schein (Ed.), *The Art of Managing Human Resources* (pp. 83–100) (New York: Oxford University Press, 1987).

4 C. D. Fisher, "Organizational Socialization: An Integrative Review," In K. M. Rowland & G. R. Ferris (Eds.), *Research in Personnel and Human Resources Management: A Research Annual, Volume 4* (pp. 101–145). Greenwich, Conn.: JAI Press, Inc., 1986).

5 G. R. Jones, "Psychological Orientation and the Process of Organizational Socialization: An Interactionist Perspective," *Academy of Management Review*, vol. 8, no. 3 (1983), pp. 464–474.

6 J. M. Brett, "Job Transitions and Personal and Role Development," In K. M. Rowland and G. R. Ferris (Eds.), *Research in Personnel and Human Resources Management: A Research Annual, Volume 2* (pp. 155–185) (Greenwich, CT: JAI Press, Inc., 1984).

7 G. R. Jones, "Psychological Orientation and the Process of Organizational Socialization: An Interactionist Perspective," *Academy of Management Review*, vol. 8, no. 3 (1983), pp. 464–474.

8 J. M. Brett, "Job Transitions and Personal and Role Development," In K. M. Rowland and G. R. Ferris (Eds.), *Research in Personnel and Human Resources Management: A Research Annual, Volume 2* (pp. 155–185) (Greenwich, CT: JAI Press, Inc., 1984).

M. R. Louis, "Surprise and Sense Making: What Newcomers Experience in Entering Unfamiliar Organizational Settings," *Administrative Science Quarterly*, vol. 25, no. 2 (1980), pp. 226–251.

P. K. Manning, "Talking and Becoming: A View of Organizational Socialization," In J. D. Douglas (Ed.), *Understanding Everyday Life* (pp. 239–256) (Chicago: Aldine, 1970).

J. Van Maanen, "Experiencing Organizations: Notes on the Meaning of Careers and Socialization," In J. Van Maanen (Ed.), *Organizational Careers: Some New Perspectives* (pp. 15–45) (London: Wiley, 1975).

9 D.C. Feldman and J. M. Brett, "Coping with New Jobs: A Comparative Study of New Hires and Job Changers," *Academy of Management Journal*, vol. 26, no. 2 (1983), pp. 258–272.

10 D.C. Feldman and J. M. Brett, "Coping with New Jobs: A Comparative Study of New Hires and Job Changers," *Academy of Management Journal*, vol. 26, no. 2 (1983), pp. 258–272.

11 R. S. Bhagat, "Effects of Stressful Life Events on Individual Performance Effectiveness and Work Adjustment Processes Within Organizational Settings: A Research Model," *Academy of Management Review*, vol. 8, no. 4 (1983), pp. 660–671.

L. M. Brammer and P. J. Abrego, "Intervention Strategies for Coping with Transitions," *The Counseling Psychologist,* vol. 9, no. 2 (1981), pp. 19–36.

N. K. Schlossberg, "A Model for Analyzing Human Adaptation to Transition," *The Counseling Psychologist*, vol. 9, no. 2 (1981), pp. 2–18.

12 R. M. Ingersoll, "The Problem of Underqualified Teachers in American Secondary Schools," *Educational Researcher*, vol. 28, no. 2 (March, 1999), pp. 26–37. Available online at <http://www.aera.net/pubs/er/arts/28-02/ingsoll01.htm>. Accessed June 1, 2003.

13 R. Evans, *The Human Side of School Change* (San Francisco: Jossey-Bass, 2001).

14 M. Fullan, *The New Meaning of Educational Change* (New York: Teachers College Press, 2001).

Chapter 18
Show Your Teeth Now and Again

"And now," as Monty Python used to say, "for something completely different." It's not really different, though. It only appears that way because, unlike most everything else in the book, it encourages you to go beyond assertiveness to plain aggressiveness. As unpleasant as this may feel for some, it sometimes is a necessity. As helpful as you can and should be in every way, and as much as influence depends upon others' impressions of you, the impressions must include an element of strength.

Sooner or later, someone will attack the way you run your library. It's only a matter of time, and the time shortens every time you cast your net wider in your school and district. There was a discussion in Chapter 2 about the additional attention you'll attract as you emerge as an informal leader in your school. The gist of it was that not all of the attention will be positive. You'll draw some criticism because you'll be perceived as a threat for one reason or another. You'll draw some criticism because not everyone understands what libraries and librarians are about in today's schools. You'll draw some criticism because other educators simply have differing perspectives. And you'll draw criticism simply because there will be people who just don't like you. It all comes with the territory.

In today's environment, it's altogether likely that someone may take a shot at you over the amount of money you spend on print as opposed to electronic resources. It might be some other topic, but that's a likely one and will serve as a good example for the general principles of professional response. Let me offer some tactical advice in repelling that or any other assault on you and your program: Respond vigorously, even aggressively. Never feed into their stereotypical image of the retiring librarian. You are the expert here. As much as this may be a criticism of your collection policy, it's much more a criticism of your expertise. Don't allow that to proceed. Display your expertise politely and respectfully but also relentlessly and mercilessly. Remember what Shakespeare had Richard III say about himself: "I can smile—and I can murder while I smile." Bombard your adversaries with fact and demand that they respond with the same. Never accept opinion without evidence, especially if you are challenged in public. Avoid defending your actions; make them defend their criticisms. Make your statement and then close with a question back to them. The goal is to put your antagonists on the defensive and make them think twice about ever attacking you again, especially in any kind of public forum.

Let's assume for a moment that you are attacked on your print budget by some self-appointed critic. How might you respond? Use the information below as a way of modeling responses on virtually any issue.

First, point out that research demonstrates the value of a balanced collection, particularly the value of print materials.[1] There isn't room here to identify studies, but you can easily find them on the Internet, through your subscription databases, and in back issues of *Book Report*, *Library Talk*, *Library Media Connection*, *School Library Journal*, *Teacher-Librarian*, and *Emergency Librarian*. Be careful, though. These publications carry articles that are mixes of opinion and experience description, along with some articles that are research-based. While these are valuable for practice, they're considerably less valuable for argumentation. It's important that you separate research from opinion. You want to challenge your critics with factual evidence, not with another librarian's opinion.

The research-based articles in these publications will have bibliographies that will lead you back to the original research reports. Track down those reports and use them in crafting your arguments. Of course, once you're familiar with the kinds of research journals that carry articles on topics likely to become contentious in your school or district, you can launch your search directly in those print and online publications.

Do your homework in advance. Put a list of supportive research article citations in your pocket calendar or PDA so they're always handy. But also memorize at least a half-dozen so you can speak without hesitation. When you're done, turn and ask your critics to cite specific evidence of electronic superiority in fostering student achievement. They won't be able to do it.

Second, someone will probably characterize print materials as a thing of the past. Challenge this immediately. Ask what evidence they have that print is in decline, then turn on them when they can't produce it. Tell them that print isn't dead, dying, or even ill. Consumers purchased more than 1.63 *billion* books in 2002, up about 1% from 2001.[2] Book sales in the United States exceeded $25 billion for the first time in 2000 and are expected to reach $43 billion by 2007.[3] Point out that even very popular sources of information about *computers*—works like *PC Magazine* and *PC World*—monthly circulate in *print* to well over a million paying readers.[4] Individual magazines die, and individual books fail, but the field is alive and well—and, ironically, it's new technology that's making print more economical, timely, and flexible.

Third, take your antagonists into areas about which they probably know little. Ask what they know about copyright. You can use some of the fascinating arguments advanced by Thomas Mann at the Library of Congress to build a thought provoking case.[5] It's naïve, he says, to think that intellectual property laws are going to disappear or that human nature will outgrow the profit motive in the next century. If a profit is to be derived from copyrighted materials on the Internet, providers must limit who has access. Copyright restrictions mean that free access to everything produced probably will *never* come to the Internet. Libraries, on the other hand, freely make copyrighted material available in their print resources.

Mann makes another point that may surprise your critics, and you can use it as a fourth argument to bolster perceptions of your expertise. It's powerful because it speaks to our educational goals. Exclusive use of electronic sources, he says, may actually undercut the student's ability to understand lengthy works. "Doing keyword searches … for particular passages is simply not the same as the much more important work of actually reading and absorbing their intellectual content as connected wholes."[6] Today's students, you can argue as he does, certainly are comfortable with computers, but that's not the same as saying that they're comfortable reading and absorbing long works on a screen. The majority of the time, Mann argues, youngsters interact with screen displays that don't require long attention spans and require less rather than more verbal interpretative skills. Because we want students to move from simple information access skills to knowledge development and application to understanding to wisdom, technology that fosters short attention spans is both dangerous and counterproductive. "Here is the important point," Mann contends, "and there is no getting around it: If the higher levels of knowledge and understanding are going to be grasped, they require greater attention spans than do the lower levels of data and information."[7]

Using Mann's arguments as a platform, you can close by arguing simple readability. No electronic medium compares with paper and ink for readability. And the first thing most students do when they locate something on a database or the Internet is print it out.[8] But don't stop there. Explain why they print it out. Claim an expertise, stress specifics, and see if your critics can keep the pace.

Three elements determine readability: light, resolution, and reading speed.[9] Electronic illumination involves light emanating from the screen. This is less engaging and more tiring on the eyes than the reflected light that illuminates a printed page. The resolution on display screens is lower than the resolution on your printer, and magazines, books, and newspapers are printed at even higher densities. This means that printed pages are much easier to read, especially when dealing with smaller fonts. Do a little research or talk with your school's tech to get some exact dpi numbers. Numbers always make your arguments sound more impressive.

Finally, reading from a screen is up to 30% slower than reading from the printed page. How much of a book or newspaper page can show on a computer screen at a given moment? We can overcome the problem of seeing a small font by increasing the magnification of the screen's text, but—when we do that—we see even less of a page. In order to read a full page, we must have our computer write and rewrite the various parts of it several times.[10]

What does all this mean? It means that print looks better; is more comfortable to deal with; and doesn't tax the mind as much in the process of resolving dots into letters and figures. Sustained reading is done more when reading is comfortable and efficient. Ask your critics to think of their own reading habits. How often and how long do any of them sit and do sustained reading at a computer screen compared to how often and how long they read in a chair with a book in their hands? And that is the whole point to be made here: The goal is sustained reading.[11] Once you make that point, you can then come full circle back to the research on the importance of reading, the link between sustained reading and library collections, and the research showing connections between collection size and student achievement.

Don't let me mislead you. Never say that we should spend our ever-short resources on print materials alone. Describe and tout the electronic resources your library provides. Spending an excessive amount on print materials makes no more sense than to spend our resources on technology alone. The key is in the balance. With luck, arguing for that balance may help to keep your critics off balance.

The aforementioned, of course, only outlines a possible response to a single topic on which you might be attacked. You need to anticipate others and prepare for them as much in advance as you're able. In effect, you need to be ready to respond to as many avenues of attack as you can. The hope is that you'll never be attacked, in which case you can use all you've learned in the most friendly and positive ways to bolster proposals and support varieties of projects. There's no wasted in effort in preparation. Part of the reason that preparation is always beneficial is because it gives you confidence that carries over into and affects your day-to-day relationships with your colleagues. Influence is, indeed, rooted in relationships. But every relationship has boundaries and limits imposed by its participants. Your ability to shape the relationships in which you participate is affected by your ability to draw those boundaries and limits by raising the price and pain level for those who would assault you with things that cannot be ignored, cannot be allowed to pass, and certainly cannot be allowed to overwhelm you.

References

1 For example, you might look at works such as the ones below, paying particular attention to their bibliographies to lead you to other research evidence

C. A. Doll, "Quality and Elementary School Library Media Collections," *School Library Media Quarterly*, vol. 25, no. 2 (Winter 1997), pp. 95–102.

K. Haycock, "School Libraries and Reading Achievement," *Teacher Librarian*, vol. 26, no. 3 (January/February 1999), p. 32.

A. McGill-Franzen and R. L. Allington, "Putting Books in the Classroom Seems Necessary But Not Sufficient," *Journal of Educational Research*, vol. 93, no. 2 (November/December 1999), pp. 67–74.

S. Krashen, "School Libraries, Public Libraries, and the NAEP Reading Scores," *School Library Media Quarterly*, vol. 23, no. 4 (1995), pp. 235–237. Significant predictors of NAEP reading comprehension scores were the number of books per student in school libraries. Software was positively associated with reading scores, but not significantly.

S. Krashen, *The Power of Reading: Insights From the Research* (Englewood, CO: Libraries Unlimited, 1993). Multiple regression analysis of data from 41 states.

J. L. McQuillan, *Access to Print and Formal Instruction in Reading Acquisition* (Doctoral dissertation, University of Southern California, 1997). Access to print via school and public libraries has significant impact on SAT Verbal test scores, even when controlling for effects of socio-economic status, teacher-pupil ratio, and computer software holdings.

W. Nagy and P. Herman, "Breadth and Depth of Vocabulary Knowledge: Implications for Acquisition and Instruction," In M. McKeown and M. Curtiss (Eds.) *The Nature of Vocabulary Acquisition*, (Hillsdale, NJ: Erlbaum, 1987). A small but statistically reliable increase of word knowledge typically occurred when students encountered unfamiliar words in print.

C. Snow, W. Barnes, J. Chandler, I. Goodman, and H. Hemphill, *Unfulfilled Expectations: Home and School Influences on Literacy* (Cambridge, MA: Harvard University Press, 1991). The richer the print environment, the better the literacy development.

2 Book Industry Study Group, <http://www.bisg.org/bisg_bulletin_5.03.html#10> Accessed June 1, 2003.

3 Book Industry Study Group, <http://www.bisg.org/pr5.03.html> Accessed June 1, 2003.

4 *PC World Marketing*, <http://marketing.pcworld.com/site/pressreleases/abc.html> Accessed June 1, 2003.

5 T. Mann, "The Importance of Books, Free Access, and Libraries as Places and the Dangerous Inadequacy of the of the Information Science Paradigm," *Journal of Academic Librarianship*, vol. 27, no. 4 (July 2001), pp. 268–281.

6 T. Mann, "The Importance of Books, Free Access, and Libraries as Places and the Dangerous Inadequacy of the of the Information Science Paradigm," *Journal of Academic Librarianship*, vol. 27, no. 4 (July 2001), pp. 270–271.

7 T. Mann, "The Importance of Books, Free Access, and Libraries as Places and the Dangerous Inadequacy of the of the Information Science Paradigm," *Journal of Academic Librarianship*, vol. 27, no. 4 (July 2001), p. 270.

8 W. Crawford, "Paper Persists: Why Physical Library Connections Still Matter," *Online*, vol. 22, no. 1 (January/February, 1998), pp. 42–47.

9 W. Crawford and M. Gorman, *Future Libraries: Dreams Madness & Reality* (Chicago: American Library Association, 1995).

10 W. Crawford and M. Gorman, *Future Libraries: Dreams Madness & Reality* (Chicago: American Library Association, 1995).

11 The importance of sustained reading is difficult to overstate. See works such as

R. Anderson, P. Wilson, & L. Fielding, "Growth in Reading and How Children Spend Their Time Outside of School," *Reading Research Quarterly*, vol. 23 (1988), pp. 285–303. Reading as a leisure activity of 5th graders was the best predictor of comprehension, vocabulary, and reading speed.

M. Foertsch, *Reading In and Out of School* (Washington, D.C.: U.S. Department of Education, 1992). 4th, 8th, and 12th graders who reported more reading outside of school performed better on reading comprehension tests. Children who have access to school libraries do more reading and score better on tests of reading comprehension.

J. McQuillan, *The Literacy Crisis: False Claims, Real Solutions* (Portsmouth, NH: Heinemann, 1998).